WHAT YOU NEED TO KNOW

bandits
on the
information
superhighway

WHAT YOU NEED TO KNOW

bandits
on the
information
superhighway

DANIEL J. BARRETT

O'REILLY & ASSOCIATES, INC.

Bonn • Cambridge • Paris • Sebastopol • Tokyo

Bandits on the Information Superhighway
Daniel J. Barrett

Editor: Linda Lamb

Production Editor: Mary Anne Weeks Mayo

Printing History:

February 1996   First Edition

ISBN: 1-56592-156-9

Table of Contents

What you need to know about this book

This book is about practical risks on the Internet.

Most people who use the Internet behave honestly. I hope you won't be too disappointed to hear this. After all, according to the media, the Internet is a slime pit, overflowing with pornography, with evil "hackers" and pedophiles lurking around every digital corner. Well, I'm sorry to report that it's simply not true. At the very least, it is blown *way* out of proportion.

So why write a book about Internet risks?

Well, the so-called dangers of the Internet might be overblown, but there are still some practical risks that users should know. They're not as sexy and intrigue-filled as the ones that make the evening news, but you're more likely to encounter them in everyday use of the Internet.

For example, do you think that your electronic mail is private? Think again. Between the time you write your "private" message and the time it is received, there are at least seven ways that somebody else can read it. Have you ever received an electronic chain letter that explained how to make truckloads of money by sending a few dollars to a list of strangers? If you were tempted to distribute it, don't bother: it's a scam, and it's illegal. Have you ever met somebody on the Net who turned out to be very different in person? You're not alone, and there are ways to prevent these kinds of misunderstandings.

The Internet mirrors our society, both the good and bad parts. Most parts of the Internet are good, fortunately, but we can't completely ignore the bad ones. There will always be troublemakers, so it's wise to take some reasonable precautions. That's what this book is about: how to deal with the (relatively few) people who use the Internet to invade our privacy, steal our money, waste our time, damage our trust, or otherwise deceive us.

Bandits on the Information Superhighway raises and answers the following questions:

- What are the realistic risks of using the Internet?
- What are the unrealistic risks, overhyped in the media, that you really don't have to worry about?
- How can you detect and avoid Internet-related risks?
- If you get ripped off, what can you do about it?

After reading this book, you'll be ready to have a safe, productive, and fun time on the Net.

This book is for all computer users.

There is plenty of information here for both beginners and experts. Even if you have never used the Internet before, the tips in this book should make sense. Some Internet scams look remarkably similar to ripoffs found in the real world (you know, that place outside our office windows, where the trees are). If you're an Internet expert, you'll find lots of reference material within these pages. Maybe even some surprises.

As you read this book, it doesn't matter what brand of computer you prefer or whether you access the Internet with a modem or a direct connection. Even if you use another network entirely, instead of the Internet, most of the book will still apply. That's why the cover says "Information Superhighway" instead of "Internet." Although the book focuses on the Internet, the risks we'll discuss can happen on any other computer network, BBS, or online service as well. The Information Superhighway is a vision of the future, in which all of these computers and networks are brought together to create the ultimate information resource. The Internet is not the Information Superhighway, but it's the closest thing we have so far.

We've kept some people anonymous.

We'll be discussing a wide variety of risks, from mild practical jokes to dangerous scams. In many cases, you'll get the details word-for-word from the users who experienced them. Because of the sensitive nature of the material, some users didn't want their names printed, so we changed them in the text. When you see a first name only, it's a pseudonym (a made-up name). When a full name is given, however, it's real. In a few cases, a pseudonym represents a composite of several people in order to illustrate a point.

This series puts technology in context.

Like other books we've published, the What You Need To Know series started with a need that we had for a certain kind of information. Tim (O'Reilly) noticed that we had nothing to give nontechnical employees about subjects they needed to understand in order to work productively. The kind of information our users need is not "Push this button"; it's more "Here's how to think about this."

When people have been using the Internet for a while, they learn that "private" electronic mail really isn't as private as it appears to be, and that messages to "make money fast" are scams. But there isn't an easy way for them to get that kind of general knowledge except through painful experience (theirs and everyone else's).

So, we developed a series of books for people who use technology as a tool for their "real" job or interests and don't have the time to become a total computer wizard. The books digest and present the kinds of information you'd come across if you worked with the technology for a while in a supportive and knowledgeable environment. These are books we give our own employees.

This book is designed to be browsable.

Depending on how you want to read the book, you can get your information from first-person stories, frequent headlines that describe each short section, the text itself, or reference sections. We have sidebars featuring users and their stories, because people learn from personal experiences. (After you've seen someone embarrass himself Internet-wide by falling for a prank, you'll be careful not to do the same.) So, we have users telling you about their embarrassing moments and their personal ways of looking at technology. The anecdotes aren't fluff to cajole you through the material. They *are* what you need to know. By reading the stories alone, you can get the gist of the material in the chapter.

Headings that summarize main points and short, standalone sections also encourage browsing. "How-to" sections are distinguished by their own format, so that you can easily skip—or find—specific procedures.

Of course, reading straight through all the chapters is also an option. We hope that when you "dip in," you'll find so much of use that you'll keep reading.

Contact us to suggest improvements or for sales information.

Please write us if you have suggestions for improving this book (or even to relate a favorite Internet ripoff story). You can find us at:

O'Reilly & Associates, Inc.
103 Morris Street, Suite A
Sebastopol, CA 95472
(707) 829–0515
Fax: (707) 829–0104
Email: *nuts@ora.com* or *uunet!ora.com!nuts*
World Wide Web: http://www.ora.com

For information on volume discounts for bulk purchase, call O'Reilly & Associates, Inc., at (800) 998–9938, or send email to *linda@ora.com* (*uunet!ora.com!linda*). For companies requiring extensive customization of the book, some licensing terms are also available.

I'd like to thank some people…

First and foremost, I thank my editor, Linda Lamb. Her expert proofreading, welcome suggestions, and keen intuition consistently improved the text, and working with her was a pleasure. I also thank Frank Willison, O'Reilly's managing editor, for believing in my initial idea.

Big thanks go to my technical reviewers for their insights and comments that helped to make the book more solid. The reviewers were Stephen Barrett, Peter da Silva, Stephanie da Silva, J. D. Falk, and Arsenio Santos.

Thanks to the production staff at O'Reilly who turned this manuscript into a finished book. Mary Anne Weeks Mayo was the copyeditor and project manager; Eric Ray converted the book from LaTeX to Frame; Mike Sierra provided expert tool tweaking; Chris Reilley created the figures; Edie Freedman designed the cover; Nancy Priest designed the interior layout; Hanna Dyer designed the back cover; Jane Ellin assisted with production; and Kismet McDonough-Chan provided final quality control on the book. Leslie Evans did the line drawings of people quoted, found in sidebars throughout the text.

I am very, very grateful to the many Internet users who shared their stories with me. To the experts, I say: "thank you for sharing your knowledge." And to the victims, I say: "thank you for helping other people to learn from your experiences." It's not easy to admit that you've been fooled.

Chapter 10 on users' rights was made possible with the kind assistance of Ethan Katsh, Professor of Legal Studies at the University of Massachusetts; Mike Botts, attorney at law in Prescott, Wisconsin; and Dan Appelman, attorney at law in Palo Alto, California. Professor Katsh, author of *Law in a Digital World* (Oxford University Press, 1995), helped me to understand some of the particulars of online law. Mr. Botts, a former assistant attorney general of Iowa, answered many of my general questions on law and the pursuit of justice, and also provided information for Chapter 11. Mr. Appelman, who represents many Internet access and content providers such as UUNET

Technologies and O'Reilly & Associates, gave the chapter a thorough technical review and helped clear up last-minute questions.

Numerous people made relatively small but extremely helpful contributions. Gregory Block was the first to point me to the Usenet newsgroup *news.admin.misc* (now *news.admin.net-abuse.misc*), where copious information could be found. Lewis McCarthy alerted me to the problem of spamming and provided several other key pieces of data. Dan King graciously allowed me to use information from his Usenet Marketplace FAQ articles. Lisa Helene Helfman suggested adding the section "Women in the Online World" to Chapter 2. Jason Andrade explained IRC operator privileges to me. David Medin provided detailed information about government auctions. Arlo West and Juan Joy checked out the classified ad groups on America Online and Prodigy. J. D. Falk created the informative Cyberporn Web Page mentioned in Chapter 9. Dave Silon offered advice about Macintosh programs. Donald Knuth, Leslie Lamport, and Jonathan Payne created the software that I used to write and edit this book. Alan Benjamin, Bill Bogstad, Dave Furstenau, Gerhard Fohler, Alan Kaplan, Herbert Nevyas, Joel Rubin, and Neil Weinstock all lent a helping hand by sending vital bits of data in my times of need.

My parents, Stephen and Judith Barrett, and my siblings, Debbie and Ben, were full of encouragement about the book, and I thank them for their warm enthusiasm and love. Mom and Dad also sent me dozens of wonderful newspaper and magazine clippings that added much diversity to the text.

Finally, my deepest thanks go to my wife, Lisa Feldman Barrett, for her love and her professional assistance with this book. As an assistant professor of psychology at Penn State University, Lisa contributed significant portions of Chapter 8. And in September 1993, when I knew her only as anonymous Internet user *acs-8981@chop.ucsd.edu*, she managed to commit the most heinous crime on the Internet...by stealing my heart.

CHAPTER 1

Welcome to the Internet!

The Internet is a vast computer network.

The Internet (aka "the Net") is the largest computer network in the world. It allows tens of millions of people around the globe to meet, work together, socialize, and help each other in ways that formerly were impossible. Until recently, the Net was accessible mainly by computers at universities, large companies, and government organizations. Nowadays, however, the electronic floodgates have opened, making the Internet accessible to anybody with a personal computer and a modem.

The Internet is filled with activity. On the serious side, you can conduct business, follow the stock market, make contacts, and collaborate with distant business partners. (This book, in fact, was developed on the Internet while my editor and I lived 3000 miles apart.) On the lighter side, you can read movie reviews, play "dungeon" games with people in other countries, listen to unreleased music, trade recipes, buy and sell personal items, and of course, make friends.

This chapter provides a brief overview of the Internet. If you are already an experienced Net user, you might want to skip the sections that introduce common Internet concepts like email and the World Wide Web. This chapter will also introduce you to the topic of this book: Internet risks. We'll

Doubling Internet

Last year the Internet as a whole doubled in size, as it has done every year since 1988.

Christopher Anderson
"The Accidental Superhighway,"
The Economist, July 1995

summarize some risks you can encounter on the Net and give you an idea of what's covered in the rest of the book.

The Internet is like a gigantic city.

In the early days of the Internet, the number of users was much smaller than it is now, and participants had a strong sense of community. The overall "feel" was that of an electronic town where people knew each other. Nowadays, with tens of millions of users, the Internet is more like an enormous city with many diverse communities. The Net is shared by computer professionals, computer novices, liberals, conservatives, pacifists, hate-mongers, adults, children.... Pick any topic of conversation, and no matter what your viewpoint is, there are sure to be people on the Internet who believe the exact opposite.

When you live in a big city, you develop an intuition about how to keep yourself safe. For instance, you learn not to walk alone in certain parts of the city at night, not to carry large sums of cash in your pocket, and not to believe everything that strangers tell you. This intuition is called "street smarts" or your "city legs." People need street smarts on the Internet too. Unfortunately, the Internet is relatively new, so many users have not had time yet to develop this intuition.

You may have heard some stories in the media about how the Internet is full of criminals. Thankfully, these stories are exaggerations. In a typical city (to continue our analogy), most people behave themselves; if they didn't, the city would collapse into chaos. There are always some troublemakers, but they are vastly outnumbered by responsible citizens. The Internet is the same way. Most users behave themselves, but there are some who use the Net to prey on other people. Some of these troublemakers are just annoying; others are a more serious threat.

This book is about the troublemakers: the *scammers*. Their numbers are small, but we can't completely ignore them. We can, however, take simple precautions to keep them away.

The Internet has risks.

The most common risks are not the ones that get all the media attention. Most of us will never run into the evil "hackers," spies, pedophiles, and bomb makers that generate such excitement in the press. In truth, such people are an *extremely* tiny fraction of the Net population. (Just as criminals are a small fraction of a typical city's population. One criminal can make a lot of headlines, but most people are not criminals.)

There are some practical risks, however, to participating on the Internet. For instance, did you know:

- The "private" electronic letters you write to friends can be intercepted and read by other people?

- A dishonest user can pretend to be you and commit rude or harmful acts in your name?

- Misleading and false advertisements are distributed on the Internet every day?

- Annoying users can waste your time and money by filling your electronic mailbox with junk mail?

Most of the people and services that you encounter on the Internet are legitimate. Nevertheless, if you go online without being aware of the risks, you might be unpleasantly surprised someday if you are the victim of an Internet scammer. The dark side of the Internet may be small, but it exists.

Scams can flourish on the Internet.

Why might the Internet be attractive to scammers? There are several reasons.

Anonymity
>Scammers can conveniently disguise their identity by hiding behind pseudonyms, making them difficult to trace.

High turnover
>New users are arriving on the Internet all the time. Eager for action and excited by the newness of the Net, these users are unaware of common scams, even ones that have been floating around the Net for years. If a scammer makes a mistake and develops a bad reputation, he knows that in a few months, there will be new users that have never heard of him, and he can begin scamming again.

Low cost
>For the first time in history, anybody can broadcast astounding amounts of junk to millions of people at little or no cost to the sender. (Frequently, the victims pay for it.) A

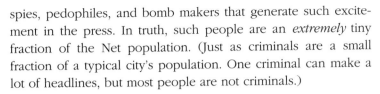

Online service providers

The Internet is often misunderstood by the media (and our lawmakers) who think it's an online service like CompuServe, America Online, and Prodigy. But it's not: it's just a bunch of wires that connect millions of computers worldwide, the same way that telephone wires connect millions of phones. Some Internet computers offer interesting and useful services, like the stock quotes and movie reviews mentioned earlier, but the Internet itself is just the means of transmitting this information.

In contrast, online services are like package deals: they give you computer access, their own set of useful services, and in many cases, access to the Internet so you can contact other computers. So, many online services are connected to Internet, but the Internet is not itself an online service. It's important to understand this distinction because news stories often get it wrong, crediting or blaming "the Internet" for events that happened on an online service.

Finding your way around the Net is like finding your way in a strange country.

There are maps—indexes like Yahoo or the Whole Internet Catalog. There are people who give you personal recommendations—a coworker points to a site that helps with a work problem or a friend recommends a site on your favorite musical group. And there are chance finds: what you see when you follow up on a link or when you read a newsgroup for the first time.

Olivia Bogdan

scammer can plunk down $14.95, join an online service, and cause a lot of grief.

Timeless tactics

Some of the scams on the Net are similar or identical to those found in other parts of life. These scams are very sneaky and have been refined for years (or even centuries). When they occur on the new and mysterious Internet, though, they may be hard to recognize.

A false sense of community

When you meet other users, you know them only through their words on the screen. As a result, it's tempting to believe that these people are a lot like you and to trust people whom you have never met in person. This trust is the foundation for many great things on the Internet, but it also provides a ripe environment for scamming.

The Internet is populated by users on computers.

Before we dive into further details about the Internet, let's cover some common words and phrases. A person on the Internet is called a *user*. Every user has a name, called a *username* or *login name*. Some examples of usernames are *amy*, *cooldude*, *wombat*, and *an54961*. Usernames can be pretty much anything you want, and your system administrator might let you choose your own, as long as it is unique on your computer system.

A username identifies you to a computer. By providing your username and a secret *password* to the computer, you "prove" your identity and are then permitted to use the computer's programs and disk space. This activity is called *logging in*.

Once logged in, you can use the computer for running programs and storing data on the computer's disks. Together, your username and your online data define your *computer account* (sometimes just called your "account"). Many users think of their account as their "home" on the computer, where they store their files and do their computing.

Every computer on the Internet has a unique name. A computer name looks like words separated by dots. Some examples are *watson.ibm.com* (a computer at IBM), *pc37.cs.umass.edu* (a PC in the Computer Science department at the University of Massachusetts), and *ftp.funet.fi* (a computer at FUNET, the Finnish University and Research Network in Espoo, Finland). For those unfamiliar with usernames and computer names, the appendix provides a crash course.

The organization that provides your computer account is called your *online service provider*. Examples of online service providers are universities, companies, and online services like America Online, CompuServe, and Prodigy.

Internet communication takes many forms.

On the Internet, communication is everything. You can interact with other users and obtain information from Internet computers in many ways. The rest of this chapter presents an overview of the major forms of communication—and the risks that they entail—on the Internet:

Electronic mail
  For sending messages directly to another user

Usenet news
  A worldwide set of public discussion groups, or *newsgroups*

The World Wide Web
  An information source in which text, images, and sound are organized into convenient "pages" for browsing

Gopher
  Similar to the World Wide Web, but containing only text

Live chat
  A forum where two or more people communicate in real time, typing simultaneously

FTP
  A method of transferring files quickly between computers

Finger
  Not really a method of communication, but a way of finding out information about other users

Electronic mail is for sending messages directly to other users.

Electronic mail, or *email,* is the most common way for users to communicate on the Internet. It works a lot like ordinary,

Users are real people

The Internet is not a game or a toy, and the other people out there are all real people. That means the risks aren't really any different from leaving your house and going out among people in real life. You could get pickpocketed, you could get hassled, you could anger people, and you could be angered. You could have an accident, or get into a fight—these things are all possible online too, and the common sense you need to exhibit in real life carries over well to the online world.

Abby Franquemont-Guillory

postal mail, except that email is much faster. On a good day, an email message can reach a user halfway across the world in a matter of seconds.

Email is like a cross between postal mail and a telephone call. Using a computer program called an *email program*, you compose a message you want to send to another user. You also specify who should receive the message by giving the recipient's *email address*. Finally, you use your email program's **send** command, and the message is sent rapidly across computer cables and phone lines to its intended recipient. The message is then stored in the recipient's *electronic mailbox,* which is a file on the recipient's computer. The recipient can then read the mail at his or her leisure.

Every user on the Internet has an email address for receiving email. An email address usually looks like a username, followed by an "at" symbol (@), followed by the name of a computer. For example, the user *zelda* with an account on the machine *apple.com* has the email address *zelda@apple.com.* The appendix has more details about email addresses if you want to learn more.

When other users send email to you, you can read it with your email program. The figure below shows a typical email message. Email programs also let you reply to messages, save them, print them, delete them, or forward them to other users.

```
From:  strand@gg.viking-products.com (Rob Strand)
To:  kc@dirdam.com (Kathy Callow)
Subject:  Meeting next Tuesday?
Date:  Wed, 19 Jul 1995 14:13:13 - 0400

Hi Kathy - it was nice to meet you at the conference
last week. Would you like to get together to discuss
those marketing reports you mentioned?  I'm free
next Tuesday afternoon if you are.  Just let me know.

-Rob
```

sender — From: strand@gg.viking-products.com (Rob Strand)
recipient — To: kc@dirdam.com (Kathy Callow)
subject — Subject: Meeting next Tuesday?

text body — Hi Kathy...

signature — -Rob

A typical mail message

Email can be sent to many users at once.

When you send an email message, you aren't limited to a single recipient. Most email programs let you send a single message conveniently to any number of users.

Some people use this idea to create *mailing lists*, in which a group of people can broadcast email to everybody else in the group by sending to one email address. For instance, if you are interested in scuba diving, you could create a mailing list for other scuba divers on the Net. Once the mailing list is set up, then whenever anybody sends an email message to the mailing list address (say, *scuba-list@your.machine.net*), it is automatically forwarded to every user on the mailing list. Setting up a mailing list might require the help of your system administrator.

Electronic mail has risks.

Because electronic mail seems to travel directly from one user to another, people mistakenly believe it is private. In fact, it is not, and we will discuss this extensively in Chapter 2. Your email can be intercepted, read, modified, or destroyed by other users.

Email carries other risks as well. Spoofing, also discussed in Chapter 2, allows other people to send email in your name, pretending to be you. Junk email, discussed in Chapter 7, can waste your time, money, and computing resources. Email also can sometimes get lost in transit, causing a misunderstanding between users who are trying to work out a deal. Chapter 11 offers advice on clearing up such problems.

Usenet news is a set of public discussion groups.

Electronic mail is fine for holding discussions when all participants are known in advance. Sometimes, however, you'd like to open a discussion to all interested people on the Net. This is what Usenet is all about. Usenet is a collection of computers worldwide that allow people to hold convenient, public discussions. These discussions are called *Usenet news*. Not all computers on the Internet are part of Usenet, but many are. Usenet news is also found on some non-Internet computers.

Tired of the hype

I wonder when they'll do a show called "Locks Can Be Picked" about how police around the world have discovered that the locks people use on their homes aren't all that safe, and can be picked or, in some cases, the doors simply forced open.

Andrew Kantor, Senior Editor,
Internet World

A variety of information

Usenet news comprises thousands of discussion groups, called *newsgroups*. Each newsgroup has a specific topic. Whether you want to talk about chemistry, alternative music, feminism, or your favorite television show, there's a newsgroup for you. Using a computer program called a *news-reading program*, you can subscribe to newsgroups, read the articles, and write your own articles. Contributing your own article is called *posting*. (The articles themselves are sometimes called *posts*.) When you post an article, copies are transmitted throughout Usenet for other people to read. A typical Usenet news article is shown in the figure below.

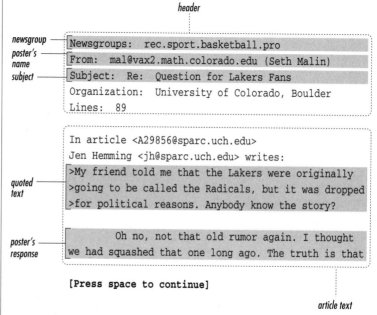

A typical Usenet news article

Newsgroup names indicate their topics. The names look like a bunch of words separated by dots. For example, *rec.music.classical* is the newsgroup devoted to classical music. As you read a newsgroup name from left to right, the topic becomes more specific. In the name *rec.music.classical*, for example, the leftmost word, *rec*, indicates the topic is a recreation. The next word, *music*, indicates that the recreation is music. The final word, *classical*, indicates that the music is classical music.

If you are a BBS user, Usenet news might look similar to the discussion groups or "boards" you'll find on BBSes. Usenet's audience, however, numbers in the tens of millions, and there are about 15,000 newsgroups. (Most computers don't carry every newsgroup, though.)

Usenet has risks.

In some ways, reading Usenet news is like reading a magazine or newspaper. Like these traditional publications, Usenet news offers "subscriptions" (to newsgroups) and contains articles on a variety of topics.

This analogy, however, should not be taken too far. Usenet news is significantly different from a newspaper or magazine for an important reason. Magazines and newspapers generally have editors who examine articles before they are published. In contrast, most Usenet newsgroups have no editor. (A small number of newsgroups have an official *moderator* who accepts and rejects articles.) In other words, people can post anything they want. It's not unusual on Usenet to see exaggeration, insults, errors, hoaxes, outright lies, and even illegal statements intended to mislead people.

Most articles on Usenet are harmless, and on the whole, Usenet news can be very entertaining and thought-provoking. In fact, the lack of editors is beneficial because it lets everybody have an equal opportunity to join the discussion. Nevertheless, it is important to be able to recognize misleading articles so you don't get fooled or scammed. What kinds of Usenet news articles are potentially harmful? Forged articles, discussed in Chapter 2, can appear in your name even though you didn't write them. "Get rich quick" schemes, discussed in Chapter 3, are designed to trick you with outlandish claims of instant wealth. Deceptive advertisers, discussed in Chapters 4 and 5, try to mislead you about products and services. Pranks and hoaxes, discussed in Chapter 7, can fool or embarrass you. Spammed articles, also discussed in Chapter 7, can waste your time, money, and disk space.

The World Wide Web combines text, pictures, and sound.

The *World Wide Web* (sometimes called "www" or "the Web") is a way of communicating words, pictures, and sound on the Internet. Information on the Web is organized into "pages,"

Sample Usenet newsgroups

Macintosh computer graphics
comp.sys.mac.graphics

Vietnamese social culture
soc.culture.vietnamese

Children's books
rec.arts.books.childrens

Fans of Madonna
alt.fan.madonna

Bicycles for sale
rec.bicycles.marketplace

Information for new Usenet readers
news.announce.newusers

called *Web pages,* that are much like the pages of a magazine. The figure below illustrates a typical Web page.

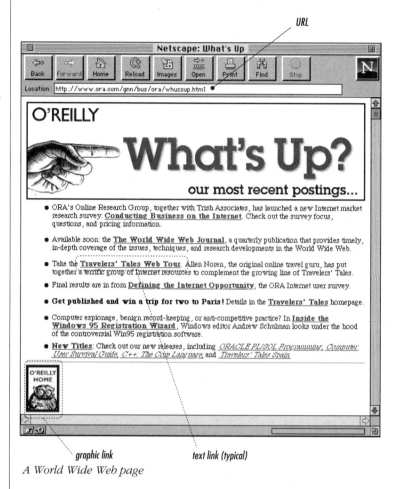

A World Wide Web page

Using a Web-browsing program (or *browser*) like **Mosaic** or **Netscape**, you can navigate from Web page to Web page using a convenient, point-and-click user interface. For example, suppose you are reading a Web page about popular music. Click on the name of your favorite band, and a new Web page appears, displaying the band's CDs. Click on an album cover, and a new Web page appears, listing the tracks on the album. Click on a track name, and the music is played through your computer's speakers.

A *link* is a word or picture you select on a Web page, usually by clicking your mouse on it, leading you to a new page. Web pages and their links are usually organized logically, as in our music example, but they don't have to be. If somebody wants to make a silly Web page combining music, wristwatch design, and lunch meat, this is perfectly OK.

Web pages are created by interested users and organizations around the world. Each Web page you view might be stored on your local computer, or it might come from another computer far away. The beauty of the Web is that you don't have to care where the pages are kept. Just select a link, and the associated Web page will pop up on your screen, even if it has to be transmitted from a computer that you've never heard of on the other side of the globe. Depending on who your online service provider is, you might be able to create your own Web pages as well, complete with links to other pages.

Every Web page has a unique name, called a *Uniform Resource Locator,* or URL, so it can be located. Usually, this locating is done automatically when you select a link, but sometimes you'll want to jump to a particular Web page directly, using its URL. URLs can look pretty cryptic. For example, the URL below leads you to the main Web page of O'Reilly & Associates:

```
http://www.ora.com
```

For the purposes of this book, you don't need to understand the language of URLs. All you need to know is how to tell your Web browser program to connect to a desired URL. Usually, this is as simple as running your browser's **Open URL** command and typing the URL. (All URLs listed in this book are correct at press time, but be aware that they often change.)

The World Wide Web has risks.

Like the information found on Usenet, the words, pictures, and sounds on Web pages are not subject to any editorial process. Any user can make a Web page containing anything he or she wants. So while the vast majority of Web pages are harmless and entertaining, some are not. If you encounter a Web page that contains strange or confusing claims, it pays for you to be skeptical.

Some of the risks found on Usenet can also be found on the Web, including "get rich quick" schemes, false advertising, pranks, and hoaxes.

The Internet has no central computer

...indeed, there is no centre at all. Far from being a hub with spokes, the Internet is more like a spider's web, with many ways of getting from point A to point B.

Christopher Anderson,
"The Accidental Superhighway,"
The Economist, July 1995

Gopher is like the Web, but displays only text.

Another information source similar to the World Wide Web is *Gopher*. Gopher is more limited, however. It uses only text, whereas the Web also has pictures and sound. Gopher links are also less sophisticated. They appear as a menu of choices, shown in the figure below, and you select from the menu.

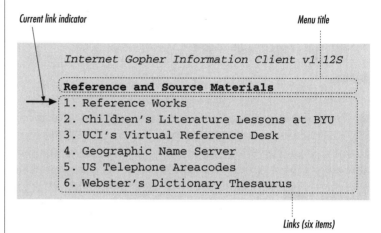

Current link indicator   Menu title

```
       Internet Gopher Information Client v1.12S

    ┌─────────────────────────────────────────────┐
    │ Reference and Source Materials              │
→   │ 1. Reference Works                          │
    │ 2. Children's Literature Lessons at BYU     │
    │ 3. UCI's Virtual Reference Desk             │
    │ 4. Geographic Name Server                   │
    │ 5. US Telephone Areacodes                   │
    │ 6. Webster's Dictionary Thesaurus           │
    └─────────────────────────────────────────────┘
```

Links (six items)

A typical Gopher display

Gopher was developed before the Web came into existence, and it is still used heavily, but the Web is likely to replace it eventually. Web browsing programs can already access Gopher data (so you don't need to learn a separate Gopher program), and many computers with Gopher data are switching over to Web pages.

Live chat lets you talk with others in real time.

All the communication methods we've discussed so far let you edit your words before other people see them. Whether you are sending email, posting a Usenet article, or designing Web pages, you can work at your own pace and correct your mistakes. In short, you produce a finished document before making it available to the Net.

Real life, however, has no backspace key. Words you say in face-to-face conversations or on the telephone cannot be erased. Along these lines, there is a way to communicate on the Net that is similar to a conversation. *Live chat* allows two or more users to speak with each other in real time by typing on their keyboards simultaneously. Imagine that you are in a crowded room, surrounded by people, all talking. Now imagine they are typing on keyboards instead, with the words appearing on a large screen for everybody to see. This is what live chat is like (though in truth, live chat is a bit more organized).

Groups of people can hold these electronic discussions in *chat groups*. Chat groups are found on the Internet itself, thanks to programs like *Internet Relay Chat* (*IRC*), and on major online services (i.e., CompuServe, America Online, Prodigy). Chat groups are discussed further in Chapter 8.

If you prefer a more personal conversation with just one other person, there are one-on-one chat programs available as well. The most popular such program, **talk**, is discussed briefly in Chapter 2.

Live chat has risks.

Chatting with other Net users is an entertaining way to meet people and exchange ideas. After you've conversed with somebody on the Net many times, it's easy to feel as if you "know" him or her. In fact, you know only the person's *Net personality*. (And you can't even be sure of the "him" or "her" part!) Important aspects of a person's behavior cannot be determined by chatting on the Net. Chapter 8 discusses these issues of knowing your Net friends.

Some parents might be concerned about having their children participate in live chat. Although some of the Internet risks to children have been overhyped by the media, live chat can be confusing to kids who don't understand how to be cautious with strangers online. Chapter 9 discusses these issues.

FTP lets you transfer files between computers.

File Transfer Protocol, or *FTP*, is one of the most common methods for sending files from one Internet computer to another. Using simple commands like **get** and **put**, users can download

and upload files between their local computer and a second, remote computer.

Normally, to use FTP, you'll need an account on both comput-ers involved. Some computers, however, are set up to let anybody download (and occasionally upload) files. These com-puters use a variety of FTP called *anonymous FTP*. The computers themselves are called *anonymous FTP sites*, or some-times just *FTP sites*. Anonymous FTP sites are generally used for uploading and downloading freely distributable files, such as freeware and shareware programs. Simply log in using the user-name *anonymous*, give your email address as the password, and you're ready to transfer files. Throughout the book, we'll mention anonymous FTP sites where interesting files can be found.

There aren't really any new risks associated with uploading and downloading files using FTP. As with Usenet news and Web pages, you should be skeptical of any information that you download that seems too good to be true. You should also use virus protection software to check out any computer pro-grams that you download.

You can locate other users with finger.

If you want to find out information about another user, the **fin-ger** program may help you. **finger** displays a user's real name, username, last login time, and occasionally other information like address and telephone number. To use it, type

```
finger person@computer_name
```

to get information about the user with the username *person* at the computer *computer_name*. You'll see a display similar to that shown below.

```
Login name: vern                    In real life: Adam Vernique
Directory: /users/vern              Shell: /bin/ksh
On since Jul 23 12:58:27 on console 12 minutes Idle time
Mail last read Jul 23 12:22:28 1995
```

A typical finger entry

Don't be surprised if **finger** fails from time to time. Some users don't have **finger** entries, and some system administrators disable "fingering" of their computers for security or privacy reasons.

Our list of Internet communication methods is not complete.

We've discussed only the methods you need to understand this book. For the sake of completeness, we'll mention a few more. *Video teleconferencing* allows a live video signal to be transmitted between computers, so you and your friends can see and hear each other as you speak. *Remote logins* let you connect one computer account to another. *WAIS* lets you search large databases on other computers. *UUCP* is another method of transferring files between computers. The list goes on and on.

For more information...

This chapter gives only a brief introduction to the Internet. If you'd like more detailed information on the Net, there are dozens of books available. A popular book from O'Reilly & Associates is *The Whole Internet User's Guide & Catalog*, by Ed Krol. If you have World Wide Web access, you can check out the online version of the catalog. Its URL is:

```
http://gnn.com/wic/
```

An excellent, hype-free overview of the Internet and its history is "The Accidental Superhighway," an article in the July 1995 issue of *The Economist*. The article is also available at:

```
http://www.economist.com/internet.htm
```

The Usenet Info Center provides an overview of Usenet and descriptions of many Usenet newsgroups. It's accessible at:

```
http://sunsite.unc.edu/usenet-i/
```

Many Usenet newsgroups have a Frequently Asked Questions (FAQ) document explaining the most common topics covered in the newsgroup. Many FAQs are available at the Usenet Info Center, and they can also be obtained by anonymous FTP from the machine *rtfm.mit.edu,* in the directory */pub/usenet.* IRC, the popular live chat service, is documented on the Web page:

```
http://www.kei.com/irc.html
```

A brief introduction to FTP can be found at:

```
http://ftp.wustl.edu/~aminet/ftpfaq
```

Net experts aren't panicking

For many years, the Internet was populated mainly by universities, large corporations, and the military. So these are the people most familiar with the Internet. Right now, while these media scares are going on, how much complaining have you heard from these experts? Almost none. All the panic is coming from the newcomers: the people who understand the Internet the least. That should tell you something.

Quick Reference

for your computer account

My username is _____ .

(Don't write down your password!)

My computer name is _____ .

My Internet email address is_____

_____ .

My email program is _____ .

My Usenet news-reading program is _____

_____ .

My Web-browsing program is _____

_____ .

My live chat program is _____

_____ .

I can transfer files between Internet computers using

the program _____

_____ .

I can locate other users with the program _____

_____ .

NOTES:

Welcome to the Internet!

CHAPTER 2

Protecting your privacy

No information is truly private on the Internet.

On the Internet, *nothing is private*. This simple statement might make you wonder if your author has lost his mind. What about passwords? File permissions? Data encryption? Don't they protect you? Well, yes and no. Each provides limited protection; perhaps enough to make you feel secure when you log into your account. Passwords, however, can be guessed by cleverly written programs. File permissions can be overridden by your system administrator. And anything you type on your keyboard (over a network) can be seen by a *packet sniffer*, a device or program used for monitoring networks, so your data can be read by someone else even before you encrypt it.

This chapter introduces the notion of privacy on the Internet. We'll begin by discussing some general issues about privacy. After that, we will raise and answer three major questions.

What is at risk?
　You might take for granted that your computer account is private, when in fact it is not. We will examine nine Internet privacy issues and their associated risks.

What is within your control, and what is not?
　Some aspects of privacy can be affected by you, and some

100% security?

The only secure computer is one that's disconnected from all networks—especially power.

Mike Meyer

cannot. (Some are controlled by your system administrator, for example.)

What can you do to protect yourself?

What safeguards can you use to help ensure your privacy, and what can you do if your privacy is violated? Keep in mind that nobody can guarantee 100% privacy on the Internet, but we'll provide many tips on how to increase your privacy.

Crackers break into computers.

A *cracker* is a malicious person who uses password-guessing programs, packet sniffers, or other means to break into another person's computer account or otherwise defeat the security of a computer. Crackers look for weaknesses in computer hardware and software to find ways to break in. Such a weakness is called a *security hole.*

The media sometimes uses the word *hacker* instead of cracker. This is unfortunate. You see, "hacker" was originally a term of respect, given only to the most creative, clever computer users or programmers. Through misuse, the word now has a derogatory meaning in the minds of the public.

There are three kinds of crackers, according to Steven Bellovin, a network security specialist for AT&T (Associated Press, February 17, 1995). The most common is the "cookbook" cracker. Cookbook crackers are not knowledgeable; they just collect tricks or "recipes" from other crackers and try them out.

The second kind of cracker is the "creative show-off." These crackers use their own knowledge to break into computer systems, but only for fun, not for profit.

The third kind of cracker is the "professional." These crackers use their own knowledge to break into computer systems for profit, espionage, or other serious purposes. There's really no way to prevent a determined, professional cracker from breaking into your account. Fortunately, there aren't many of them.

Your first defense is "safety in numbers."

Nobody knows exactly how many people use the Internet, but current estimates put the number of users somewhere in the tens of millions. With such a large population, it is unlikely your computer account will be singled out and attacked by a cracker. This fact is sometimes called *safety in numbers*; that is, because the Net is so big, the odds of anything bad happening to any one person are small.

So most of the time, you don't need to feel paranoid, looking over your shoulder, constantly wondering if an evil cracker is about to erase all your files. Some irresponsible journalists have recently overhyped the dangers of the Internet, making it seem as if crackers are everywhere. This is false. Every city has its criminals, but they are a small segment of the population. So don't stay home and cower in fear. Explore and enjoy the Net.

Safety in numbers, however, is not a complete defense against harm. In a large city, you still take precautions to lower the odds of being attacked: lock your doors, don't walk alone at night, and so on. There are similar precautions you can take on the Net, as we shall see. Also, as computers get faster, your safety in numbers gets weaker. A single cracker, using a very fast computer, can search through large portions of the Internet to find computer accounts that look easy to crack. The tips in this chapter will help you to make your account less noticeable to crackers. Finally, if you store high-risk information (credit card numbers, trade secrets) on an Internet-connected computer, and other people know that the information is online, then of course your chances of being noticed or robbed on the Net are increased.

Your second defense is "security through obscurity."

In the past, computer software was harder to use than it is today. "Ease of use" is a good thing in general, but the difficult software of the past had a hidden benefit. Because specialized knowledge was required to use computers well, the average user didn't know enough about networking and security to make problems for other users. This concept is called *security through obscurity*; that is, if software is really hard to figure out, then very few people will abuse it. (By analogy, the locks on our doors are effective because few people know how to pick them.)

Today's networking software still has some murky corners that require specialized knowledge to understand, but on the

Once I lost my temper with someone and sent email to her that was not pretty. A year later, the very email I sent ended up on an Internet computer, readable by anybody, in a file owned by the woman. It included a series of discussions we had had, and they had been changed to reflect favorably on her and very poorly on me. A friend of mine saw this file, which happened to be named with my name, and downloaded it for me. It was quite distressing.

Mara

whole, it's easier to use than before. As a result, more and more users can mess up a network, either accidentally or intentionally. Much software used for electronic mail, Usenet news, and other Internet communication still operates on the principle of security through obscurity. As a result, there has been a marked increase in certain kinds of Internet abuses. For example, *spamming,* the posting of large numbers of duplicate Usenet news articles, has increased so much it is practically a business. (Chapter 7 discusses spamming in detail.)

It doesn't take much to remove obscurity.

A single, clever user can strip away the obscurity of a program, making it easy to use for thousands of people. Take electronic mail, for example. Email travels from computer to computer thanks to a special email language all Internet computers understand. Very few users know this language because they don't need it: today's user-friendly email software hides these obscure details. If the language is abused, however, a user can send fake electronic mail.

In 1990, I was teaching an introductory computer programming course at The Johns Hopkins University when I got a telephone call from the computer system staff. *Dozens* of my students were sending fake electronic mail! How could this happen? Well, one clever person on the Internet figured out how to send fake email and wrote an easy-to-use program to let anybody do it. The program spread rapidly on the Net, and half my class had copies, even though none of them understood how it worked. In effect, I had a class full of cookbook crackers.

Such cookbook methods can cause much more serious problems than a bit of fake email. Consider computer viruses. Thousands exist nowadays, even though they require some special knowledge to create. Or at least they used to require it. George C. Smith, in his book *The Virus Creation Labs: A Journey into the Underground,* discusses how one anonymous programmer removed the obscurity. The programmer wrote and distributed an easy-to-use software package called Virus Creation Laboratory that lets just about anybody create a virus. Gee, thanks. I've also heard that cookbook viruses occasionally are advertised in electronic hobbyist magazines.

Another serious example occurred in April 1995, when Dan Farmer and Wietse Venema released a novel computer program called "Security Administrator's Tool for Analyzing Networks," or SATAN. SATAN helps computer operators locate security holes so they can be repaired. Farmer and Wietse, however, did two controversial things with this program. First, they gave SATAN a very simple user interface so even novices could use it. And second, they released the program freely on the Internet for anybody to download and use. This meant that just about anybody could use SATAN to find and exploit security holes in other people's computers. Needless to say, many security experts were angry with Farmer and Wietse for effectively putting guns in the hands of children. But what's done is done.

The days of relying on security through obscurity are nearly over. It is time to build more secure networking software to replace what we have now.

Privacy comes in all shapes and sizes on the Net.

Some privacy concepts are obvious even to beginning users, such as the secrecy of your password, but others might surprise you. To guide our discussion of privacy for the rest of this chapter, here are nine important issues that you should be aware of on the Internet. These privacy issues are not rights; that is, they are not completely guaranteed by law or by the software you use. Instead, they are important categories of privacy every Internet user should know.

Your email address
This is usually publicly available on the Internet.

Your real name
This is often publicly available, though you might have the option of making it private.

Your address, telephone number, and other personal details
These can almost always be kept private, except from your system administrator. If you are not careful, though, this information can be made public without your knowledge.

Your password
The most private piece of data you own. Even your system administrator doesn't know it (though he or she can access your files without it).

Revealing information

Every communication reveals a little bit about yourself. For instance, it may reveal what you're interested in or what kind of computer you own. And more often than not, somebody is collecting that data, or has the potential in the future to collect that data, or is inefficient today at collecting data but will be efficient tomorrow.

Ethan Katsh

Monitoring postings to Usenet

There are now companies who monitor Usenet, chat groups, and Web pages to capture the participants' email addresses. Lists of these addresses are then sold for marketing purposes.

Consider this junk email message sent by a well-known publishing company:

Greetings! We welcome your participation in the following survey. We have selected your email address because it appeared on one of the adult-oriented Usenet newsgroups.

Apparently, the company gathered users' email addresses by scanning postings in the *alt.sex* newsgroups and created a mailing list. Some users call this an invasion of privacy.

Gathering email addresses like this is legal, and there doesn't seem to be anything we can do to prevent it.

Your electronic mail

You might think email is private: you're in for a surprise.

Your files

As long as your password is a secret, your files are relatively safe from crackers outside of your computer. Other users on your computer, however, can read your files unless you learn to protect them.

Your possessions

Some people put lists of their belongings online in a public place. This is a bad idea.

Your time

Your time is valuable. Other users can bother you by making messages appear on your screen. You can often prevent this.

The computer itself

If you leave yourself logged in and walk away from your terminal, somebody else can use your computer account. There are ways to prevent this.

These issues are discussed in the sections that follow.

Your email address is public information.

Usernames and email addresses are almost always publicly available. Every email message you send or Usenet article you post has your email address enclosed. Users around the Internet can sometimes use the **finger** program to find your username. If you interact on the Net, you probably can't keep your username and email address completely private, unless you are a system administrator who can create and delete computer accounts.

Publicly available usernames and email addresses are generally good things, for the same reason that telephone directories are good: so you can locate people that you want to reach. Unfortunately, just as in real life, some people collect names and addresses for other, less desirable purposes, such as building junk mailing lists. Right now, there are companies that monitor particular Usenet newsgroups, record the email addresses of all people who post there, and send them electronic junk mail. For example, a company that sells Macintosh software might build mailing lists of all users who post to the *comp.sys.mac* newsgroups. Fortunately, the junk mail contains the return address of the sender, so you can conveniently tell the company how annoyed you are by its junk! (Assuming that the return address has not been forged; we'll discuss this later in the chapter.)

An anonymous address can provide some privacy.

Sometimes, users have a real need to keep their identity secret. Suppose you want to post a personals ad looking for a romantic partner in the Usenet newsgroup *alt.personals.ads*. You might feel embarrassed if somebody recognizes your name, or you might feel afraid that some creep will harass you. Or suppose you want to participate in a heated Usenet discussion about IBM computers, but you happen to work for an IBM dealership. You might want your identity hidden so people will judge your argument by your words, not by your job. In such cases, it is possible to use an *anonymous address* to disguise yourself.

You can obtain an anonymous address by requesting one from a computer service called an *anonymous remailer*. An anonymous remailer allows you to post Usenet articles with an anonymous return address (e.g., *an19237@anon.penet.fi*) in place of your real email address. If anybody responds to your article by email, the response is automatically sent to your true email address. (Often, the response will be automatically made anonymous too.) To learn how to get an anonymous address, look in any Usenet newsgroup where anonymous addresses are common (such as *alt.personals.ads*). Typically, you'll find instructions at the bottom of every anonymous article.

Note that an anonymous address isn't used for logging in. It is simply an *alias,* or *nickname,* as explained in the appendix.

Anonymous addresses are controversial.

Anonymous addresses provide a way to hide your name for legitimate reasons, such as the ones we discussed above, but they are sometimes used for less honorable purposes. Dishonest users have been known to use anonymous addresses to annoy other people and get away with it. Even worse, they're sometimes used for illegal purposes. Copyrighted materials, such as articles and digitized images from magazines, are regularly posted on Usenet by anonymous users without permission.

Another controversy is that anonymous addresses might not be private after all. In February 1995, one of the most popular anonymous remailers, the computer *anon.penet.fi* in Helsinki, Finland, was raided by the Finnish police with a search warrant. The owner of the machine, Johan Helsingius, facing the seizure of the entire computer, agreed to reveal the identity of one person who used the anonymous remailer. Nobody knows how this incident will affect the use of anonymity on the Net in the future. A Usenet newsgroup, *alt.privacy.anon-server*, is available for discussion of these issues, and a Frequently Asked Questions (FAQ) document is posted there regularly.

Your real name may be public or private.

When you get a computer account, you will almost definitely have to tell your real name to the system administrator before you can use the account. Beyond this, though, you might be able to choose whether your real name is available to other users or not. By default, your real name will probably be accessible via **finger** or similar commands. If this concerns you, talk to your system administrator to find out what options you have.

Some computers allow you to specify a *nickname* (also called a *nick* or *handle*) that is displayed instead of your real name. Some UNIX machines have a program called **chfn** (change finger) to let you alter your online personal information, including your real name. In addition, some Usenet news-posting software lets you specify an alternative "real name" to be used in your articles, though your true email address will still be used.

Choose a good password and keep it secret.

Your password is the most important and effective way to keep your computer account private and safe. I know you've probably been told this a million times already, but please: choose a good password and keep it a secret.

Women in the online world

On the Internet, there are plenty of public forums where people get to know one another through posted articles and electronic chatting. In a noticeable number of these forums, however, the number of men contributing to the discussion appears to be much higher than the number of women. There are exceptions, of course; but in plenty of forums, the participants occasionally scratch their collective heads and wonder why there aren't more women around.

The reasons for this imbalance are not clear. Some people believe that it's because more men use computers. Others maintain that the Net started out male-dominated, and as women now trickle in, they get treated as oddities and quickly leave. Still others say that more women *are* on the Net, but they use male-sounding pseudonyms to draw attention away from their gender and onto their words. I have seen some preliminary studies, but nothing definitive.

Whatever the reasons, when a woman speaks up in a traditionally male-dominated newsgroup or chat group, sometimes she finds herself the target of unwanted attention. Some men will respond to her not only to discuss her words, but also to ask about her age, her address, her physical appearance, or just "how great it is finally to have a woman participating." She might feel singled out for her gender, not her ideas, and this can be uncomfortable. (Men can be harassed similarly, but in my experience, this is quite rare online.)

In an ideal Internet, everybody would be treated equally, regardless of their gender (or nationality, or religion, or favorite brand of personal computer, etc....). For the most part, the Internet works pretty well as a raceless, classless, genderless society dedicated to the free exchange of ideas. But when it doesn't work this way, some women use other means to get equal treatment.

One popular idea is to choose a username that does not reveal your gender: either a last name, a nongender-specific first name like *sandy* or *lee*, or a genderless word like *chaos* or *wombat*. (My friend Lynn has received quite a few suggestive email messages from men. They quickly give up after discovering that Lynn is male.) On some computer systems, it's also possible to disguise your real name in addition to your username; ask your system staff for details.

Some men "cruise" the Internet using the **finger** command, looking for women who are logged in, and then send bothersome messages to the women's screens (using the **talk** command, for example). There is a women's college in my area whose students regularly complain about such interruptions. If you are the target of this kind of abuse, be aware that many computer systems allow you to disable these messages so people can't bother you. We'll talk more about this in the section, "You can prevent on-screen interruptions."

It is a sad commentary on our society that some women aren't taken seriously on the Internet unless they hide their names or other personal information. Let's hope that more users learn to coexist politely and respectfully with the opposite sex.

What does it mean to choose a good password? It means to pick something that is not in the dictionary, is at least six characters long, and contains some digits or other nonalphabetic characters. If you don't choose a good password, it can be cracked (guessed). People have actually written *password-cracking programs* that are designed to guess passwords. Some of these programs are freely available on the Net. Why? Because security through obscurity is not going to protect people's passwords. Crackers already have these programs, so it makes sense for the good guys to have them too. System administrators can use them defensively by checking the security of their own users' passwords. Any user who has an easily cracked password can be notified to change it.

What does it mean to keep your password a secret? It means not telling it to anybody, not writing it down, and taking care not to be tricked into giving it away. On many machines, passwords are kept online in an encrypted (secret code) format. Modern encryption methods are pretty reliable as long as you choose a password that is hard to guess, as described above.

Maybe you aren't worried about keeping your password a secret because you don't have any files worth stealing. Unfortunately, stealing files is only the beginning of what a cracker can do with your computer account. For example, a cracker can:

- Change your password so you can't log in.

- Post obscene articles on Usenet in your name.

- Send annoying email to anybody on the Net (including your boss and your mother).

- Leave security holes in your account, so the cracker can break in again later, even if you change your password.

- Roam around the entire computer, not just your account, reading other people's unprotected files.

Keep this in mind when somebody "just wants to borrow your account for a few minutes."

Crackers use tricks to steal your password.

Even if you fully intend to keep your password a secret, crackers can try to trick you into revealing it. Here are a number of common password-snatching scams you should know about.

Protecting your privacy

Don't change your password for "testing"

Ellen, a computer professional at a well-known corporation, was sitting at her company workstation one day when she heard a familiar beep, announcing the arrival of new email. To her surprise, it was a letter from her computer system administrator, asking for help.

> Hi El, this is Nancy over in system administration. A few days ago, someone tried to break into our computers, and I'm doing some security testing. Would you mind changing your password to "ABCDEFG" for two minutes so I can run a test? You can change it back to whatever you want afterwards. Thanks a bunch! – N.

Ellen examined the email message carefully. The return address showed that the message was truly from Nancy. In addition, Ellen thought, "There's no harm in changing my password for Nancy. As system administrator, she has access to my files

anyway." So, Ellen dutifully changed her password. Two minutes later, she changed it back and replied to Nancy's email asking how the test went. Nancy's reply was puzzling: "I didn't send you any message, Ellen; what are you talking about?" Confused and suspicious, Ellen hurriedly checked her computer account, but it was too late. The thief had needed only 30 seconds to break in and take a copy of the system password file.

Ellen's experience is an example of a serious privacy violation. By faking an electronic mail message, an anonymous cracker gained access to Ellen's account. Even though Ellen is an experienced computer user who thought carefully before believing the message, she still was fooled. Her mistake was believing that a return email address is always accurate. As we'll see later, this is definitely not the case.

Watching you while you type your password

Simple as it sounds, this is the most common method crackers use to snatch a password. The technique is sometimes called "shoulder surfing."

If somebody is looking over your shoulder while you type your password, just ask them politely to look away.

Fake email from the "system administrator," asking for help

This is what happened to Ellen in the sidebar, "Don't change your password for 'testing.'" When she changed her password as requested, the cracker broke into her account. I know of another user who received mail from the "system administrator" asking him to email the computer's entire password file for "testing." The user believed the mail at first, but then became suspicious and contacted the real system administrator, so no damage was done.

A competent system administrator *never* needs to ask for your password, nor suggest that you use a particular password. If you receive email asking for "help" with "testing" that involves revealing your password or any sensitive information about the computer, contact your system administrator immediately—preferably by telephone or in person.

These kinds of cracker tricks, in which people are fooled into revealing or changing their password, are sometimes called "social engineering" tricks.

A fake command in someone else's computer account

Have you ever borrowed another user's account so you could connect to your own account on another computer (or even on the same computer)? On a UNIX machine, this means running **telnet, ftp, rlogin,** or **su** from somebody else's account. All of these programs have something in common: they can require you to type your password.

If you have ever done this, you took a risk. When you use another person's account, that person can sneakily substitute his *own* versions of the programs you normally use. For example, if you use **telnet** to connect to your account and type your password, the other person could have created his own version of **telnet** that remembers your password after you type it! In other words, when you use another person's account, you have no guarantee that the programs you run are the same as those you normally use. They could be clever fakes: sometimes called "trojan horses" because they contain an unexpected surprise.

To be safest, do not use another person's account. If you must use one, do not run any program that requires you to type your password.

A fake login prompt

When you are ready to log in, most computers prompt you for your username and password:

```
Login:
Password:
```

Suppose, however, that a cracker wrote a computer program that *looked just like* the login prompt above. If you typed your username and password, the cracker's program could remember them for the cracker's later use. Does this sound farfetched? Well, it has actually been done; see the sidebar, "The cracking of a university computer system."

There are two ways a cracker can accomplish this trick. The first method is to replace the system login program with a fake, as illustrated in "The cracking of a university computer system." This requires the cracker to gain superuser privileges on the system, which can be quite difficult. As a user, you can't do anything to protect yourself against this risk; you have to trust your system staff to prevent such break-ins.

For the second method, the cracker doesn't have to be a superuser: just have a login account. The cracker simply logs in, runs a fake login program, and walks away from the terminal, hoping the next person who uses it will be fooled by the fake prompt. If you work in public computer rooms, you are at risk from this kind of trick, so here are some safety tips. If you log in using a PC, make it a habit to reboot the PC before you use it. If you use a terminal, however, rebooting won't have any effect on such a program. Instead, disconnect the terminal's network connections before using it. On many terminals, this is done by pressing the `Break` key. (Ask your system staff how to do it at your site.) Afterwards, you can begin a brand new login session.

A packet sniffer

A packet sniffer is a device or program that monitors the data traveling between computers on a network. Crackers can use these devices to watch for the `Password` prompt that

Mitnick's tricks

Kevin Mitnick, the infamous cracker arrested in early 1995, used several ploys for breaking into computer systems. He sent phony "emergency security patches" (bug-fixes) in authentic-looking, shrink-wrapped packaging, to sites that he wanted to invade. When the system staff installed the patches, a security hole was created that Mitnick could exploit.

*Another ploy was to use **finger** to find users who had not logged in for a long time. He would then telephone the Computer Help Desk at a site and hassle the poor user consultant into changing a password for one of these accounts, and then break in.*

Peter Tokmaktchiev, UNIX Systems Support, Imperial Cancer Research Fund, London

Packet sniffers

We continue to receive new incident reports daily about sniffers on compromised hosts. These sniffers, used to collect account names and passwords, are frequently installed using a kit. In some cases, the packet sniffer was found to have been running for months.

Computer Emergency Response Team (CERT) Summary CS-95:02, *The Risks Digest*, Volume 17, Issue 37

appears before you type your password, and then watch whatever you type (even if it does not appear on your screen). Your network administrator is responsible for making sure that sensitive information is kept away from packet sniffers. You can't do anything about them yourself. Luckily, packet sniffers are not commonly used and require specialized knowledge to program.

You might be surprised that I'm revealing these cracker tricks in print. What if a dishonest person reads this book, learns the tricks, and uses them to steal passwords? Wouldn't it be better to keep these tricks secret? This is a controversial point, but as we've seen already, "security through obscurity" doesn't work any more. These cracker tricks are already being used on the Internet, so people are learning about them anyway. Presenting them here helps to educate you, the honest user, so you will be more prepared to avoid them.

Be careful how much personal information you reveal.

A friend of mine (let's call him Dave) is a respected computer science professor at a top-ranked university. One day, I needed to ask Dave a question but couldn't remember his username. So, I used **finger** to find out.

```
finger dave@famous.university.edu
```

A few seconds later, the information I wanted appeared on my screen:

```
Login name: dsmith              In real life: Dave Smith
On since Dec 20 11:17:54        1 hour 15 minutes Idle Time
Plan:
    Office: 234 Hallowed Hall   Home: 123 Hackhaven Blvd
           Famous University          Anytown, MA  01234
           (617) 555-9876             (617) 555-3141
I'll be out of town from January 3-10, so contact my
secretary, jones@famous.university.edu, if you need to get
in touch with me.
```

Thanks to the power of the Net, I now knew some important information about Dave. His username is *dsmith*, he'd been logged in since late this morning...and January 3-10 is a great time to rob his house at 123 Hackhaven Boulevard. Whoops!! Luckily for Dave, I'm not a burglar, so I sent him an email

The cracking of a university computer system

The break-in began in July 1994. The cracker entered through our computer science department computers, and from there he used a packet sniffer to explore the campus, pulling in every password transmitted over our part of the network. Sometime in August, he migrated to our central machine, replacing the system's **login** program with his own (to grab people's passwords) and installing another packet sniffer.

He then used our machines as a staging ground for attacks on others. From what he left behind, he seemed to be a professional. (He'll probably turn out to be a 13-year-old kid.) He knew what he was doing, and he was picking his targets with care. From the organizations and companies that he hit, I suspect that he was trying to obtain data on the construction of nuclear weapons. Welcome to the Internet.

We should have recognized that something was wrong when it happened. Our password propagation software, which lets a user have the same password on multiple machines, had suddenly stopped working. Normally, we would have noticed, but by coincidence, another department on campus had just installed some buggy software that messed up the whole university network. When the network problems were finally repaired, we noticed that our password propagation software was now broken. My partner and I figured that we had screwed something up. But what had really caused the problem, unknown to us, was the break-in.

I spent the rest of the semester, on and off, trying to figure what we had done wrong. Just as we were entering the final exam period, we got our first hint of what had actually happened. We received a frightening message from a large aerospace firm in Tennessee

that had discovered a break-in several weeks ago. They had already been through a cleanup and had left online boobytraps for our friendly neighborhood cracker. The traps didn't work; he was smart enough to realize something was wrong, and he backed out quickly. But they traced him back to my desk.

I started going through the system files on our computer. Among the goodies I found were log files from the cracker's packet sniffer. They contained passwords from machines in every department on campus! I started calling other departments to tell them about their corrupted accounts. I was amazed at how blasé some of the administrators were, as if they figured that nothing could ever hurt them. They turned pale when they actually saw the logs.

Not long afterward, calls started to reach our university from the rest of the world. People across the country were reporting break-ins from our computers. From there, it snowballed. Within two hours, we cut off our computers from the campus network to prevent them from further use by the cracker.

I put in about 90 hours of work in the next five days, reinstalling operating systems from scratch, running programs to check for known security holes, and connecting machines back to the network after they were declared "clean." Install, plug, verify. Install, plug, verify. I really have no clear recollection of the order of events during that week. I don't think I could have kept working without the appreciation and the pizzas that a few professors kept fueling us with. It took another week or so to get everything up and running again.

Jeff, a system administrator

Don't put anything in your finger entry that you wouldn't put on your telephone answering machine.

Peter da Silva

warning about this unwise combination of facts in his **finger** data.

In everyday life, common sense teaches us not to tell strangers the dates that we'll be away from home. The Internet is new and exciting, however, and it's fun to design fancy **finger** information and World Wide Web pages to tell the world all about ourselves. Some users, however, do not think enough about the risks involved. Dave, for instance, simply wanted his colleagues at other universities to be able to reach him during his vacation. Even though he is a computer professional, he didn't realize that unscrupulous people on the Net might use the information to take advantage of him. After all, the majority of the Internet used to be populated by computer professionals. Nowadays, there is no way to predict who is out there looking at you.

Know what to reveal and what to keep private.

It is important to be aware of the risks of revealing too much about yourself to strangers on the Internet. Here are some common examples.

Home address and telephone number
Treat these on the Internet as you would in a telephone book that is distributed to the entire world. I recommend that you don't make this information public. If somebody on the Net needs your home address or phone number, he or she can request them from you by email.

Work address and telephone number
These are generally safe to make public, as long as your employer does not object.

Photograph
Many people put photos on their World Wide Web pages. It's fun to show your Net friends what you look like. Is this risky? It's hard to say. Some women who put their photos on the Web find that they get harassed by men more often. Also, a public photograph can be copied exactly and used by other people, which you might not want. It's up to you. I've decided to put my photo on the Web.

Vacation dates
Never reveal your vacation dates on the Net, since they tell

a thief the ideal time to rob your home. Even if your home address is not available on the Internet, a determined thief can probably find it in the telephone book (if it's listed) or by craftier means.

Credit card number

I strongly recommend that you do *not* send your credit card number to anybody over the Net—not even to legitimate businesses. If you send your credit card number by email, a cracker with a packet sniffer can grab it. (Crackers can use packet sniffers to watch for sequences of digits that look like credit card numbers: e.g., 16 digits separated into four groups of four digits.)

Some people say that this is a small risk when compared with, say, giving your credit card number to an unknown business over the telephone. In my opinion, that's an unconvincing argument. Even if there are larger risks, that doesn't make the smaller ones irrelevant. And if we rely too heavily on "security through obscurity" or "safety in numbers" to protect our credit card information online, eventually we're going to get burned.

Some businesses on the Internet have begun using safer methods for transmitting credit card numbers on the Net so you can purchase things more easily. These methods use *encryption* to convert your credit card number into a secret code that crackers (presumably) cannot decode. Until these methods are proven through widespread use, however, you might want to be cautious about using them. Even if the encryption techniques themselves are unbreakable, the programs that use them may still have loopholes that allow a cracker to capture your keystrokes before they get encrypted.

Social security number

Never reveal this on the Internet. Think of how many companies (your bank, your investment broker, your credit card company, and so on) use your social security number to verify your identity on the telephone.

The safest policy is not to reveal any personal information on the Internet except your email address. If you really want to make it easier for people to contact you by postal mail or telephone, I recommend limiting the information to your work address and work telephone number.

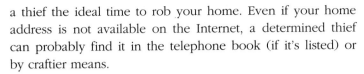

Credit card numbers

Some scams and legitimate advertisements request that you email your credit card number to pay for things, as in this ad from Usenet's *misc.forsale* newsgroup:

> Order Now!! Guaranteed discreet delivery within 4 days. E-Mail Credit Card details to....

Emailing your credit card number to a stranger is asking for trouble.

Electronic mail is not private.

Do you think electronic mail is private? Many people do, and it's easy to understand why. Email messages seem to be sent directly from one user to another. When you send an email message to a friend, you expect that only your friend will receive it. And when you receive an email message, it is kept in your own electronic mailbox.

This might surprise you, but electronic mail is most definitely *not* private. If somebody wants to read your email, there are at least seven ways to do it (not counting just looking over your shoulder). The following figure, "Email can be snooped," illustrates a typical path taken by an email message that you send to a friend.

Rather scary, isn't it? And most users are completely unaware of these risks.

To be fair, it's worth mentioning that system administrators usually behave responsibly and don't snoop into their users' files. (At least this is true of system administrators at major sites, who presumably were hired because they are responsible people. At smaller sites, this might not be safe to assume.) And again, since the Internet is so huge, it isn't likely that your mail will be singled out for snooping. But don't believe that email is private. It isn't. If you have truly secret information to send, ordinary email is not guaranteed to protect your secrecy.

Electronic mail and Usenet news can be spoofed.

Here is another reason that today's electronic mail software is not secure. Another user can pretend to be you and send email in your name. In other words, when the recipient of this email looks at the return address, it appears to be yours. This practice of sending email with a fake return address is called *spoofing* or *forging,* and the resulting mail is called *spoofed mail.*

Some spoofing is done as a practical joke, such as the time my friend Matthew sent me email that was addressed from *God@heaven.com.* Other spoofing can be destructive. In one well-publicized story from late 1994, a cracker pretended to be Professor Grady Blount of Texas A&M University and sent rac-

Email can be snooped

User — User's Terminal — Backup Device — Friend's Terminal — **Friend**

Spool Area — User's Computer — Friend's Computer

Unknown Computer — Unknown Computer — **Internet**

❶ *Using a mail writing program, you compose a letter.* As you type, a packet sniffer can monitor your keystrokes, allowing a cracker to read what you type.

❷ *You send the letter.* Before the letter leaves your computer, it sits in a temporary area of the disk, called a spool area, waiting to be sent. While it sits there, it is possible for your system administrator to read the letter. If the mail software is improperly set up, anybody can read your letter.

❸ *Your letter is sent from your computer to a sequence of other computers and gateways.* Mail probably is not sent "directly" from your computer to your friend's computer. More likely, the letter will travel through a series of other mail-routing computers on the way to its destination. An unscrupulous user on any of these computers can intercept your mail and read it.

❹ *Your letter arrives on your friend's computer.* Until your friend logs in and reads the mail, your letter will sit in an "unread mail" file. It is possible for the system administrator of your friend's machine to read this file.

❺ *Your friend reads the letter.* Eventually she logs in and reads your mail, removing it from the "unread mail" file. As the words of your letter travel from the computer disk to your friend's screen, they can again be captured by a packet sniffer and read.

❻ *Your friend saves your letter in a file.* Did she remember to protect the file? If not, any user on her machine can read it.

❼ *The hard disks on your friend's computer are backed up weekly.* This means that a copy of your letter might get backed up too, probably onto an archive tape. Anybody with access to the backup tapes can transfer your letter back onto disk and read it.

Forgery victim

ist messages to tens of thousands of users. Professor Blount's reputation was seriously hurt. The story about Ellen earlier in this chapter also involves spoofed mail.

Many users are not aware of the risks of spoofed mail. In March 1995, an advertisement was posted on Usenet for a faculty position at a major university. It actually requested that all letters of recommendation should be submitted by email! Can you imagine the potential for abuse? An unscrupulous faculty candidate could spoof some glowing letters of recommendation. I certainly hope this university verifies an applicant's letters before scheduling an interview.

Electronic mail is not the only material that can be spoofed. A malicious user can post Usenet articles in your name as well. I know several users who found their electronic mailboxes full of angry letters after somebody maliciously spoofed a Usenet article in their names, containing the "Dave Rhodes" money-making scam (described in Chapter 3).

How is spoofing done? The hard way is for a cracker to break into your computer account and send email or post articles in your name. Access to your account is not necessary, however, for spoofing to occur. This is because the major email and news software is not secure. It was written at a time when the Net was much smaller; now that the Internet is so huge, security is an increasing problem. Eventually, email and news will be made more secure through better software, but until then, the problem remains.

You can sometimes trace spoofed email back to the spoofer.

It is sometimes possible to locate the true author of a spoofed email message. To do this, you need to look at the complete *mail headers* that accompany the spoofed email. Mail headers are the lines at the top of the email that start with To, From, Subject, and other words followed by colons. Here is an example. Suppose you receive spoofed email from someone pretending to be The Pope. The headers might look like this:

```
Received: by your.computer.net (5.57/Ultrix3.0-C)
    id AA21004; Sat, 4 Sep 93 14:13:58 -0400
Received: by gateway.computer.net (5.57/Ultrix2.0-B)
    id AA17465; Sat, 4 Sep 93 14:13:18 EDT
Received: by bad.cracker.org (5.65c/Spike-2.0)
```

```
        id AA13946; Sat, 4 Sep 1993 14:13:13 -0400
Message-Id: <199309041813.AA13946@bad.cracker.org>
From: pope@vatican.org (The Pope)
To: you@your.computer.net
Subject: Your appointment as Bishop of East Anglia
Date: Sat, 4 Sep 1993 14:13:13 -0400
```

You don't have to understand every word in these headers, but you can learn to look for key phrases. According to the `From` line, the message came from the user *pope* on the machine *vatican.org*. Look at the three `Received` lines, however, and read them from bottom to top (that is, from earliest to latest, based on the dates and times given). They demonstrate that the message actually was sent from the machine *bad.cracker.org*, passed through *gateway.computer.net*, and arrived at *your.computer.net*. The `Message-Id` line also indicates that *bad.cracker.org* was the originating site. Armed with this information, plus the fact that the message was sent on Saturday, September 4, at 14:13 (2:13 p.m.), you can email the postmaster of *bad.cracker.org*, who might be able to figure out which users were logged in at that time. (Contacting a postmaster is discussed in Chapter 11.)

Spoofed Usenet articles can sometimes be traced.

Once again, the headers of the article provide the clues. Let's look at an example of a spoofed article posted in *comp.sys.mac.announce*, a newsgroup for users of Macintosh computers.

```
Newsgroups: comp.sys.mac.announce
Path: your.computer.net!news.your.computer.net!
     gateway.ibm.com!newsfeed.cs.berkeley.edu!
     bad.cracker.org!news
From: gates@microsoft.com (Bill Gates)
Subject: Microsoft Word has been discontinued
Sender: spoofer@bad.cracker.org
Message-ID: <1994Jul29.140845.2989@bad.cracker.org>
Date: Fri, 29 Jul 1994 14:08:45 GMT
Nntp-Posting-Host: bad.cracker.org
```

Although the `From` line indicates the article was posted by Bill Gates at the machine *microsoft.com*, the `Sender` line reveals the true poster to be *spoofer@bad.cracker.org*. The `Message-ID` and `Nntp-Posting-Host` lines also point to *bad.cracker.org* as the originating machine. In addition, the `Path` line confirms *bad.cracker.org* as the originating machine. It lists the computers that the article passed through, in reverse order, before it reached your computer, *your.computer.net*. This is much like the `Received` lines in our email example.

If your mail-reading (or news-reading) software does not display all of the headers in a message, then check your documentation to see if there is an option or command to display them. If not, then save the message to a file, and the full set of headers will probably be saved in the file as well.

Unfortunately, header information might not be reliable.

A knowledgeable spoofer can make every header line look legitimate. Even worse, the spoofer can insert the names of other computers and users, leaving false clues to throw you off the track.

As spoofers get better and better, so do the people who catch spoofers. It is a constant battle.

Your articles can be deleted without your permission.

Have you ever posted an article on Usenet and then wished you hadn't? Perhaps your article contained a mistake or an embarrassing statement that you wanted to remove. Usenet news articles expire (get automatically deleted) eventually—usually after a few days—but what if you want your article to vanish immediately?

Most news-reading software has a **cancel** command that lets you delete an article after you post it. This command sends a special *cancel message* to all the computers that have received your article, causing them to delete their copies automatically.

Unfortunately, cancel messages are not a secure feature. A dishonest user can send a cancel message in your name, much like forging a Usenet article, and delete your articles. Usenet history is filled with stories of "cancel wars" between users who repeatedly tried to silence each other by deleting their Usenet articles. A well-publicized example began in December 1994, when members of the Los Angeles-based Church of Scientology allegedly began canceling Usenet articles that were critical of the Church or that allegedly contained copyrighted Church information. The Church reportedly went so far as to try to remove the entire newsgroup *alt.religion.scientology.* At press time, the issue has not yet been resolved.

If somebody cancels your Usenet articles, there isn't much you can do. With the help of your system administrator, you might be able to locate and examine the cancel message that deleted your article and trace it back to its source, but crackers with enough knowledge to make cancel messages often know enough to make them difficult to trace. The real need here is for better news software that prevents such abuses from happening.

You can usually protect your files from prying eyes.

Do you know whether the files in your computer account are private or if they can be read by other users? If you aren't sure, it's important to find out, either by reading a computer manual or by asking your system staff.

Many computers allow you to choose which of your files are private and which are available to other users. On UNIX, for example, the **chmod** (change mode) command lets you choose which of your files can be accessed by other people. This is called changing the *permissions* on your files. Your computer manual should tell you how to change file permissions on your computer. Don't ignore file permissions: if you do, all your files might be readable by everybody else on your computer…without your knowledge.

Encryption provides more powerful data protection.

Changing the permissions on your files protects them from most other users. The system administrator of your computer, however, has the ability to read or change any file on the computer. Although system administrators are generally responsible people who will not snoop into your files, you may want to increase the privacy of your data. You might also want to send email that only the intended recipient can read. If so, then you should look into *encryption*.

A UNIX privacy tip

*Sometimes I don't want other people on my UNIX machine to know what file I'm editing. Unfortunately, the **ps** command reveals this information. To get around this, I run my editor without any arguments and then load the file from inside the editor. Now **ps** shows only the name of the editor.*

*Similarly, if I don't want people to know what file I'm reading, instead of typing "more filename" I type "more < filename." This makes only "more" show up in the output of **ps**.*

Dan Barrett

Encryption lets you convert your files into a secret code that looks like random garbage. Decoding the files (this is called *decryption*) requires a password. This password can be—and should be—different from your login password. The most popular encryption program is PGP, which stands for Pretty Good Privacy. It is available for many computers. UNIX machines have a program called **crypt** that does the trick too, but it is less secure than PGP. Ask your system staff about the encryption programs available on your computer system. Encryption can also be used to make your email more private. If you and your friend want to exchange encrypted email so nobody else can read it, even if it is intercepted, PGP makes it possible. PGP also allows you to "sign" your email with a special code guaranteeing that you are the real sender. This can help cut down on spoofing, since a spoofer will not be able to sign your email properly. (If you want more details, see the section "For more information" at the end of this chapter.)

In the future, it is likely that all computer data will be encrypted automatically before it gets sent on a network, and decrypted automatically when it arrives at its destination. If this were done, then even packet sniffers could not read what we type. The U.S. government has proposed a special chip for this purpose, called the Clipper chip, that would be installed in computers to do encryption and decryption. The Clipper chip is very controversial, however, because it has a special "back door" that lets the government decrypt anybody's data. In other words, if the Clipper chip is adopted as a standard, the government will be able to listen in on any computer communication. Many computer professionals are opposed to the Clipper chip for this reason. The basic idea, however—automatic encryption that users don't have to think about—is a good one that might prove the solution to a number of privacy issues.

Don't make public lists of your possessions.

In newsgroups devoted to computers, stereo equipment, and other possessions, users often discuss their equipment. In one music newsgroup, the participants regularly upload lists of their compact disc collections onto a public FTP site so they can trade discs. Some users also put lists of their equipment into the signatures at the ends of their public postings and email messages, like this one:

```
*** Cindy Hackhead, hack@cs.mit.edu
*** IBM 100MHz Pentium PC, 2 GB hard disk, 16 MB RAM
*** Hackers make better lovers
```

In these examples, users are freely revealing information about their possessions, some of them quite valuable. I find this strange. Most people wouldn't display a list of their belongings on the front door of their house. Even fewer people would circulate lists of their belongings at the local shopping mall. So why are people so casual about announcing their possessions to the whole world? A dishonest person might see what you've got and decide that it would be nice to rob your home.

"Oh, come on," some of you will say. "That is ridiculous. People talk about their possessions all the time in these public forums. Nobody is going to read about my stereo system and then come and steal it. Most users live hundreds or thousands of miles away from me, anyway."

Well, perhaps that is true…for now. But what will happen in the future, when *everybody* is online, including people who live geographically close to you? Describing your valuables on the Net isn't any different from shouting them into a megaphone in the center of town.

My point is this: if you want to tell the world about your belongings, that's your decision. But please be aware that there is a risk and make a conscious choice about revealing this information. Even if you decide the risk is too small to worry about, at least you've thought about it.

You can often prevent on-screen interruptions.

Your computer time is valuable. Whether you are doing work or just relaxing, your computer time is your own. Certain kinds of programs allow other users to interrupt your work, however. Some new users don't realize these interruptions can be prevented, and they silently suffer through them. Here are the details.

Many Internet computers have a program that lets you "chat" interactively with other users on the same computer or other computers. On UNIX, the programs **talk** and **write** serve this pur-

Harassing messages

*I think most women on Internet have had this joy: a bored guy finds a user with a female-sounding name and starts sending **talk** requests. One time while working on my thesis, I got a series of these **talk** requests, which I ignored, but they kept on coming. Finally, the guy sent me an obscene message, and for a few weeks, he sent me that same lovely message every time I was logged in. I learned how to block **talk**, and I have never heard from the charmer again.*

Lisa Helene
Helfman

pose. When somebody wants to chat with you, a message will appear on your screen, announcing an invitation to chat. This chatting can be a lot of fun, but it can be annoying if people interrupt your work with chat requests. Fortunately, most computers provide a way to prevent all such invitations from appearing on your screen. On UNIX computers, the **mesg** program does the trick. On other computers, the program names may be different. Ask your system staff to find out how to disable these invitations at your site.

Beware of leaving yourself logged in.

Sometimes when you are working in a public computer room, you might leave your computer for a moment while still logged in: perhaps to pick up a printout at the other end of the room. If you do this, beware. An experienced cracker needs only 15 to 30 seconds at your keyboard to create a security hole in your computer account. After this, the cracker can get into your account any time.

So, should you log out every time you go to pick up a printout? No, that is a waste of time. Instead, find out if there is a *lock program* available on your computer. A lock program temporarily locks your keyboard and mouse with a secret password so nobody else can use them. To unlock things later, you type the password. On UNIX machines, the **lock** program serves this purpose. On personal computers, many screen saver programs have this feature. Ask your system staff what lock programs are available at your site.

If you find a security hole, tell your system administrator.

Security holes are bugs or oversights in software or hardware that allow a cracker to defeat the security of a computer. For example, email software has a security hole that allows users to send spoofed email that appears to come from somebody else, as we have seen.

If you use computers frequently, someday you may discover a security hole. If this happens, the best thing to do is tell your system administrator immediately. That means *now*, not tomorrow morning. Your rapid response might mean the difference between a safe computer and a break-in.

Above all, do not experiment with the security hole yourself! In other words, don't try it out "just to make sure" it's really a hole. (If you discovered that your neighbor's front door was unlocked, would you walk in and take a few items, just to make sure it could be done?) If it's a real security hole, and you experiment with it, you might cause damage. Worse, you might alert your system administrator's "watchdog" software that watches for security problems, and you could be mistaken for a cracker and wind up in deep trouble. Just report the problem and let the system administrator do the rest. Even if you are mistaken about the security hole, the system administrator won't mind. If you are curious about the security hole, ask your system administrator if you can watch while he or she checks it out.

Be informed, not fearful.

The intent of this chapter is *not* to reduce you to a quivering mass of flesh, terrified to touch a computer keyboard lest the Evil Crackers steal your very soul. Cracking does happen on the Net, but it is not as widespread as some sensationalistic media reports would have us believe. This chapter exists to help you identify and avoid some common methods crackers use to invade your privacy.

You should come away from this chapter thinking about four basic themes:

Be safe
Choose a good password, protect or encrypt your sensitive files, and don't reveal too much personal information on the Net.

Be aware
Some of your information is public and some is private, so know which is which. Know that email is not as private as people think.

Be critical
Know about spoofing and password-snatching scams so you don't fall for such tricks.

Be realistic
Don't let the fear of crackers stop you from enjoying the many good features of the Internet.

A bizarre security hole

A fascinating privacy violation used to be possible on Sun workstations with built-in microphones. Because of a bug in the operating system, the microphone was active when the user didn't know it, and his speech could actually be heard by other users on the Internet! It sort of gives a new meaning to the term "computer bug."

The safety of your computer account is ultimately your responsibility. Your system administrator can help a certain amount, but beyond that, it's up to you. By remaining informed about Internet privacy issues, you increase your odds of having a safe and happy computing environment.

For more information…

There are many online sources of privacy-related information. Some relevant Usenet newsgroups include *alt.privacy* for general privacy discussion, *alt.privacy.anon-server* for discussion of anonymous remailers, and *alt.privacy.clipper* for discussion of the Clipper chip. *news.admin.net-abuse.misc* also gets some discussion about online privacy issues.

The *Computer Privacy Digest* is an electronic publication with articles contributed by its readers. You can read the digest on Usenet in the moderated newsgroup *comp.society.privacy*. Alternatively, you can subscribe to the digest and receive it by email; simply send the message Subscribe to *comp-privacy-request@uwm.edu*. Back issues are available via Gopher from *gopher.cs.uwm.edu*, via FTP from *ftp.cs.uwm.edu,* or on the Web at the URL

```
gopher://gopher.cs.uwm.edu
```

If you'd like to learn more about using PGP to encrypt your electronic mail or files, check out the PGP FAQ at the URL

```
http://www.smartpages.com/faqs/pgp-faq/top.html
```

For a more thorough discussion, a good book is *PGP: Pretty Good Privacy*, by Simson Garfinkel (O'Reilly & Associates, 1994). This book also describes the history of PGP and the controversy over its use.

Quick Reference

protecting your privacy

My system administrator's name is _____ _____. He/she can be reached at the email address _____ _____ and the telephone number _____ .

I can change my password using the program _____ _____ .

I can change my personal information online using the program _____ .

Anonymous addresses are available from the anony-mous remailer machine _____ _____ .

I should beware of using another person's account to connect to my own account, especially if I must type

my password. Such programs that require me to type my password are _____ _____ .

In our public terminal room, I can disconnect a terminal's network connections by _____ _____ .

I can change my file permissions using the program_____ _____ .

I can encrypt my files using the program _____ _____ .

I can disable other users' invitations to chat using the program _____ .

I can lock my keyboard and mouse using the program _ _____ .

NOTES:

CHAPTER 3

"Get rich quick" schemes

Schemes abound on the Net.

Everybody can use a few extra dollars now and then. How about a few thousand? Advertisements for "money-making opportunities" are widespread on the Internet. These "get rich quick" schemes are not new—some of them have been around as long as we've had mass communication. Probably all of us have seen or received a chain letter at some time, promising great wealth or good fortune, or dire consequences if you break the chain. These schemes play on our desires, promising huge sums of money for very little work and no risk. Such claims are very tempting, but are they true? In many cases, they are not.

Thanks to the plummeting prices of computers and network services, just about anybody these days can get a computer account with Internet access and blast out electronic "get rich quick" ads by the thousand. Several Usenet newsgroups in particular have become fertile ground for these ads. In *misc.forsale.non-computer*, at any given time, it's not hard to find half a dozen or more "get rich quick" offers lurking among the usual ads for cars, skis, and pets. The worst offender for these ads, however, is *misc.entrepreneurs*, a group originally intended for the discussion of business methods and tips. It is positively overflowing with scam advertisements. (Check it out sometime, purely for entertainment value.)

Scams have been around forever

The scams aren't new, just the medium. Some con artists who always used telemarketing, infomercials, newspapers and magazines, and the mail to attract consumers to their investment schemes, now have turned to the Internet and the online services of Cyberspace as the new medium to promote their scams.

Federal Trade Commission
Online Scams: Road Hazards on the Information Superhighway (pamphlet)

Some of the oldest scams on the books are beginning to appear in the new technology of the online world these days, officials warn, posing pitfalls for the unwary traveling along the Information Superhighway.

Ted Sherman, "Snake Oil '95," *New Jersey Star-Ledger*, January 8, 1995

This chapter will help you to identify and avoid these common and cleverly worded "get rich quick" scams. We will cover pyramid and Ponzi schemes, 900 number scams, Internet advertising scams, busy-work scams, and gambling scams. Let's begin with the most famous example on the Net.

Don't believe "Dave Rhodes" can help you "make money fast."

By far the most widespread "instant wealth" method advertised on the Internet is the "Make Money Fast" letter, written by someone calling himself "Dave Rhodes." The letter says that you can make $50,000 or more by "developing mailing lists" and selling them. Inside the letter are the names and addresses of ten people. You are instructed to send one dollar to each of the first five people on the list. After that, you remove the first name from the list, add your name to the end of the list, and then spread ten copies of the updated letter electronically. As the letter spreads, your name will (theoretically) keep moving upward in the list until you are one of the top five people, and then you will start receiving $1.00 contributions from thousands of people. "I have NEVER failed to earn $50,000.00 or more whenever I wanted," says "Dave."

Simple, isn't it? Tempting, too. But it's a fraud.

The "Dave Rhodes letter" is an example of a *pyramid scheme.* It has been widely spread by electronic mail. You'll find it on BBSes and FTP sites in a file called *MAKE.MONEY.FAST* or *QUIK-CASH.* On Usenet, the letter is posted so often (about three times per week, at press time) that it's commonly known as the "MMF" article.

In the following sections, we examine pyramid schemes in detail and see why they cannot work.

Pyramid schemes can be identified by their pyramid shape.

All pyramid schemes are based on the same structure: one person sends money to some number of people (say, five), who each send money to five more people, who each send money to five *more* people...and so on. The figure below illustrates how this structure resembles a pyramid of people. The participants in each *level,* or *generation,* of the pyramid send money to those above them and receive money from those below them. At least in theory. In reality, it doesn't work.

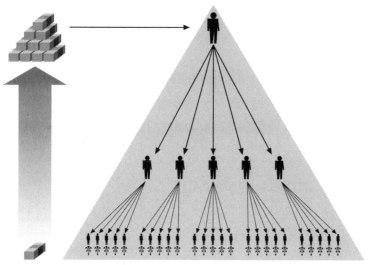

A pyramid with three levels or generations

The amount of money varies, depending on the pyramid scheme. Some of them ask for only a dollar. Others require an expensive "entry fee."

Pyramid schemes cannot work.

Although they sound enticing, pyramid schemes cannot possibly work. Some simple math will show you why. Suppose you send 10 "Make Money Fast" letters to your friends, and they dutifully pass on 10 letters to their friends, and so on. By the time your name reaches the top of the list, nine generations of letters will have been sent. Look how many people are in the pyramid now:

$$(10 \times 10 \times 10 \times 10 \times 10 \times 10 \times 10 \times 10 \times 10) = 10^9 = 1{,}000{,}000{,}000$$

Yes, that's one *billion* people! And one generation later, it will jump up to ten billion people, almost twice the world's population. So, if the pyramid worked as advertised, every person in the world would have to participate, *and* would eventually become rich. You can't have both; where would all the money come from? Space aliens?

Some schemes use smaller pyramids: for example, payment after five generations, with each person recruiting five friends. This pyramid needs to contain only

$$(5 \times 5 \times 5 \times 5 \times 5) = 5^5 = 3{,}125$$

people. Now, three thousand people is a more manageable number, and it becomes almost believable that you can make money, right? Think again. Many people who receive these letters ignore them, breaking the chain. In short, it is very unlikely that all 3,125 of those people are going to make huge bucks.

Pyramid schemes promise quick wealth but don't deliver.

Pyramid schemes promise to make people rich with little or no effort. They often contain fancy "profit charts," like the one in the following figure, to demonstrate that you can earn hundreds of thousands of dollars easily. What they don't tell you, however, is that these profits are almost impossible to achieve.

Profit chart: pyramid scheme with $20 entry fee

Sell to five people	5 × $20 =	$100
First generation	25 × $20 =	$500
Second generation	125 × $20 =	$2,500
Third generation	625 × $20 =	$12,500
Fourth generation	3,125 × $20 =	$62,500
Fifth generation	15,625 × $20 =	$312,500
Earnings		$390,600

Even if enough people could be found to fill in the whole pyramid, these charts assume that nobody ever drops out. This is very unrealistic, because most people who receive pyramid literature ignore it. Let's see what happens to your "profits" in the previous figure as participants drop out. Suppose you send your letter to five people, but three of them are familiar with pyramid schemes and ignore it. Oh well, there goes $234,360 (60%) of "your" money. Maybe one of the remaining people decides to participate, but she erases your name and inserts hers instead. Kiss another $78,120 goodbye. And if the fifth person is forgetful and never gets around to sending the letter, there goes the last $78,120. Easy come, easy go….

"Get rich quick" schemes

Only the scammers profit.

"So," you ask, "if these pyramid schemes don't work, why do scammers start them?" The little-known answer is: because the scammers don't play by the rules. Instead of sending out five or ten letters, scammers send out *thousands* with their name placed first on the list. (This can be done on the Net at almost no cost to the scammer.) The first generation of victims responds by sending money to the scammer's post office box. The scammer closes the box after a short time and then moves on before he can be caught. The letters continue to circulate, but they will not make money for future generations of victims who diligently follow the directions.

Other scammers take a slightly different approach. They charge each participant an "entry fee" that can range from a few dollars to hundreds of dollars. The scammer then disappears with the entry fees, leaving the pyramid to propagate itself into nothingness.

Pyramid schemes are illegal. They promise great wealth to all participants, when only the participant on the first level—the scammer—is likely to make any money.

If you are tempted to participate in a pyramid scheme, don't do it. If you help to spread a pyramid advertisement on the Net, even innocently, it's very likely that somebody will complain to your system administrator, and you might lose your account…or worse!

The "get rich quick" fantasy

Some people perpetually believe in these "get rich quick" methods. But the only people who make money are the ones who start them. That's why they're illegal.

Mike Botts

Pyramids come in many guises.

Pyramid advertisements never say, "Hello, welcome to my pyramid scheme." A scammer will try hard to fool you by describing the pyramid as a different kind of business. Here are examples of some of the many disguises that have used on the Net to camouflage pyramid schemes.

Mailing list sales

This is the classic pyramid. You send money to people on a list, add yourself to the list, and "sell" the list to other people. An advertisement for this type of scam typically discusses how mailing lists are legal and are commonly bought and sold by companies. Don't be fooled: this "mailing list" idea is not legitimate.

Gift giving

Some pyramids try to hide the "mailing list" scheme by calling it "gift giving." One advertisement I received spent several pages complaining about politicians, the national deficit, the economy, and lost jobs. Afterwards, it offered a pyramid scheme as a patriotic solution to protecting our hard-earned tax dollars. By exchanging "monetary gifts" with our friends and families, we could "control the politicians' access to our money" and improve our "economic status."

Advertising by fax

This appears to be a business for sending advertisements via fax machine. On closer inspection, however, it is just the "mailing list" pyramid being operated by fax.

Make money stuffing envelopes

These advertisements claim you can make big bucks by putting letters into envelopes. Guess what's being put inside? Could it be…"mailing lists?" You got it!

Electronic mailing list sales

Welcome to the computer age. "Mailing list" pyramids are now being run with people's names on a computer disk instead of on paper. One recent scam of this type even included a program for printing official-looking "purchase orders" to enclose with your payments to other people in the pyramid. Unfortunately, there was nothing to be purchased….

Shareware sales

This is a variation of the electronic mailing list. You first purchase a computer disk or CD-ROM full of "valuable soft-ware." Each program on the disk is "locked," so a secret code number is required before you can run it. Code numbers can be purchased from your "supervisor" (who sold you the disk). This technique is used legitimately in the software industry, for example, on font CD-ROMs that let you unlock individual fonts for a price.

What happens next, however, exposes the pyramid. Once you have unlocked some software with your supervisor's code number, you can use your *own* code number to "lock" the software and sell it to other people…who will then buy *your* code number, get their own code numbers, and continue the process. So what do we have? A bunch of people buying and selling worthless code numbers. The "valuable software," incidentally, is usually freeware or shareware that is widely available.

Printed reports

These are reports that cover a wide variety of topics, and they are usually offered at a "special discount" price. When you buy them, you are given "unlimited reproduction rights" so you can sell them to other people, who will also have "unlimited reproduction rights," and so on, into infinity....

Worldwide "lotteries"

To enter the lottery, just buy a ticket. In addition, if you pay a special "membership fee" (typically $100 or more), you will receive a percentage of every lottery ticket sale. (Hmmm...) On top of this, you can "sponsor" other lottery members and receive a percentage of their winnings as well. (Voilà: the pyramid reveals itself.) One of these advertisements contained the most outlandish financial claim that I've seen in a scam: a billion dollars a week in ticket sales! (Incidentally, it is against U.S. law to purchase foreign lottery tickets by mail.)

T-shirts

This is one of the most creative pyramid ideas around. At first, it looks like an advertisement for T-shirts. The ad mentions a code number that you must include with your order. When you receive your T-shirt, you are given your *own* code number and permitted to advertise T-shirts. Anytime someone orders a T-shirt using your code number, you're given a percentage of the profits. (A-ha!) Oh, guess what is printed on the T-shirt? Your code number, and an advertisement for the T-shirt. It's funny to imagine a room full of people, each wearing a T-shirt with a different code number, trying to sell T-shirts to each other.

Telephone tricks

A variation of the previous scam uses telephone calls instead of T-shirts. Your job is to convince people to make a toll call to a central telephone number and speak your "code number." Every time somebody does it, you (supposedly) earn a commission, and the caller gets his or her own code number to advertise. The last time this scam was spread on Usenet, the ad claimed that the telephone number was in Canada, but the area code was really from an island off the coast of Africa. No doubt the victims had a big surprise on their phone bills.

A central clearinghouse.

Some pyramids hide their shape by having all the money go to a "central clearinghouse" where it (supposedly) will be distributed later to everybody involved. Sure, sure. You can bet that the "central" address is a post office box that will vanish, along with your money, faster than you can say "Federal Trade Commission."

Some pyramids are disguised as multi-level marketing.

Multi-level marketing, sometimes called MLM or *network marketing,* is a business technique that has a pyramid-like shape. MLM participants, called *distributors,* work as both salespeople and recruiters. As a salesperson, you sell such merchandise as jewelry, cosmetics, and health products to consumers. As a recruiter, you can turn your customers into distributors who, in turn, can sell and recruit more distributors. This network is called your *downline.* To sweeten the pot, you are promised commissions on sales made by the distributors in your downline. The more merchandise they sell, the more money you can make—at least in theory.

Although some MLMs are legitimate, others are nothing more than pyramid schemes, and some fall into a gray area where the distinction is fuzzy. How can you tell the difference? The key question is whether the merchandise has a legitimate market. In other words, is it possible for you and others in your downline to make retail sales (a sign of a legitimate business), or are your profits generated solely or primarily by selling distributorships (a pyramid scheme)?

The Usenet newsgroup *alt.business.multi-level* is dedicated to the discussion of MLM. Many pyramid advertisements are posted there too, unfortunately, and this tends to anger the regular participants.

Ponzi schemes give the illusion of a good investment.

Pyramids are the most widespread "get rich quick" schemes on the Internet, but they are not the only game in town. A similar scheme is called a *Ponzi scheme,* named after the con artist who popularized this scam in the days before computers.

Seven ways to spot a pyramid scheme

Pyramid schemes are often disguised. Watch out for the following telltale signs:

1. Watch out for the phrases "MAKE MONEY FAST," "QUICK CASH," "make money with your PC," or "home business opportunity."

These words are commonly used by pyramid schemers on the Net.

2. Look for a pyramid shape.

Are you supposed to send cash to several people from a list of names? Soon after, will thousands of people supposedly send you money? Then watch out.

3. Look for a product.

Is any actual product or service being sold, or are people just mailing money around? If there's no product or service, there isn't really a "business." Some pyramid schemes include a token product like a printed report, a "mailing list" (the names of other people in the pyramid), a recipe, or a floppy disk full of shareware, but they are still pyramids.

4. Every customer is a salesperson or "distributor."

Look closely: do ordinary customers ever enter the picture, or do all your customers turn into salespeople? If there are no consumers, there is no business.

5. Watch for the phrase "unlimited reproduction rights."

You'll see this phrase in pyramid schemes that use nearly worthless, token products like printed reports and computer disks. It's just an upbeat way of saying "every customer is a salesperson."

6. Look for a profit chart.

These charts are often separated into "levels" that show how much money you will supposedly make as the pyramid grows.

7. Look for claims that "this isn't a pyramid scheme."

Scammers often try to throw you off the track in their literature. They'll say, "all those other offers are just pyramid schemes, but ours really works!" They might even quote a law that (supposedly) makes their business legal. A legitimate business, however, doesn't need to reassure you like this. When was the last time you went to a job interview and were told, "Oh, by the way, we aren't breaking the law." Get real!

In a successful Ponzi scheme, the scammer advertises a terrific-sounding (but fake) "investment" that has a very high rate of return: say, doubling your money in a week. As more and more people send money, the scammer uses the later people's investments to pay the earlier people. Because the early participants actually receive the promised money, the "investment" appears to be legitimate. The scammer gets a great reputation, and the early participants recommend the investment to their friends and even reinvest what they've earned. The number of participants grows and grows until one day, the scammer simply disappears with all the money!

A Ponzi scheme needs a lot of participants in order to pay off the early investors and look legitimate. The Internet provides scammers with a convenient way to advertise to large numbers of people. If you see a "get rich quick" scheme advertised on the Net that promises a huge and rapid return on your investment, remember Mr. Ponzi and be suspicious.

"900" numbers do not equal instant wealth.

Another popular scheme involves "900" numbers: telephone services that charge the caller a high rate (typically one to three dollars per minute) for specialized information. Some Internet advertisements say that running your own 900 number is like owning a miniature gold mine. "Estimates show that 95% of the American public has never called a 900 number," wrote one company in response to my query. "Just consider the awesome business potential." (Oh yes, a business ignored by 95% of the population is a *great* investment. Sign me up immediately!) This ad went on to say that you could rent a 900 number for an unspecified price. "The longer the call and the more times the caller uses your 900 number, the richer you become," it said.

Truth be told, there are thousands of 900 numbers in operation today, so competition is stiff. Some 900 numbers make money; others lose money. As with most businesses, unless you advertise heavily, it's hard to get people interested in calling you. So don't believe that a 900 number will automatically make you rich.

Internet advertising is not a road to riches.

As the Internet becomes more commercialized, advertisements are increasing. Some recent scams are taking advantage of Internet advertising as a hot topic. "REALLY earn MONEY on the Information Superhighway! ...earn up to $500/day with your PC, working from home. This is ABSOLUTELY, POSITIVELY TRUE!" These familiar-sounding phrases begin a letter I received from the creators of a book about "ELECTRONIC MARKETING...THE WAVE OF THE FUTURE!" For $20, you can buy their book on how to get rich posting advertisements on CompuServe, Prodigy, and similar online service providers. (Comparable information has been sold for "OVER $2,000," they claim.)

Another company says that "you, too, can earn at least $100,000 per year (or even more) with your computer, working from your home just a few hours each day." Once again, they insist that Internet advertising is the key to great wealth. "It is so easy—virtually ANYONE CAN DO IT!" Their kit is guaranteed to work, or you get your money back. (Sure, sure.) In addition, you get a "FREE distributorship" for the information that you'll be sent. (Does anybody smell a pyramid here?)

The fact is that advertising is a complicated subject. Companies spend billions of dollars annually studying the population and creating advertisements to boost sales. If a company claims that "anybody" can get rich quickly by posting ads on the Internet, don't believe it. Also, some of the advertising methods described by these companies, such as spamming and junk email (discussed in Chapter 7), are very annoying to users. They're likely to turn off more people than they attract. I've even seen companies lose their Internet access after hundreds or thousands of angry users complained about these advertising techniques.

You won't make millions by doing busy work.

Some "home business opportunities" offer you large sums of money for doing simple tasks at home. "How would you like to earn between $300 and $500 within a short period of time?" asks one. "Well, it can be done easily by simply clipping news-

Practice what you preach

If your "get rich quick" book is so great, why aren't you using it instead of selling it?

Steve Wechsler, in response to a scam ad on Usenet

paper articles part-time from the comfort of your home or dorm." Another advertisement shouts that you can "RECEIVE A PAYCHECK FOR $400.00 PER WEEK AND MORE" for household tasks like assembling stuffed animals.

When you see advertisements like these, take a moment and think about them from a business perspective. What company could afford to pay people "$252.00 a week" for "painting wood calendars?" More than likely, the company will require you to purchase the materials from them in advance, and if you don't paint calendars fast enough, you won't make enough money to cover your costs. Alternatively, they may require you to sell those calendars yourself, and the market is likely to be so small that you'll never recoup your costs.

A computer can't pick winning lottery numbers any better than you can.

Many people dream of winning the lottery. What could be simpler: plunk down a dollar and walk away a millionaire. When computers hit the scene, it didn't take long for people to start writing programs to pick winning lottery numbers. You'll see advertisements for these programs on the Net, filled with promises that they can make you rich. The ads might even have testimonials from people who have used the program and won the lottery.

On the surface, a lottery program can look pretty scientific. It might draw graphs that represent the winning ticket numbers over the years. It might offer you the choice of several different lottery "systems" for picking a number based on previous winners. Some of them are based on the so-called "statistical principle" that if a number has not won for a long time, then it is "due" to win soon.

Unfortunately, all the fancy charts, graphs, and statistics in the world won't allow a computer program to predict which number will win the lottery tomorrow. In fact, *no* computer program can increase your odds of winning the lottery. All such programs are fakes. The winners who gave their "testimonials" are either lying or just got lucky, or the testimonials themselves may be fakes.

Here is an analogy to help you see why a computer program cannot help you win. Imagine that you are in a *gigantic* room,

Eight general tips for spotting a scam

1. Anonymous email addresses.

If the return address of the sender begins with "an" or "anon" followed by a number, like *an98475*, be wary. This is an anonymous address, so the sender's identity is hidden. Anonymous addresses have legitimate uses, but you should be suspicious of anybody who uses one to ask you for money.

2. Post office box addresses.

Sending money to a stranger is risky; sending money to a stranger's post office box is even worse. Sending money to a stranger who uses a P.O. box *and* an anonymous email address is… well…it would be simpler if you just tossed your cash off a cliff.

3. Uncheckable references.

Some scam artists cite newspaper articles and talk show interviews that "prove" their methods. Unfortunately, you are almost never given enough information to find these references. One author of a "home study course" stated that he'd been on "Donahue, Regis, and over 1000 other radio and TV shows." When I asked the author politely for more specific information, it never arrived. Another ad boasted of being awarded "Business Opportunity of the Year." But by *whom*?

4. Lots of CAPITAL LETTERS, dollar signs, and exclamation points!!

This might sound funny, but a surprising number of scam advertisements are loaded with capitalization and punctuation. For three months, I examined the Usenet newsgroup *misc.forsale* and read every article with a capitalized subject line. Between 30% and 40% of them were "get rich quick" advertisements. "MAKING MONEY ON THE INTERNET…I WILL SHOW YOU EXACTLY HOW!!!" shouts one ad. "BUY BELOW WHOLESALE—SELL RETAIL—MAKE THOUSANDS OF $$$," cries another.

5. Hidden costs.

Watch out for advertisers who say that their services are "free" in one breath and then ask you for money in the next. "It won't cost you a penny to get started," states one such advertisement that later asks for $29.95.

6. The offer is available "only to the first 50 people" who respond.

The ad says that only people who are "serious about making money" (who isn't?) need respond, and that later applications will be rejected. What's the real story? The scammer wants you to respond quickly so he can close up shop and skip town with the money.

7. Lots of details about wealth, but few details about the job.

"Get rich quick" ads often spend pages talking about how happy you will be when you are rich. When you look for information about the job itself, though, you'll find little or nothing. Some ads even refuse to reveal any details until you send payment. It's a good bet that your payment will vanish into thin air, or that the information you bought will turn out to be worthless.

8. Very obvious, rhetorical questions.

You won't believe how moronic some of these questions are. "Are you serious about making money?" (No, I'd rather be poor.) "Have you ever wondered what it takes to be a millionaire?" (Let me guess: eating enough dietary fiber?) "Wouldn't you be happier if you could be totally independent and free to call all of your own shots?" (No thanks, I'd rather be a slave to my boss.) "Are you familiar with Coca-Cola, Gillette, GM, Ford, Visa, Magnavox, MCI, and Xerox, all of whom use our method?" (Sorry, I've lived in a closet for the past 25 years).

like a sports arena or huge warehouse. Fill the room with millions of lottery tickets, each with a different number on it. This represents every possible lottery ticket number available for a single day. (Did you know that if you stacked up all the possible tickets for a single day, the pile would be several miles high?)

Next, reach in and pull out one of the tickets, and declare that this is today's winner. This is just like the way that the winning lottery number is drawn and publicized every day (except that they use a more efficient method than filling a stadium…). Note that your choice was completely random.

Now, here is the proof. Toss that "winning" ticket back into the room, mix up the millions of tickets, and draw one ticket as tomorrow's winner. Is this second ticket related in *any* way to the first ticket? The answer is no. The conditions under which you picked the first ticket and the second ticket were identical and completely random. This is true regardless of whether the number is picked by you or by a computer program. Therefore, all of the information in the world about previous lottery winners cannot help predict today's winner. End of story.

Actually, there is one way that a computer can help you "win" with the lottery. It can calculate your odds of losing. Then, when you see how bad they are, you'll stop wasting your money on lottery tickets. The odds of winning a typical jackpot can be well over 100,000,000 to 1 against you. A typical human being lives fewer than 100 years (about 36,500 days). If you work out the math, you'll find that even if you play the lottery every day, from the minute you are born until the day you die, your odds are still 2500 to 1 against *ever* winning the jackpot. And you'll have wasted $36,500 buying tickets. (Does investing $36,000 at 2500-to-1 odds sound like a good bet?)

Some lotteries offer other, smaller prizes in addition to the jackpot, but the odds are still designed so that the average player loses more than he or she wins.

For more information…

A free pamphlet on pyramid schemes, entitled *Pyramid Schemes: Not What They Seem*, is available from the Direct Selling Education Foundation. Just send a self-addressed stamped envelope to:

Direct Selling Education Foundation
1666 K Street NW
Suite 1010, Washington, DC 20006
(202) 293-5760

Another free pamphlet, *Online Scams: Road Hazards on the Information Superhighway*, discusses all kinds of "get rich quick" scams. It is available from the Federal Trade Commission by mail and on their World Wide Web page.

Federal Trade Commission, Correspondence Branch
6th Street and Pennsylvania Avenue, NW
Washington, DC 20580
(202) 326-2222
World Wide Web: `http://www.ftc.gov`

"Make Money Fast" pyramid schemes are commonly discussed in the Usenet newsgroup *news.admin.net-abuse.misc.* Multi-level marketing is discussed in *alt.business.multi-level.*

The U.S. Postal Inspection Service maintains a terrific Web site with descriptions of dozens of schemes, scams, and frauds. Check it out at the URL

`http://www.usps.gov/websites/depart/inspect/`

The Consumer Law Page contains over 100 online brochures, some of which discuss common scams.

`http://www.seamless.com/talf/ftc/ftc.html`

For a look at the latest scams in action, check out *misc.entrepreneurs*, the newsgroup with the highest number of ripoffs posted on Usenet. (Don't fall for them, though.) You can also find scam ads in some of the "classified ad" areas on major online services, such as Prodigy's "Money Makers" classified area.

A thorough discussion of health-related MLM schemes is available in "The Multilevel Mirage," a chapter in *The Vitamin Pushers: How the Health Food Industry Is Selling America a Bill of Goods* (Prometheus, 1994) by Stephen Barrett and Victor Herbert.

Sometimes you can't help laughing

Some of these stupid scammers remind me of a bad Beavis and Butt-head television episode: "Yeah, uh, send me five bucks, and I'll, like, tell you stuff. Huh huh."

Jeff Goslin

CHAPTER 4

Appearances can be deceiving

Things are not always what they seem.

Years ago, an advertisement appeared in numerous magazines, selling genuine, copper engravings of President Abraham Lincoln for the bargain price of only one dollar. Interested buyers sent in their money, and in return, they received…a shiny, new penny.

Things are not always what they seem to be; and on the Internet, the same rule applies. As you explore Usenet newsgroups and World Wide Web pages, you will come across advertisements and offers that seem really great, and indeed, some of them are bargains. But while the majority of Net users behave honestly, there are some who will try to deceive you about goods and services they want to sell you. Some users will also pretend to be unbiased about products when in fact they are financially connected to their sale.

One of the lessons of this book is: if a deal seems too good to be true, it probably is. The previous chapter discussed "get rich quick" schemes that illustrate this lesson. The schemes discussed in this chapter don't offer you wealth; instead, they offer you a product or service in a misleading way. We'll talk about:

Pricing on the Net
  Are the "bargains" offered on the Net actually cheaper than what you'd find in a store?

Online deception isn't unique

Would you believe one of these articles if it had arrived unsolicited in your mailbox? Do you believe those outrageous ads in the backs of magazines? Why should we expect the Net to be any better?

Peter da Silva

Hidden commercial interests

Is that "unbiased" Net user secretly a paid consultant? Is that "informational" user survey actually a marketing tool?

Opportunities for fame

Can a Net talent agency make you famous?

"Beat the system" tricks

Is it true that you don't have to pay income taxes? How about sending U.S. mail for only four cents?

Phony requests for help

When are users' questions not as innocent as they seem?

Prices on the Net can be higher than elsewhere.

"State policeman tells all!" shouted an advertisement in the Usenet *misc.forsale* newsgroup. "Accurate, insider's information on avoiding speeding tickets and the fines and increased insurance premiums that go with them." Intrigued by these claims, I sent email to the poster for more information. In return, I received a 300-line advertisement for the book, *A Speeder's Guide To Avoiding Tickets.* For only $19.95 (plus $4.00 shipping and handling), I could "stop worrying forever" about speeding tickets. To some people, this probably seemed like a good deal, considering the high cost of speeding tickets, until another Usenet reader posted a telling response. "I just want to point out that this book can be bought in paperback at your local bookstore for $3.99."

Another Usenet advertisement offered Thermoscan instant ear thermometers for sale. "These units wholesale for $399.99," said the ad. Another user quickly responded, explaining that these thermometers cost only $79 at his local drug store.

It is a common belief that prices on the Net are generally cheaper than those you will find in a store. In fact, they often are cheaper, because many are for used items offered by individuals, not businesses. (Chapter 6 covers buying and selling in detail.) As you can see from the above examples, however, prices on the Net can also be significantly higher than store prices. This is particularly true for items that people are not likely to have encountered before, so users don't have intuition about store prices. (When was the last time you went shopping for an ear thermometer?)

When a price is really out of line, it's common for other users to pipe up and say so. When an unusual advertisement is posted, sometimes it's worth waiting a few days to see what other people say about it.

Some newsgroups have established price lists for relevant products. For example, the readers of *rec.music.makers.synth* (devoted to music synthesizers) keep track of the best known prices for new and used instruments, and the most current price list is posted every month. Some of the computer-related newsgroups have similar lists. Such lists are usually mentioned in the FAQ article, if one exists. (And if nobody has created a product price list, then consider volunteering. Lots of other users will thank you for it.)

Coupon books are no bargain.

Instead of selling products, some Net businesses sell coupon books and catalogs. Here's the basic idea. You first purchase a coupon book and a catalog from the company. Later, when you want to buy something from the catalog, you use the coupons to get merchandise at (supposedly) discount prices. The advertisements for these coupon books make them sound like a great way to buy things. When you add up all the costs, however, coupon books look less attractive.

Compact discs are a frequent subject of coupon book schemes. You can find advertisements for these books in Usenet newsgroups like *rec.music.marketplace.cd*. The ads claim that you can get "discount CDs" or "two-for-one CDs" if you order the company's coupon book. Each time you buy a CD at "regular prices," you can use a coupon to get a second CD for free. Sounds great, right? Well, not necessarily.

These companies typically use two tricks to reduce your savings, as illustrated in the table below. The first trick is to sell CDs for an unnaturally high price. For example, if a CD's official list price is $15, the catalog might list it for $30. So even when you use a coupon to get a second CD free, you're still paying $15 per CD. Add the cost of the coupon book (generally between $5 and $20), and you're really losing money, especially since many stores sell CDs for less than list price.

Buy CDs from	Two CDs	Coupon cost	Shipping /tax	Total
Tricky coupon club	30.00	2.00	8.00	40.00
Discount store	25.00	—	1.30	26.30
You lose	5.00	2.00	6.70	13.70

The other trick is to charge artificially high "shipping and handling" fees. The cost of shipping one CD via first class mail is about a dollar, but the coupon-related fees might be as much as $3 to $4 per disc. If you also get charged shipping and handling fees for your free discs, then your total cost could be higher than store prices.

Some companies have unidentified representatives on the Net.

Jeff Preston is a regular participant in several music-related newsgroups and mailing lists. Back in 1993, he noticed something unusual about the CD reviews being written by one particular user. A large number of the reviews were glowingly positive. That in itself wasn't anything to be alarmed about, but the reviewer was also writing his reviews under several different nicknames, which seemed odd. So, Jeff searched through some online archives to see what this guy had been writing about for the past year. Guess what he discovered? In one of the mailing lists, all 85 CDs reviewed by this user were produced or distributed by the *same* record company. Perhaps, thought Jeff, this "reviewer" was really an advertiser in disguise.

In June 1994, Jeff publicly announced his suspicions on Usenet. The reviewer responded, calling Jeff "deceitful." Not long afterward, however, the reviewer reluctantly admitted that he was a paid consultant working for the record company. Even so, his glowing reviews continued. In January 1995, Jeff filed a formal complaint with the Federal Trade Commission, claiming that the consultant had violated sections of the FTC's Deception Policy Statement. The FTC has yet to respond.

Some companies disguise their advertisements to look like ordinary news. Television has "infomercials," in which paid actors are used to portray satisfied customers. Newspapers and magazines have ads that look like articles, except for the word "advertisement" at the top in small print. Disguised ads are now appearing on the Net too, and some are very hard to detect, thanks to the anonymity of usernames. Jeff Preston's incident is unusual only because it was discovered. There are plenty more examples.

Some businesses pretend to be ordinary users.

A common tactic is for a business to post an advertisement on Usenet, pretending to be an individual. "Brand new modem, only $75," read an ad posted in late 1994. "You can't beat that price on this modem at ANY store." The article was simply signed "Thanks, Bill." The phone number provided, however, belonged to a computer store in California.

You'll see plenty of these hidden advertisements in health-related newsgroups. Be skeptical when a newfound Net "friend" recommends a non-standard health product and then just happens to sell it too. (People involved in multi-level marketing do this all the time.)

A related type of misleading advertisement is called a *timeshare scam*. You'll typically see these in the newsgroups *misc.for-sale.non-computer* and *rec.travel.marketplace*. The article looks like it's from an individual who is trying to rent out his vacation home, typically in Florida or the Bahamas. When you respond, however, you find that the article was really posted by a company, and they use high-pressure sales tactics to try to convince you to rent or purchase a timesharing unit (such as a condominium or apartment).

Another scheme offers a vacation package for sale by an "individual." The usual story is that the person bought the vacation package but suddenly can't use it because of other plans, so the package is now for sale. When you respond, however, you find that the "individual" is really a travel agency. There is also a similar-looking scam that offers a "free" vacation, but requires that you join a "travel club" and pay a high "membership fee." Avoid these offers.

Some companies don't directly hide their identities, but they don't exactly come out and admit them either. In December 1994, several mysterious Usenet articles were posted with the

"Accidental" email

I remember when one advertiser with a severe shortage of brain cells sent out a deceptive email message to a massive list of people all over the Net. The message itself was supposedly meant for "Bill" (a made-up person), and it urged "Bill" to buy a certain "hot Canadian investment." The idea, evidently, was to fool the recipients into thinking they'd accidentally received misdirected email containing valuable investment information. You'd have to be the dumbest thing on four feet to fall for this completely transparent scam.

Mark Eckenwiler

I received a similar "misdirected" advertisement (as did thousands of other users) from a company selling a "learning machine." The writer pretended to be an unbiased user who just happened to find an "amazing" Web page advertising the machine. But the return address clearly showed that the writer was an employee of the company! Brilliant. The company, Zygon International Inc., was eventually sued by the Washington attorney general.

Dan Barrett

subjects "LOVE THIS ONE" and "OH BABEEEEE FACE." The articles themselves contained only two lines: a World Wide Web URL, and the words "kiss me sweet cheeks" or "it's excellent!" What was on the Web page? An advertisement for bathroom products. (Oh yes, of course. That was my first guess too.) When I spoke with a company representative, she called the ad "informative and creative—not sneaky at all." You be the judge.

Some businesses pretend they already know you.

In August 1995, I received a friendly looking email message from somebody whose name I didn't recognize. That's not unusual, since I often get responses from new people about my Usenet articles. But this letter was mysterious, because the person seemed to know me. "Here's the interesting World Wide Web site we discussed earlier," said the writer, who then listed a Web URL and signed the letter "P."

What was on the Web page? An advertisement for an eye care clinic. The email was obviously a marketing gimmick. The sender and I had never discussed any Web site "earlier," and the identity of "P" was left up to my imagination. By pretending to know me, the writer hoped to fool me into checking out the Web site. And in fact, I did check it out, but the ploy backfired. Not only will I never give my business to dishonest advertisers, but also I will recommend that my friends stay away from them.

To see what would happen, I emailed the company, criticizing their advertising methods. In response, they wrote: "The previous message sent to you regarding the web site was in error. It was meant for another address. I apologize for any inconvenience this may have caused."

Do you think this was an honest apology? A quick check in the Usenet newsgroup *news.admin.net-abuse.misc*, where Internet junk mail is discussed, revealed that other people had received the same, mysterious advertisement. What's the verdict? Not only did the company broadcast misleading ads by email, but also their "apology" was bogus.

User surveys aren't always what they seem.

Almost every day on Usenet, somebody posts a survey form for users to fill out. It can be a lot of fun to ask your newsgroup friends to vote for their favorite author, most recommended mailorder computer dealer, most hated political candidate, or whatever. Users respond to the survey by email, and the results are often tallied and posted for the readers' enjoyment and education.

Some surveys, however, are not conducted just for fun. As more and more marketing organizations discover the Internet, increasing numbers of commercial surveys are being conducted on Usenet. I'm not going to argue whether commercial surveys are good or bad, but there is one kind that everybody should be aware of: the kind that is disguised as a "fun" survey and does not reveal its commercial purpose. These surveys are intentionally misleading about their purpose.

Before you respond to a survey on the Net, I recommend you ask the following four kinds of questions. A well-designed survey article will contain answers to all of them. If not, then ask the survey taker directly.

Who is sponsoring the survey?
An individual? A company? The Nazis?

What is the purpose of the survey?
Is the survey just for fun? For an academic research project? For commercial purposes? What are they?

What will be done with my response?
Will your answers be made public? Will your personal information (name, email address, etc.) be kept confidential? Or will your name and address be put on a list and sold to other companies?

What will be done with the results?
Will they be public or private? Will they be reported on the Net? When? In which newsgroups? Will a copy of the results be sent to you?

If you cannot get satisfactory responses to your questions, then I recommend not participating in the survey unless you are eager to have your name and address added to a hundred junk mail lists.

Appearances can be deceiving

Some surveys on the Net are individually posted to large numbers of newsgroups—sometimes thousands—at once. This practice, which is not limited to surveys, is called *spamming*. (Chapter 7 discusses spamming in detail.) People should be discouraged from using spamming as a cheap way of collecting data, since it clutters up the Net and wastes other people's computer resources. I recommend not responding to spammed surveys at all, except perhaps to tell the poster that spamming is very wasteful and rude.

By the way, the Usenet newsgroup *alt.usenet.surveys* is devoted to surveys. Unfortunately, most people on Usenet don't read this newsgroup, so any survey posted there isn't going to be very statistically valid. (In fact, any survey conducted on Usenet has a similar problem, since the responses aren't a random sample.)

Beware of phony talent searches.

Do you want to be famous? There is no shortage of people who are willing to help you try! Or so it seems. "Hollywood production company seeks talented and interesting men and women for movies and television," reads one ad in the Usenet newsgroup *rec.arts.movies.production.* "Acting experience is not essential." For a mere $100, this company offers to send your biography and photo "along with our endorsement to all major movie and television productions studios."

"Show your talent on TV world-wide," says another ad that was spammed on Usenet in January 1995. "Everyone is accepted, no one is rejected." Just send $50 to the post office box (*hmmm...*) given in the ad, or mail your credit card number (*HMMM...*) to the poster.

Don't waste your money, folks. What kind of credibility do you think the first company has, if it sends an "endorsement" for anybody who pays the fee? What kind of TV show accepts "everyone," regardless of their talent?

Some scams offer to help you "beat the system."

Other types of scams focus on "beating the system." For a fee, these scams will (supposedly) teach you how to avoid paying for government-related services such as taxes and postage. In

Appearances can be deceiving

general, you must pay the fee before you actually know what you're getting, so the ad-writers work hard to convince you. Once they have your money, they don't care if the methods work for you or not.

One scam that resurfaces every few months offers a way to eliminate your income tax payments. According to the U.S. Constitution, the scammers insist, federal income taxes are "voluntary" for "natural born free citizens" of the United States. As a result, you can decide not to pay your taxes. Just send for their book, and tax freedom can be yours. Or can it? The answer, of course, is no. These arguments against taxes are typically based on bizarre or outdated interpretations of the Constitution. For example, they may conveniently forget about the Sixteenth Amendment ("The Congress shall have power to lay and collect taxes on incomes…"). Other arguments use outlandish definitions of the word "income" to prove that people don't actually have income. Don't waste your money replying to these scam artists. Above all, don't follow their advice unless you enjoy going to prison for tax evasion.

Another scam claims that you can send first class mail via the U.S. Postal Service for free, or for a few cents per letter. "Wouldn't you like an easy and completely legal way to cut your own mailing expenses by 88%!?" says one advertisement. "For only $20, this valuable report" will explain how to do it. A variety of "methods" are explained in such reports: using too little postage and leaving off the return address, sticking the stamps upside down, or writing the recipient's address as the return address (hoping the letter will be returned to "sender"). Don't be fooled: these techniques are illegal, and people who use them have been federally prosecuted for mail fraud. Not only that, but the methods often don't work anyway. If there is insufficient postage on a letter, it could just wind up in a dead-letter office, or it could be delivered "postage due" so the missing postage is collected upon delivery. The bottom line is not to believe these scammers. Attempting to defraud the Post Office is illegal, and the cost of a stamp is a lot less than the cost of defending yourself if you get caught. Don't do it.

Taxes aren't voluntary

The IRS generally takes a very harsh attitude towards people who attempt to use this concept to avoid paying taxes. In fact, most authors of these books make absolutely sure that their own tax returns are complete and correct.

Scott Pallack

Beware of these schemes to get out of income taxes—they are hoaxes, and illegal. If you don't believe me, ask a tax accountant or lawyer. Hundreds of people have tried to cheat the system with these phony methods, and they've failed miserably. These scammers just want you to buy their books; they don't care if the information in them sends you to jail.

Tracy

Appearances can be deceiving

Students might ask you for homework solutions.

"Could someone please send me the solution to the 'Towers of Hanoi' problem?" asked an article posted in a Usenet newsgroup devoted to computer programming. "I'm tutoring someone and need to look at it so I can help him."

The *Towers of Hanoi* is a famous problem in computer science that is taught in almost all college computer curricula. The problem is to figure out a way to move a stack of objects from one location to another without ever placing a large object on top of a smaller one. (The exact details aren't important for our discussion.)

It seemed odd that a "tutor" wanted the answer to a problem found in virtually every introductory computer programming textbook. A quick check with the **finger** program revealed that the poster was a sophomore at a well-known university. It didn't take much deduction from there to figure out that the "tutor" was in fact a student who had been assigned the Towers of Hanoi as a homework problem. He was posting the homework question on the Net with the hope of getting an answer.

Another similar post appeared with the subject "I am taking a poll." The poster asked all "PC fans with much experience in computer organization" to "describe in detail, without using comparisons to other machines, why by itself the IBM PC family of computers are excellent examples of a microcomputer." Now, if that doesn't sound like a word-for-word homework question, I don't know what does! And **finger** revealed the poster to be a university graduate student. Tsk tsk.

The Net is a fantastic place for getting questions answered. In ten years of Usenet participation, I've almost never failed to get an answer to even the most obscure questions, and I've answered hundreds of other users' queries. Sometimes, however, a question is asked with an ulterior motive, as in these two examples. Students who are newcomers to the Net sometimes do this with the hope of getting a free answer to a tough homework question. This is ethically shaky, to say the least, and would likely result in disciplinary action against a student if it were discovered.

These examples of deceit on the Net are relatively mild when compared with others we have seen, but they illustrate an important point. The Net has a wonderful spirit of helpfulness that has grown over the years through the free exchange of facts and opinions. When somebody exploits the Net for personal gain like this, disguising unethical motives behind an innocent question, this spirit of helpfulness is tarnished. What would the Net be like if everybody viewed each others' questions with suspicion instead of curiosity?

For more information...

The Federal Trade Commission is responsible for investigating deceptive advertising at the national level. They have a very informative and readable World Wide Web page at the URL

```
http://www.ftc.gov
```

We'll talk more about the FTC in Chapter 11.

If you have questions about CD coupon books, you can raise them on Usenet in the newsgroup *rec.music.collecting.cd*. You can also find plenty of cheap, used CDs in the newsgroup *rec.music.marketplace.cd*.

CHAPTER 5

Free information…for a price

Beware of scammers who sell freely available information.

What would you do if a stranger in a trenchcoat walked up to you on the street and said, "Pssst! Hey buddy, wanna buy some free information…cheap?"

It's a rather ridiculous sales pitch, isn't it? After all, you shouldn't have to pay for free information. But this same sales pitch is repeated every day on the Internet, though it is sometimes disguised quite well.

Let's look at an example. In the Usenet newsgroup *rec.music.cd* (now *rec.music.collecting.cd*), an advertisement was posted offering brand new, famous-artist compact discs for only four dollars each. The ad wasn't actually selling CDs, though: it was selling information on how to buy them at such a bargain price. For just $10, the secret method could be yours.

On the surface, this looks like a great opportunity, but what do you get for your $10? You get a printed sheet that says:

> Join a compact disc club, like Columbia or BMG, that gives you ten CDs for a penny when you agree to buy several more at "regular club prices." After you finish buying the minimum number of discs, quit the club. Your average cost will be less than four dollars per CD.

Free information

One of the guiding principles of the Internet is free exchange of information. Many users do this out of the goodness of their hearts—people helping people, just for the sake of it. It's ironic that some scammers try to profit on the Net by selling freely available information.

Dan Barrett

This information is hardly a secret; you could have figured it out yourself by adding up the total cost and dividing by the number of discs. Basically, you've wasted ten bucks on information you could have gotten for free.

This kind of advertisement is commonly found on Usenet, particularly in the *misc.forsale* newsgroups. An ad offers to sell you wonderful information to help you save or make money, get out of debt, or succeed in some way. The ad implies that the information is kept secret or at least is very hard to come by. For a fee—sometimes as little as one dollar, but other times over $100—the secret can be yours, and you'll be on your way to success. The unspoken punchline, however, is that the secret information is really available for free, if you know where to look.

The theme of this chapter is: "don't pay for free information." The following sections will help you spot some of the more common scams of this type, including:

Personal credit reports
   Do you need to pay for them?

Credit repair
   Can you pay to have a bad credit history erased?

Government auctions
   Can you really purchase a car for five dollars?

Wholesaler lists
   Is there a secret to buying from wholesalers?

Pen pals
   Do you really need to buy a list of names and addresses?

Don't pay for a personal credit report.

Did you know that there are companies that keep a record of your credit history? Every time you open a new credit card account or take out a loan, an entry is made on your credit report. The report also shows whether you've been "naughty or nice" when making your credit or loan payments. Other companies look at your credit report all the time to decide whether they should offer you more credit, or to accept or reject your applications for financing.

How much would you be willing to pay to get a copy of this report? Numerous ads on Usenet have offered these reports for as little as $12.95 or as much as $89. Well, don't waste your money; you can get a copy of your credit report for free.

Free credit reports are available from several organizations. The best-known is TRW Information Services of Orange, California. You can receive a free credit report from them once each year, or whenever an agency takes a negative action against you because of your credit report. For information, call TRW toll-free at (800) 682-7654. You can also find lots of information on TRW's World Wide Web page at

```
http://www.trw.com
```

It is a good idea to check your credit report every few years to make sure that there are no mistakes in it. At the very least, check it before you apply for a loan. If you can clear up any credit report errors first, you might save yourself a hassle later.

Finally, beware of any credit service that offers to send you a credit report by email. If your credit card number is included in the report, then you risk having it intercepted and read by other people, as we saw in Chapter 2.

You can't erase bad credit by paying for it.

Credit-related ads on Usenet are not limited to offers of credit reports. Some people and companies advertise that they can help you "erase" bad credit. In other words, if you have a bad credit history, these folks claim they can rapidly restore your credit rating to good standing. For a fee, of course.

Is it possible to erase bad credit? Yes it is, but not as easily as these ads imply. All you can really do is pay off your debts and wait for them to be removed from your credit report. It takes about seven years for a bad credit item to be removed. Yes, that is a long time, but unfortunately there is no magic method to make these items disappear.

If it's not possible to erase a bad credit history "instantly," then what are these companies selling? Sometimes they are simply lying, hoping that you'll send some money to their post office box before they close up shop and skip town. But some of these ads have a grain of truth to them. If you see ads offering "guaranteed credit cards regardless of your credit history" or "no-interest credit cards," then they are probably talking about secured cards.

A *secured card* looks and acts just like a credit card, with one twist: there is no credit involved. Before you can use a secured card, you have to deposit a chunk of money into a bank account. Then, each time you charge to your secured card, the money is automatically withdrawn from the account to pay the bill. So unlike credit cards, you aren't borrowing into the future; you're spending what you already have. Virtually anybody can get a secured card, even if one's credit history is bad.

Few companies who place these ads actually offer secured cards. Most of them just want to sell you information on how to get one. There's no need to buy this information, though. Even though one Usenet ad called it "secret information that banks and financial institutions don't want you to know," you can get free information on secured cards at virtually any bank.

Government auctions are no secret.

"Fellow Investors and Entrepreneurs," read a Usenet advertisement in January 1995, "there is money to be made in GOVERNMENT AUCTIONS!" The article advertised a financial package that supposedly gives you "STRATEGIES ON HOW TO WIN AT AUCTIONS and A LIST OF ADDRESSES AND PHONE NUMBERS OF GOVERNMENT AUCTIONS IN YOUR STATE OR AREA OF INTEREST." (Ouch, my ears.)

What is a government auction? It is an auction run by a U.S. government organization, such as the military, the Government Services Administration (GSA), the Customs Service, or the Internal Revenue Service (IRS), in which surplus, confiscated, and used items are sold. Local government also runs similar auctions called "sheriff's auctions" or "sheriff's sales."

Ads related to government auctions are very common on Usenet. They usually boast about how cheaply you can buy a car at a government auction. There are "thousands of government vehicles for auction each month," insists one of these ads, such as an Oldsmobile Cutlass that sold for five dollars and a Mercedes that sold for $350. The ad does not, however, mention when or where these sales occurred.

Most of the government auction ads you see on Usenet do not actually advertise auctions. Instead, people try to sell you the dates and locations of auctions, as if this information were some big secret. Don't pay for it! Information on government auctions is available for free from many sources. For starters, just check the classified ads in your local newspaper, or a newspaper from your closest major city. Auction announcements are quite common.

If you are serious about participating in government auctions, your next step is to get onto the mailing lists maintained by the organizations holding the auctions, and they'll notify you as auctions are announced. Local military auctions are run by Defense Reutilization and Marketing Offices (DRMO), and larger ones are run by regional and national offices. Call (800) 222-3767 to find out how to contact your local DRMO. For information on many nonmilitary auctions, contact your regional GSA office. You can also try the GSA World Wide Web site at

    http://www.gsa.gov

Can you really buy a new car for five dollars at a government auction? Long ago, government auctions were not well known to the public, and rumor has it that such purchases were sometimes possible. Nowadays, however, these auctions are heavily attended by both consumers and resellers (such as car dealers), so it's unlikely you'll get a car for pennies on the dollar. You may find some bargains though.

Wholesaler lists are in your telephone book.

Some Usenet ads offer to sell you a list of sources for wholesale products. With such a list, supposedly, you can make lots of money by buying wholesale and then reselling the items for big profits. "You can buy literally hundreds of products at low wholesale prices," proclaimed one such advertisement in early 1995. "It took me years to assemble this list and it is tried and true," said another ad.

Want a free list of wholesalers? Simply pick up the Yellow Pages of your closest major city. Then look up the type of item you want, and there should be a separate heading for wholesalers and manufacturers of that item. Some telephone books even have a "Wholesalers" heading under "W."

Before you jump headfirst into the world of wholesale, be aware there are a few "gotchas" to working with wholesalers. First, not all wholesalers will sell to consumers, especially if you want to buy only a small number of items. Second, for dealing with some wholesalers, you might need to have a

Wholesaler lists

I can tell you that this wholesaler list IS NOT A SCAM! You WILL get valuable information from this list and it is worth every cent and then some.

Usenet advertisement posted in numerous *forsale* newsgroups reseller's license, and to sell the items you buy, you might need a business license.

Don't pay to get a pen pal.

Sometimes, an Internet advertisement is so pointless that you just have to sit back and laugh. The most ridiculous ad category has to be "pen pal" ads. Would you like a pen pal? A list of names and addresses of potential pen pals is available for a fee. Would you like to be a pen pal? Your name and address can be added to the list, again for a fee.

Can you see why these ads are so ridiculous? Because pen pals are the most common free commodity on the Internet! During ordinary use of the Internet, you are almost guaranteed to gather more email pals than you know what to do with. In a sense, all of Usenet is one huge pen pal club. Simply post an article, get responses, reply to the responders, and...voilà, instant pen pals. The concept of actually paying for pen pals on the Internet is ludicrous.

There are many more examples.

Here are a few examples of free items I've seen advertised for sale on the Internet. I present a quote from each advertisement and then explain why it isn't necessary to pay a middleman for the information.

Beer and wine making
"EASY to follow instructions on how to make beer at home," read an advertisement that was spammed on Usenet. "This packet will take you through simple step by step procedures to making home-brew. Just $6.99...." You can get free information on beer and wine making by reading the Usenet newsgroups *rec.crafts.brewing* and *rec.crafts.winemaking*. Or just stop by your local home-brewing shop and purchase a starter kit, and you'll find instructions inside.

Counterfeit money detection
"Businesses lose a lot of money on account of counterfeit currency because they lack a way to spot the fakes before accepting it. We can provide you with detailed information about a fantastic product that can save you a lot of money...." What is the secret product? An ordinary counter-

feit-detection pen that you can buy at any well-stocked office supply store.

Recipes

"I have tons of recipes for everything from appetizers to desserts and everything in between. I would love to share them with you, but I do ask for one thing in return: one dollar." A dollar a recipe might not seem like a bad deal, but if you think about it, buying a cookbook is cheaper. Also, you can find thousands of free recipes in the Usenet newsgroup *rec.food.recipes*. The entire recipe archive is available on the World Wide Web at the URLs

```
http://www.neosoft.com/recipes/
gopher://spinaltap.micro.umn.edu/hh/fun/Recipes/
```

For all you know, the advertiser is selling recipes from these very archives!

Also, be aware that recipe sales are a common disguise for pyramid schemes on the Net, as we discussed in Chapter 3. If you are asked to send money to a list of people in exchange for recipes, and thousands of other people will (supposedly) send you money later, then watch out.

Government information

"Now you can order the first complete directory of government resources on the Internet...only $17.95." Or you could simply connect to the World Wide Web URL

```
http://www.whitehouse.gov
```

and get all the information for free, directly from the U.S. government!

To spot a fake, ask an expert.

As you can see, there is a lot of free information in the world, but it's hard for one person to be aware of it all. So when you are in doubt about an ad of this type, try asking an expert in the field.

For example, suppose you see a suspicious advertisement offering "secret" information on how to save big dollars on your mortgage payments. Rather than risk your money for the secret, print out the advertisement and bring it to a local bank, accountant, or real-estate agent. From the text of the ad, they might be able to figure out what is really being offered. (There are some fairly well-known "secrets" of mortgage payments

Use a Web search engine

Now that the World Wide Web has been in existence for a while, many people and organizations have created Web pages that help you search the Internet for information on any topic. Whenever you see an advertisement for "secret" information on the Net, use one of these "search engine" Web pages to see if there's already an archive of free information on the subject. Many Web browsers come with built-in "search" buttons or menu items, or links to popular search engines.

that can save you money, like paying 13 payments per year instead of 12.) Or maybe they'll recognize the ad as a more serious scam that's gunning for your money.

Some free information is worth paying for.

Some people legitimately charge a fee for "free" information. These people have spent long hours gathering the information from many sources and organizing it carefully. You are paying for their time and effort.

For example, if you want a list of all the telephone numbers in the United States, this information is freely available, but you'd have a heck of a time collecting all the data yourself. Sure, you could ask your friends around the country to mail you phone books. (And then build an extra wing onto your house to store them....) But it would probably be simpler to pay $49.95 for a CD-ROM with the same "free" information.

For more information...

One of the best ways to find free information on a topic is to look on the World Wide Web. Some good, well-organized starting points are Yahoo, at the URL

    http://www.yahoo.com

the Whole Internet Catalog, at the URL

    http://gnn.com/wic/

and Lycos at the URL

    http://www.lycos.com

There are many more Web-searching pages, and they often have links to one another.

Also, you can look for Usenet newsgroups on the topic, using your news-reading program, and check for Frequently Asked Questions (FAQ) documents in the newsgroups. FAQ documents are also available by anonymous FTP from the machine *rtfm.mit.edu* in the directory */pub/usenet*.

CHAPTER 6

Buying and selling on the Net

Most online sellers and buyers are honest, but some are not.

In early December 1994, an individual calling himself "Trieu Le" and "T. Le" posted a dozen advertisements in the *misc.for-sale.computers* newsgroups on Usenet. The ads were highly detailed and listed a wide variety of computer hardware and software at very reasonable prices. Over a four-day period, approximately 50 users responded to Le's advertisements and sent him checks and money orders as he requested. Not long afterwards, Le sent them their packages.

Unfortunately, the packages were empty. And Le's postal address turned out to be a Mailboxes Etc. store. Le vanished with over $13,000 of other users' money, and at press time, he has still not been caught. (The story appeared on NBC News on May 5, 1995.)

Hundreds of users engage in buying and selling items on the Internet and commercial online services every day. Most people involved in these sales behave honestly, and most of the transactions work out fine. A small proportion of these deals go bad, however. The reasons range from simple misunderstandings to email delays to out-and-out fraud. Large-scale ripoffs like the one involving "T. Le" are rare but quite frightening.

Most transactions work fine

For the vast majority of users, transactions in the Usenet Marketplace are successful, as long as you take reasonable precautions.

Dan King, *Usenet Marketplace* FAQ

This chapter is designed to help you conduct individual-to-individual sales on the Internet in the safest possible manner. (Some of the information applies to business sales too.) Usenet is the largest network where these sales occur, so we'll focus our attention there. We'll also discuss the "classified ad" areas of commercial online service providers, like America Online, CompuServe, and Prodigy, where similar buying and selling occurs.

When you conduct business with a complete stranger over the Net, there is no 100% effective method to guarantee honesty, but the guidelines in this chapter will help you avoid the most common pitfalls. We'll begin with general information about buying and selling on Usenet. Next, we'll present "The 10 commandments of safe buying and selling" and examine various methods for conducting small, medium, and large transactions safely. After that, we'll talk about what to do if you think something has gone wrong with a sale. Finally, we'll touch on the subject of online blacklists.

Buying and selling on the Net can be risky, but it can also be very rewarding. You'll reap the benefits when you finally locate a copy of an out-of-print book, or find a buyer for your XV9000 Obscuro-Tron Celery Slicer.

Buying and selling on Usenet is like using electronic classified ads.

Usenet is a popular place for individuals to buy and sell personal items. Hundreds of new ads are posted daily in over 50 newsgroups dedicated to individual sales. These newsgroups are easily identified because their names contain the words *marketplace, forsale, wanted,* or *swap.* The largest set of related newsgroups for buying and selling have names beginning with *misc.forsale.* Some users also post ads in discussion newsgroups, but this is frowned upon. It is unfortunate that there is not a standard way of naming all the newsgroups dedicated to buying and selling, but that's the way Usenet has evolved.

Articles in these newsgroups are a lot like electronic classified ads. A typical "for sale" ad contains a list of items for sale, their prices, and sometimes a description of the seller's terms and conditions. Users also post want ads to buy or trade particular items. Articles contain mainly facts and not much advertising hype. Unlike classified ads, however, you don't have to pick up a telephone to respond. Simply press a key or click a mouse button while reading an ad, and you can send electronic mail directly to the advertiser. Good news-reading software also lets you conveniently browse ads by their Subject lines.

Usenet is not the only place on the Internet where buying and selling goes on. As the World Wide Web becomes more popular, classified ad Web pages are sprouting up with convenient user interfaces for placing and responding to ads. Right now, however, Usenet is a much larger and more popular means of connecting private buyers and sellers.

Other online service providers have classified ads.

The three major online services provide classified ad services for their subscribers. Most of the tips in this chapter will apply to these classified ads as well.

America Online

> Use your mouse to select GO TO from the top row of commands, and when prompted, type CLASSIFIEDS. Ads are separated into several "boards" for different types of items: Macintosh-related items, PC-related items, other computer-related items, general merchandise, and business and jobs.

CompuServe

> Type GO CLASSIFIEDS to enter the classified ad area for general buying and selling. Some of the more specific forums (such as AMIGAUSER, DTPFORUM, NOVUSER, TENNIS, and PHOTOPRO) have their own classified sections as well.

Prodigy

> Type the JumpWord classifieds, and you'll be taken directly to a menu screen that lets you browse and place ads. There are about 25 categories for ads, including computers, audio/video, vehicles, household items, appliances, sports, crafts, and more.

Notice how the online services use different words to describe their forums for advertising (newsgroups, boards, areas). For the rest of this chapter, we'll just call them "newsgroups."

The Usenet marketplace

The Usenet marketplace is a fragile thing. I'm sure a very large percentage of Usenet readers refuse to trade on the groups because of risks both real and perceived. The place is seen by many to be teeming with thieves, pickpockets and cutpurses. In fact, of course, the percentage of loss to such thieves is probably still quite small. But their mere existence, and the loud and immediate shrieks of their occasional victims, magnifies their importance, ultimately jeopardizing the viability of the marketplace itself.

Jay Brown
GuaranTrade escrow service

Advertise in the most appropriate newsgroup.

With so many newsgroups available for posting ads, which one should you use? If you want to reach interested buyers quickly, your best bet is to post your ad in the most specific newsgroup possible. Advertising in an inappropriate newsgroup, like trying to sell your fish tank on Usenet in *misc.forsale.computers.work-station*, is a waste of everybody's time. Similarly, an advertisement for IBM PC computer games won't attract much attention in a general newsgroup like *misc.forsale.comput-ers.other.misc*, especially since the more specific group, *comp.sys.ibm.pc.games.marketplace*, exists.

If you are selling a computer-related item on Usenet, see Table 1 for a list of relevant newsgroups. If your item is not computer-related, check out the list in Table 2. In addition to the world-wide newsgroups listed in the table, there may be local Usenet newsgroups at your site for buying and selling. For example, in my area of western Massachusetts, there is a local newsgroup, *5col.forsale*, for buying and selling items in the "5 College Area." Selling in one of your local newsgroups is an especially good idea if the merchandise is heavy or otherwise difficult to transport, such as refrigerators or glass sculptures.

If you feel you must post your advertisement in more than one newsgroup, remember not to post a separate ad in each news-group. Instead, use your news software's *crossposting* feature. Crossposting causes a single article to appear in multiple news-groups. Less disk space and computer time are used by crossposting than by posting several identical articles, so you are being more Net friendly. Excessive multiple postings are called *spams,* and this abuse of the Net is discussed in Chapter 7.

Individual and commercial sales are conducted in different newsgroups.

Traditionally, Usenet has had an informal policy against commercial advertising. The spirit of Usenet is the free exchange of information, and commercial ads are seen as intrusive. In order to keep Usenet as free of commercialism as possible, a separate branch of Usenet has been formed, sometimes called *Biznet,* that is dedicated to commercial purposes. Newsgroups

Usenet "for sale" newsgroups

1. Computer-related ad newsgroups

IBM PC and Clones

Software	*misc.forsale.computers.pc-specific.software*
Games	*comp.sys.ibm.pc.games.marketplace*
Complete systems	*misc.forsale.computers.pc-specific.systems*
Portable systems	*misc.forsale.computers.pc-specific.portables*
Motherboards	*misc.forsale.computers.pc-specific.motherboards*
Audio equipment	*misc.forsale.computers.pc-specific.audio*
Video cards	*misc.forsale.computers.pc-specific.cards.video*
Expansion cards	*misc.forsale.computers.pc-specific.cards.misc*
Other equipment	*misc.forsale.computers.pc-specific.misc*

Apple Macintosh

Software	*misc.forsale.computers.mac-specific.software*
Games	*comp.sys.mac.games.marketplace*
Complete systems	*misc.forsale.computers.mac-specific.systems*
Portable systems	*misc.forsale.computers.mac-specific.portables*
Video cards	*misc.forsale.computers.mac-specific.cards.video*
Expansion cards	*misc.forsale.computers.mac-specific.cards.misc*
Other equipment	*misc.forsale.computers.mac-specific.misc*

Other Computer Makes and Models

Apple II	*comp.sys.apple2.marketplace*
Commodore Amiga	*comp.sys.amiga.marketplace*
NeXT	*comp.sys.next.marketplace*
Sun workstations (want ads)	*comp.sys.sun.wanted*
Other workstations	*misc.forsale.computers.workstation*

Non-Brand-Specific

Software	*misc.forsale.computers.other.software*
Complete systems	*misc.forsale.computers.other.systems*
Modems	*misc.forsale.computers.modems*
Network hardware	*misc.forsale.computers.net-hardware*
Memory	*misc.forsale.computers.memory*
Monitors	*misc.forsale.computers.monitors*
Printers, plotters	*misc.forsale.computers.printers*
Storage media	*misc.forsale.computers.storage*
Miscellaneous	*misc.forsale.computers.other.misc*

Discussion About Computer Sales (no ads permitted)

Discussion	*misc.forsale.computers.discussion*

2. Non-computer ad newsgroups

Transportation and Travel

Bicycles	*rec.bicycles.marketplace*
Boats	*rec.boats.marketplace*
Cars	*rec.autos.marketplace*
Planes	*rec.aviation.marketplace*
Tickets, vacations	*rec.travel.marketplace*

Music-Related Items

Audio components	*rec.audio.marketplace*
Musical instruments	*rec.music.makers.marketplace*
Compact discs	*rec.music.marketplace.cd*
Vinyl record albums	*rec.music.marketplace.vinyl*
Other recordings/memorabilia	*rec.music.marketplace.misc*

Games

Board games	*rec.games.board.marketplace*
Fantasy role-playing games	*rec.games.frp.marketplace*
Video games	*rec.games.video.marketplace*

Trading Cards

Magic The Gathering sales	*rec.games.trading-cards.marketplace.magic.sales*
Magic The Gathering trades	*rec.games.trading-cards.marketplace.magic.trades*
Magic The Gathering auctions	*rec.games.trading-cards.marketplace.magic.auctions*
All other game cards	*rec.games.trading-cards.marketplace.misc*
Non-sports cards	*rec.collecting.cards.non-sports*

Reading Material

Books	*rec.arts.books.marketplace*
Comic books	*rec.arts.comics.marketplace*
Science fiction	*rec.arts.sf.marketplace*

Other Specific Interests

Antiques	*rec.antiques.marketplace*
Craftwork	*rec.crafts.marketplace*
Electronics	*misc.industry.electronics.marketplace*
Genealogy	*soc.genealogy.marketplace*
Ham radio, CB	*rec.radio.swap*
Japanese animation	*rec.arts.anime.marketplace*
Photography	*rec.photo.marketplace*
Sex-related items	*alt.sex.erotica.marketplace*
Skiing	*rec.skiing.marketplace*

Miscellaneous

Any other non-computer items	*misc.forsale.non-computer*

3. Commercial ad newsgroups (Biznet)

Computers	
IBM PCs and clones	*biz.marketplace.computers.pc-clone*
Apple Macintosh	*biz.marketplace.computers.mac*
Workstations	*biz.marketplace.computers.workstation*
Other computers	*biz.marketplace.computers.other*
Computer services	*biz.marketplace.services.computers*
Non-computer Items	
Non-computer items	*biz.marketplace.non-computer*
Non-computer services	*biz.marketplace.services.non-computer*
International sales and service	*biz.marketplace.international*
Discussion About Sales (no ads permitted)	
Computer items	*biz.marketplace.computers.discussion*
International sales and service	*biz.marketplace.international.discussion*
Anything else	*biz.marketplace.discussion*

in Biznet have names beginning with *biz*. A list of *biz* newsgroups for buying and selling can be found in Table 3. (Note that not all sites carry the Biznet groups.)

Be a courteous buyer or seller.

When posting an advertisement and conducting a sale, please remember to use common courtesy. If you are a seller, here are some guidelines:

- Post a fair price. This might require some investigation on your part to find out what other prices are being asked for similar merchandise. If your price is unreasonable, you are almost guaranteed to get irate email.

- Once you have reached a final agreement with a buyer, honor it. Even if someone else comes along and offers a higher price, you should keep your original agreement. If you don't, other users will remember your name and might stop doing business with you.

- Send the merchandise promptly. Then send email to the buyer immediately, explaining how you shipped the merchandise and estimating how long it will take to arrive.

- When the payment arrives from the buyer, again send email to acknowledge it.

Likewise, there are similar guidelines for buyers:

- Send your payment promptly. Afterwards, send email to the seller, saying that you have sent payment and estimating when it will arrive.

- Once the seller has shipped the merchandise, don't change your mind and refuse the shipment (unless the box is visibly damaged). A refusal will cost the seller some money. If you must refuse the shipment, offer to pay for half or all of the seller's wasted shipping cost.

- When the merchandise arrives from the seller, again send email to acknowledge it.

Don't post "sold" messages.

When you complete a sale, you might be tempted to post a new message in the newsgroup, announcing that "the item has been sold." This is not a good idea, for two reasons. First, these messages are rather wasteful. On average, only a few readers out of tens of thousands will be interested in your sale to begin with. Imagine what would happen if every seller posted a "sold" message; you'd have to wade through hundreds of them every day.

Second, if you are trying to prevent more people from responding to your ad, posting a "sold" message won't help. Many users read articles in a newsgroup from first to last. Therefore, they will encounter your original ad—and respond to it—long before they see your "sold" message. A much better idea is to *cancel* your "for sale" message. This is done using your newsreading software. For example, the programs **rn** and **trn** allow you to cancel an article by displaying the article and typing a capital C. Consult your local system staff for more help with canceling articles.

For small transactions, a check or money order is simple and sometimes acceptable.

Now that we've covered the basics of where to buy and sell on the Net, let's talk about specific methods. As we've said, most online sales work out fine. When dealing with inexpensive items like compact discs or computer games, if you are willing to take a small risk, you can send payment in advance (if you are the buyer) or merchandise in advance (if you are the seller). Some buyers and sellers arrange to mail their respective pieces simultaneously so they cross in the mail.

Because these methods of conducting business are so simple, plenty of things can go wrong.

- You have no guarantee that the other person will obey the rules. He or she can simply send you nothing and can even claim that your money or merchandise never arrived. You can avoid the "never arrived" problem by sending things via certified mail with a return receipt, but this won't solve everything.

- If you are the seller, the buyer's check can bounce. This means you lose the money from the sale, and your bank might charge you a fee for depositing a bad check. You can avoid this problem by insisting on a money order instead of a check, but some buyers will be reluctant to send a money order to a stranger. Alternatively, you can accept a check

Prepayment is sometimes OK

For small items like CDs, I don't mind sending a personal check or money order to a stranger. It's a small amount to risk in the name of trust. In the other direction, I've been on Usenet for ten years, so people in my favorite newsgroups know my name pretty well and are usually willing to mail me a check or money order in advance.

Dan Barrett

The 10 commandments of safe buying and selling

1. **Thou shalt not conduct business with an anonymous user.**

   If a user will not reveal his or her full name, take your business elsewhere, no matter how good the deal sounds.

2. **Thou shalt ask for a street address and telephone number.**

   If something goes wrong with the deal, an email address might not be enough to trace the other person. Insist on being given an address and telephone number, and call the telephone number to verify that it is legitimate.

3. **Thou shalt not send money or goods to a post office box.**

   Although people use these boxes for legitimate business, a thief can easily close one and disappear. If for some reason you must deal with a P.O. box, be sure to obey Commandment #2 and get a street address and telephone number.

4. **Thou shalt ask about the physical and working condition of all goods.**

   Don't forget to ask whether an item is in *both* good cosmetic condition and good working order. When buying expensive items like jewelry, high-end audio gear, or fine china, ask for photographs of the items. Photos can be faked, of course, but the average ripoff artist probably won't go through the trouble.

5. **Thou shalt not send large amounts of money in advance.**

   The convenience of prepayment sometimes outweighs the risk if the deal is small, like $6 for a used compact disc. For larger transactions, however, prepayment is risky.

6. **Thou shalt use COD or escrow for large orders.**

   Cash on Delivery does not guarantee complete safety, but is safer than sending money or goods in advance. Escrow is best for expensive items.

7. **Thou shalt prefer to do business with users from reputable Internet sites.**

   In general, it is less risky to conduct a transaction with someone from a well-established site like *microsoft.com* or *harvard.edu* than someone from *bobs-cool-pc.bbs.org*. Well-known companies and universities are less likely to give computer accounts to fly-by-night individuals, whereas public-access sites will give an account to almost anybody who pays their fee. Further, if a company employee or university student rips you off, you can call their boss or department head. There are exceptions to this commandment, of course—anybody can register a reputable-sounding domain name for $50 a year—but it's a reasonably good rule of thumb.

8. **Thou shalt pack your goods properly for shipping.**

   Don't leave fragile items loose in the box. When packing any item, you should *expect* that the package will be dropped—hard—sometime during delivery. Shake the box after you pack it to make sure that nothing is moving around. If you want to pack electronic components in styrofoam peanuts or shredded newspaper, be sure to wrap the components in airtight plastic; otherwise, particles from the packing material can get into the electronics.

9. **Thou shalt not sign for a visibly damaged package.**

   If the outer box is damaged, refuse delivery, or you could get stuck with broken merchandise.

10. **Thou shalt save copies of every document involved in the sale.**

    This includes the posted advertisement, email, printed correspondence, registered/certified mail receipts, UPS tracking numbers, canceled checks, money order receipts, and anything else you can think of. Don't throw anything away; keep the documents for a year after the deal is done, just in case.

and wait for it to clear, but it still might bounce and cost you a bad check fee.

- If you are the buyer, the seller can ship you a "box of rocks": that is, a package containing something worthless, like a brick, instead of the promised merchandise. In this case, you lose your entire payment. Similarly, the seller can send you damaged or incomplete goods.

If you follow "The 10 commandments of safe buying and selling," and you believe you can trust the other person, then prepayment might be OK for small transactions. But don't use it for anything substantial. We'll examine safer (and more complex) methods next.

For medium-sized transactions, use COD.

Cash on delivery is a relatively low-risk method of transporting and selling merchandise. When using COD, the seller ships the merchandise to the buyer in a package. When the merchandise arrives, the buyer gives the payment to the delivery person in exchange for the package. The COD provider then mails the payment to the seller. COD services are provided (for a fee) by the U.S. Postal Service, United Parcel Service (UPS), Federal Express, and other private couriers.

COD prevents the other person from claiming that something did not arrive. Similarly, it can eliminate bounced checks because you can require the buyer to pay cash to the delivery person. You *must* tell this to the COD provider, however, or they might accept a personal check from the buyer. Ask your COD provider for more details.

Although COD is safer to use than simply mailing money or merchandise, it is not flawless. Several things can go wrong with the transaction.

- If you are the buyer, the seller can still send you a box of rocks, as described in the previous section. Sometimes you can convince your delivery person to let you open a package to make sure it contains what you expect (hey, it can't hurt to ask), but this is against the official policies of the U.S. Postal Service, UPS, and Federal Express. All of them forbid you to open a COD package until you pay for it. I've seen a rumor on the Net that Federal Express has an option

that allows the recipient to open the package before paying, if the sender preapproves it, but according to Federal Express, this is false.

- If you are the seller, the buyer can refuse your package. The COD provider then returns it to you. In this case, you lose the shipping fee you paid the COD provider.

- If you are the seller, the COD provider can take a long time to send you the payment. Payment should arrive at best within a few days, and at worst within a few weeks. I had one bad COD experience in which payment took almost four months, but this is very unusual.

For large transactions, an escrow service can act as a middleman.

A cautious buyer and seller can enlist a trustworthy third party, called an *escrow service,* to help conduct an expensive sale. Instead of sending things to each other, the buyer and seller send their money and merchandise to the escrow service. Once both items have been received, the escrow service forwards the merchandise to the seller, who then has a few days to make sure that the merchandise is the same as what the seller claimed. If all is well, then the escrow service forwards the money to the seller. If either the buyer or the seller backs out of the deal, or if the merchandise is not acceptable to the buyer, the escrow service returns the items to their senders. Regardless of how the deal turns out, the escrow service collects a fee.

The key word in the previous paragraph is *trustworthy.* If the escrow service does not keep its promises, it isn't worth using. If you are uncertain about a particular escrow service, ask the company to provide references. You can also check with the Better Business Bureau (BBB) to see if any complaints have been lodged against the escrow service. (The BBB is discussed in Chapter 11.)

Escrow services are offered by lawyers and by specialty companies. You will find the names of some escrow services in Dan King's *misc.forsale* Frequently Asked Questions (FAQ) articles. (See "For more information" at the end of the chapter.)

Lack of communication is a common problem.

No matter how you conduct your transaction, be sure that you and the other person completely understand the details of the sale. Neither person should send any money or merchandise until both of you have asked all the questions you want. Make sure you agree on the merchandise, the price, the shipping method, the shipping dates, the shipping addresses, and any special terms and conditions such as warranties. Make sure you save copies of all your communications for later reference. When you are finished asking questions, if you are not satisfied with any of the details, don't go through with the sale.

Don't rely on electronic mail to clear up problems.

Electronic mail is a wonderful method of communication that has revolutionized the world, but it is not the best medium for solving problems. If a computer or electronic gateway crashes somewhere between you and the other user, email can be delayed for a long time, leading each of you to believe that the other is not responding. Email can also be delayed or lost because of software bugs or intermittent telephone connections. In addition, email does not convey emotions and subtlety very well. A single ambiguous sentence can lead to a major misunderstanding between the buyer and the seller. (Does the phrase "yeah, sure" mean yes or no?)

When in doubt, reach for the telephone. (You *did* obey Commandment #2, right?) While it might cost you a little money in long-distance charges, it's cheaper than talking to a lawyer later.

Blacklists have pros and cons.

Every few months, somebody in a *forsale* or *marketplace* newsgroup posts a message asking, "Why doesn't somebody keep a list of all the buyers and sellers who ripped people off and post it once a month?" Such a list is called a *blacklist*. Blacklists are sometimes the subject of heated debate in these newsgroups. On one hand, blacklists are good because they might prevent other users from being ripped off by known thieves. On the other hand, if an innocent person's name winds up on

The condition of items

I bought or sold about 50 items over the Net between 1991 and 1995, with prices from $2.50 to $150, and all of these transactions worked without a hitch. I've been careful about whom I do business with, though. My only small problem was that I once broke "Commandment #4" and forgot to ask about the physical condition of a synthesizer I purchased. Its sides were totally bent out of shape. The seller must have rack-mounted it incorrectly with a huge weight on top. Since the synth otherwise worked perfectly, I decided not to bother doing anything about it.

Dan Barrett

No public blacklists

a blacklist by mistake, that person's reputation could be damaged, and the user maintaining the blacklist might even get sued for it.

Publicly posted blacklists are a bad idea. Suppose you decide to maintain a blacklist by collecting horror stories from Usenet, or by having victims email you about the users who ripped them off. Since you probably won't know the victims nor the accused ripoff artists personally, you won't be able to guarantee the accuracy of the information. For example, if user Larry is angry at user Susan, Larry could mail her name to you just to be malicious. If you then make the blacklist public—say, by posting it on Usenet, or distributing it by email—you can be sued by someone whose name appears on the list. *Even if that person really is a ripoff artist!* The ripoff artist might not *win* this lawsuit, but you can still be sued, and that could waste a lot of your time and money...much more than you are likely to lose through dishonest Net transactions.

There is nothing wrong with making a private blacklist, however. Whenever you see a posted complaint about a ripoff, save the names of the poster and the alleged ripoff artist. Do *not* distribute list to anybody else. Instead, any time you want to buy an item advertised on the Net, or you receive an offer to buy one of your items, check your list for a match. This is completely legal for you to do, as long as you don't distribute the list. Even if the information on your private blacklist is not completely accurate, at least you won't accidentally damage an innocent person's reputation in public (or risk a lawsuit).

For more information...

I strongly recommend that you read Dan King's excellent FAQ before buying or selling anything online. It contains the most up-to-date information about buying and selling on the Net, including the current list of Usenet newsgroups, tips for carrying out transactions safely, tips for handling international sales, and guidelines for individual versus commercial selling.

The articles are titled ADVERTISING FAQ—INFO FOR NEW USERS and TRANSACTIONS FAQ—INFO FOR NEW USERS and are available from at least three sources:

- They are posted regularly in *misc.forsale.non-computer, news.answers,* and other relevant Usenet newsgroups. Your news-reading software very likely has a command for

The victims speak

Most transactions work out fine, but occasionally they go wrong. Here are some examples of transactions gone wrong.

I responded to T. Le's Usenet posting, and offered him $250 for a monitor. Like others, I received only an empty envelope. First, I reported it to my university's police department. They seemed interested at first, but found that the local district attorney was not, because of the small amount involved. I also spoke extensively with the Loss Prevention Dept. of UPS. They were sympathetic, but have no enforcement powers. I filed a report with the postal inspectors. They're probably not interested because UPS was used. I filed information with the San Diego branch of the FBI. As you'll hear from others, they are only interested in white-collar crime cases totaling much larger amounts. If the guy had stuck up a convenience store for $100, the police would launch a manhunt. T. Le stole over $13,000, and no law enforcement agency seems interested. (At least not until they started getting calls from NBC News.)

Richard Kershenbaum

I feel kind of stupid that I sent money to T. Le in advance. It's just that I've dealt with so many other people on the Internet that I wasn't worried. I was wrong.

John Lockwood

On November 22, 1994, I purchased a money order and mailed it to a user to buy his hard drive. On November 28, I sent him an email message asking if he had received the money order. The next day, I received a message from him saying that he had not received the money order. I contacted American Express, however, and found out that the money order was cashed on the 29th. As of now, I still have not received the hard drive from him.

Mario D'Alessio

I purchased what I thought were 50 original Nintendo games from a user for $65. However, the merchandise turned out to be a 50-games-in-1 cartridge of pirated games. The jerk claimed that he had delivered what he advertised and would not give me a refund.

After many successful Net deals, this is the first time I've had a problem. Unfortunately, I don't have the time or money to take legal action against this scammer.

Maureen

A company requested my CD want list. I sent it. They replied and confirmed what was in stock. I sent a money order, and they have refused to answer my mail. They took me and ran. IBM is helping to track down this CD con-artist who has taken a lot of our dollars. Be cautious on the Internet. It is like the wild west with outlaws like these taking advantage of little or no police or law and order.

Zack

I bought some trading cards from a guy on Usenet and never received them. He did cash my check though. He sent me some lame excuse, and now he ignores all my email. I've since discovered that several other people had the exact same problem with him. I wish I'd known beforehand.

Leo

The cost of trust

I have bought and sold a lot of stuff on the Net, and I've had only one major problem. I know I'm honest; but if I distrust the unknown person on the other end and require shipment before I pay or money before I ship, the whole process breaks down. As a Christian, I am comfortable treating the other person only with respect and with the same expectation of honesty that I expect them to have for me. If it costs me $200 or more to treat someone as an honest person, then that is the way it goes.

Lamar Frederick

searching through article subjects, so search for "FAQ" to locate these articles quickly.

- They are available by anonymous FTP from *rtfm.mit.edu* in the directory */pub/usenet/misc.forsale.non-computer.*

- They are available via the World Wide Web at the URL

```
http://www.smartpages.com/bngfaqs/misc/forsale/
   non-computer/top.html
```

If you have any information that might help solve the "T. Le" case, please write to *ripoff@ipoint.vlsi.uiuc.edu.*

CHAPTER 7

Pranks, spams, and time wasters

Your time is valuable.

Whether you use the Internet for business or for fun, your time is important. When you're busy working, you don't need pointless distractions. And when you're busy playing, you don't want your leisure time wasted by annoyances.

Unfortunately, some people on the Internet don't seem to care about the value of your time. Advertisers send you electronic junk mail. Practical jokers spread hoaxes designed to make you worry. Selfish users clog thousands of Usenet newsgroups with duplicate articles, forcing you to wade through garbage to find articles of interest. All of this is even more relevant if you are paying for your Internet link by the minute or by the megabyte.

This chapter is about events on the Internet that can suck up your time. Some of them are funny, and some are malicious. They're like false alarms to a fire department: they make a lot of noise and get your attention, but the time that they take up is largely wasted.

This chapter covers:

April Fools' Day pranks
Every year, hundreds of misleading messages are spread around the Internet on April 1. Don't be too quick to believe them, or you might find yourself the butt of a joke.

Junk email

I don't like junk phone calls, but I can deal with them by letting the answering machine get them, or by saying "I'm not interested" and hanging up. Junk email is worse because I have to pay for it, since I pay for email access and disk space. It costs me money, and I hate that.

Nita

Hoaxes and urban legends

These bizarre stories can be entertaining, but they can also be destructive.

Flames

Arguments on the Net can be enjoyable or frustrating, but watch the clock to make sure you don't throw away your entire day.

Trolling

Some people intentionally try to start arguments or make other people look silly. We'll discuss how to spot these tactics.

Junk email

Unsolicited advertisements are arriving in people's electronic mailboxes with increasing frequency.

Spamming

This practice of posting duplicate articles to large numbers of Usenet newsgroups (sometimes thousands) wastes everybody's time and computer resources.

In some ways, this is the most lighthearted chapter of the book. An April Fools' joke can make you laugh, even if you fall for it and are laughing at yourself. Some hoaxes and urban legends can be amusing too, once you know the truth behind them. As long as you are enjoying yourself, your time isn't being wasted. But it's another story entirely if a prank causes you to waste effort, lose money, or distrust something unnecessarily. In addition, some of the topics covered represent very serious issues. Intrusions like junk email and spamming threaten the future of the Net as we know it.

April Fools' Day is an active time on the Net.

April Fools' Day is a grand tradition on Usenet. Every year on April 1, hundreds of practical jokers post misleading articles in scores of newsgroups, hoping to fool or entertain their fellow users. The topics of these pranks range from reasonably believable ("Microsoft has just purchased WordPerfect") to outright silly ("Microsoft has just purchased the Vatican") and everywhere in between.

For the most part, April Fools' jokes on the Net are a lot of fun. So why mention them in a book about Internet risks? Because sometimes a joke can be realistic enough that people believe it, causing them to waste time and possibly make fools of themselves in public (which is the point, I suppose). If you don't want to be the butt of a joke, then watch out every April 1.

Traditionally, the authors of April Fools' articles will leave clues in the headers or the text, indicating that the article is not what it seems. Common clues include:

- A posting date of April 1 at midnight, as indicated in the `Date` header line:

  `Date: 1 Apr 95 00:00:00 GMT`

- Imaginary computer names in the `From` and `Path` header lines. One name that regularly pops up is *kremvax*. This is a homage to the first Usenet April Fools' joke in 1984, when a European user spoofed a posting from an imaginary computer at the Kremlin in the Soviet Union.

- Anagrams of "April Fools." For example, one joke posting mentioned a rock band named Slirp Aloof, and another was posted by the user *prail@folos.yda*.

- Postings that appear to come from famous people, living or dead.

An urban legend is a story that "everybody knows."

Have you ever heard that the childhood rhyme "Ring Around the Rosie" was inspired by the Black Plague? How about this one: if you draw on a compact disc with a green magic marker, the sound quality will improve? If so, then you have heard *urban legends:* stories that "everybody" seems to know or that your friend heard from her brother's boss's aunt.

Some urban legends, like the ones we just mentioned, are relatively harmless. It doesn't really matter whether or not you believe that all snowflakes are different, or that a penny dropped from the top of the Empire State Building will crack through the sidewalk. Some urban legends, however, can make people take unnecessary action or precautions, or distrust something that is really harmless.

For example, an urban legend that has made the rounds on email is the *gangster headlight initiation* hoax. In a new initiation ritual, gangsters were supposedly driving around with their

Urban legends

An urban legend:

- *appears mysteriously and spreads spontaneously in varying forms;*

- *contains elements of humor or horror (the horror often "punishes" someone who flouts society's conventions);*

- *makes good storytelling;*

- *does NOT have to be false, although most are. Urban legends often have a basis in fact, but it's their life after-the-fact (particularly in reference to the second and third points) that gives them particular interest.*

Terry Chan and Peter van der Linden, *alt.folklore.urban* FAQ

headlights off. Whenever helpful drivers would flash their headlights to indicate that the gangsters' lights were off, the gangsters would kill them. Although the story is false, the Illinois State Police actually issued an official warning about it, lending credence to the story. They later retracted the warning (and were probably quite embarrassed).

In the next few sections, we'll look at a few of the more notorious urban legends. When repeated on the Internet, they spread rapidly, thanks to the speed of email and Usenet news. As a result, they cause problems for users, system administrators, and even government agencies.

Craig Shergold doesn't need any more get-well cards.

One of the most famous urban legends on the Net is the story of Craig Shergold. Craig, the legend goes, is a seven-year-old British boy dying of a brain tumor. Craig is supposedly trying to get into the Guinness Book of World Records by receiving the most get-well cards in history. Everyone who reads the story is asked to send a card to help Craig realize his goal.

This sad yet heartwarming tale did not originate on the Net; it has been bouncing around the world for many years. It is based on truth, but the story is many years out of date. Craig set the world record long, long ago, so he doesn't need any more cards from well-wishers.

Unfortunately, the story keeps spreading. To this day, get-well cards are still pouring into the hospital where Craig was originally treated. And nobody really knows what, if anything, can be done about it. The Craig Shergold story has propagated so long and so far that it has proved difficult to stamp out, even after public announcements in the *New York Times, People Magazine,* and Ann Landers' column.

So if you hear this story on the Net (or anywhere else), please don't send any get-well cards, and please tell your friends that the story is outdated and should not be spread any further.

Incidentally, Craig was eventually cured. A sympathetic billionaire heard Craig's story and paid for specialized medical treatment that saved Craig's life.

There is no FCC modem tax.

Another long-standing urban legend says that the Federal Communications Commission (FCC) is considering legislation to make modem users pay extra money for their telephone connections. When this gets spread on the Net, you can imagine how much chaos it causes. Think of how many Internet users have modems! People start calling and writing letters to the FCC and Congress, urging them not to support this plan.

Unlike the Craig Shergold story, this one is a complete hoax. If you see it on the Net, please don't call the FCC about it. They are familiar with this hoax and wish people would ignore it.

There is no Good Times virus.

In the Fall of 1994, a scary article was widely distributed on the Net, alerting thousands of Internet users to a terrible danger. The article claimed that a destructive computer virus, called the *Good Times virus,* was being spread throughout the Internet. This virus was unlike most others because it was spread by simple email, in a message with the subject line "Good Times." If you receive such an email message, said the article, you should delete it immediately without reading it, or else your computer will catch the virus, which would then erase your hard drive.

Experienced computer users and programmers recognized that this was a hoax. It isn't possible for a computer to become infected by a virus simply by receiving and displaying an email message. A virus can be caught only if you run a program that contains a virus or if you boot your computer with a virus-infected disk. But many less-experienced users were fooled. People who believed the message forwarded it to their friends. System administrators worldwide were deluged with questions from users who feared the worst.

On December 6, 1994, the Computer Incident Advisory Capability (CIAC) of the United States Department of Energy released a statement to combat this spread of misinformation. "The Good Times virus is an urban legend," it stated. "Upon investigation, the CIAC has determined that this message originated from both a user of America Online and a student at a university at approximately the same time, and it was meant to be a hoax. As of this date, there are no known viruses which can infect merely through reading a mail message."

The Good Times virus

Here is some important information. Beware of a file called Goodtimes... There is a virus on America Online being sent by E-Mail. If you get anything called "Good Times", DON'T read it or download it. It is a virus that will erase your hard drive. Forward this to all your friends. It may help them a lot.

The original Good Times virus hoax—
author unknown

The Good Times virus is an example of a destructive hoax. The total amount of time, computing resources (disk space, email traffic), and human worry that resulted from this hoax was significant enough that the government got involved. If you receive a copy of this "warning," please ignore it, and do not pass it on to others. In addition, you should alert the sender of the message that the story is untrue.

The ironic part of the Good Times hoax is that in the end, the email "warning" itself behaved rather like a virus. A virus infects a computer and makes copies of itself so it can spread to other computers. Similarly, the "warning" was duplicated thousands of times and spread to computers around the world via email and Usenet news. Strange, eh?

Flames are online insults.

A *flame* is an online message intended to insult or provoke other users. Sending a flame is called *flaming*, and people who do it are called *flamers*. If you've read Usenet news for any length of time, you're probably already familiar with flames and flaming, but here's an example:

```
Wayne:    "Gilligan's Island" used to be my favorite TV
          show.
Kev:      <gag> No way... I can't believe anybody
          actually liked that piece of trash, except
          maybe total dweebs with an IQ of 37.
Wayne:    Hey, well at least I have a brain at all,
          idiot.  What was YOUR favorite show - "The
          Brady Bunch in Outer Space??"
```

Flames can be more subtle, of course:

```
XYZ Inc.: Buy our product today!  It dices!  It SLICES!
          Only $47.95!!
Carol:    <Yawn...>  Hellllp, someone stop me before I
          post my credit card number....
```

Depending on your mood, your personal involvement with the topic, and the phase of the moon, flames can be either fun or annoying. Sometimes it's fun to blow off a little steam by "toasting" somebody in the newsgroup. But when a newsgroup fills up with flames, the other articles get obscured, and readers might have to waste a lot of time wading through the junk to locate on-topic material. (Good news-reading software can make a big difference here.)

Flames can also waste your time if you get caught up in responding to them. A big flaming argument in a newsgroup is called a *flame war*, and getting involved in one can really suck away your time. In general, before you flame somebody, take a moment and consider whether it's going to be worth the effort. Will you be contributing something valuable to the newsgroup or just adding noise?

Flames can also hurt others' feelings, and some flames might even get you in legal trouble. Chapter 10 discusses issues of online libel.

Trolling is the art of putting out bait for unwary readers.

A *troll* is an online message, typically posted on Usenet, whose purpose is to attract responses and make the responders look stupid. If the intended responses are flames, the message is sometimes called *flame bait*. People who troll want to make you waste your time responding to their pointless statements.

For example, suppose you are happily reading the literary newsgroup *rec.arts.books* when you come across an article that says, "There's no point to reading so-called 'non-fiction' books any more, since today's publishing companies are all controlled by the government—particularly the CIA."

You might have several different responses to this claim (assuming that you don't believe it). You could ignore it. You could reply by email to the author. Or, you could post a followup article. If you picked the last choice, then congratulations: you have been trolled!

The typical troller posts once and then disappears, letting the arguments flare while he watches from the sidelines (or completely ignores the responses). Some trollers instead participate in the resulting argument and continue to make intentionally ridiculous or inflammatory comments, laughing all the way.

How can you avoid becoming the butt of a joke by responding to a troll? Here are some common warning signs can help you recognize trolling in an article:

- *Very obvious factual errors*, intended to draw huge numbers of corrections. For example, if someone posted an article in the Star Trek newsgroup, *rec.arts.startrek*, that intentionally

What is a troll?

The well-constructed troll is a post that induces lots of newbies and flamers to make themselves look even more like idiots than they already do, while subtly conveying to the more savvy and experienced that it is in fact a deliberate troll.

The Jargon File, version 3.1.0,
15 October 1994

Q: Somebody just posted that
Roman Polanski directed Star Wars.
What should I do?

—smartaleck@some.site

A: Post the correct answer at once!
We can't have people go on
believing that! Very good of you to
spot this. You'll probably be the only
one to make the correction, so post
as soon as you can. No time to lose,
so certainly don't wait a day, or
check to see if somebody else has
made the correction.

Brad Templeton, "Emily Postnews
Answers Your Questions on
Netiquette," *news.announce.newusers*

mixed up two of the characters (say, Kirk and Spock), legions of fans will be tempted to post corrections. That's exactly what the troller wants to happen.

- *Highly controversial topics*, sometimes presented in a fanatical manner. For example, if somebody posts an article in *soc.women* saying that married women should be required by law to take their husband's last name, that is almost surely flame bait. Other favorite troll topics are abortion, politics, and religion.

- *Insults directed against the main topic of a newsgroup, or against the readers.* An example would be an article in a computer programming group that simply says, "Computer programming is for geeks; all you losers need to get a life!" This sort of article tends to appear from out of nowhere, posted by a user who doesn't usually hang out in the newsgroup and just wants to make trouble.

- *Old arguments that refuse to die.* For several years in the Commodore and Atari computer newsgroups, any article comparing the two computers would invoke a flame war. It was prime troll material to crosspost an article in both newsgroups, claiming that one of the computers was clearly better than the other, especially for ridiculous reasons.

- *Strange or hostile crossposting.* If a strange or antagonistic article is crossposted to unrelated newsgroups—say, *talk.politics.libertarian* and *alt.pets.hamsters*—it may be a troll. If the newsgroups are devoted to opposing topics, the probability of trolling is even higher.

- *Anonymous addresses.* Trollers like to post once and then disappear, and anonymous addresses make this easier.

- *Followups directed to "test" newsgroups.* Check the `Followup-To` line in the article header to see if it contains the newsgroup *misc.test* or another "test" newsgroup. This is very bad, because anybody who posts a response to the troll will be automatically deluged with unwanted email. You see, *misc.test* is a special newsgroup for testing a computer's Usenet connection. If your response is sent to *misc.test*, dozens of computers around the world will automatically respond by email, telling you that your "test post" was successful. Ouch!

The best thing to do with a troll is ignore it. While it might be momentarily satisfying to voice your disagreement, you're doing just want the troller wants you to do: wasting your time and energy.

Internet advertising has good and bad points.

"CYBER SALES!" cried the cover of the May 1995 issue of *Internet World*, a special issue on Internet advertising. Like it or not, advertising and commercialism on the Internet are increasing steadily. Many vendors see the Internet as a vast, untapped market. Users, however, see the Internet as an environment for working, playing, and communicating. Can these two views coexist comfortably?

For consumers, Internet advertising can be annoying or enjoyable. If a vendor bombards our electronic mailboxes with ads for a new laundry detergent, that's nothing but a headache for us. But on the other hand, suppose you're a big fan of musical artist Billy Joel, and his record company sent you a polite announcement every time Billy released a new album or scheduled a concert in your area. You might really appreciate the information. To be even less intrusive, the company could maintain a World Wide Web page about Billy's activities.

The challenge of online advertising is to straddle the line between vendors' interests (selling their products and services) and our interests (privacy, and the need for certain products and services). Will vendors learn to advertise in a way that is not annoying and takes into account the unique aspects of the Net community? Let's hope so.

Two techniques—*junk email* and *spamming*—have recently become popular for online advertising. These methods are almost universally hated by users; they invade our privacy, clutter our newsgroups and mailboxes, and cost us time and money. And yet, they are increasingly used because they are cheap (for the advertiser, not the consumers) and are believed to reach huge numbers of users quickly (which may not be true, as we'll see). The remaining sections in this chapter discuss these two methods in detail.

Junk email is an increasing problem.

If there are any people on earth who enjoy receiving junk mail, I haven't met them. In today's advertisement-ridden society,

Robomailers

I once received a really stupid, automatically generated junk email advertisement. The guy apparently skimmed my email address from a Usenet article I posted in misc.consumers. His software quoted the first two lines of my posting, appended his advertisement, and emailed it to me. He never bothered to proofread his ad before sending it to me, so he never knew that my posting was a criticism of another stupid advertisement. The two lines that his software quoted were part of the ad, not my words.

Andrew Green

When I post articles as the moderator of comp.sys.amiga.reviews, the Usenet headers list my name as "comp.sys.amiga.reviews moderator." Several robomailers have sent me junk email that begins "Dear comp.sys.amiga.reviews," assuming that this must be my first name. Duhhh....

Dan Barrett

Myths and facts about junk email

MYTH   Junk email isn't a problem because there's so little of it right now.

FACT   Junk email is increasing. New junk mailings are discussed daily in the Usenet newsgroup *news.admin.net-abuse.misc*. In my own mailbox, junk email has gone from "almost zero" in the late 1980s to two or three messages per week in late 1995. (People who belong to a lot of mailing lists get even more.) As more and more advertisers discover that the Internet is an extremely cheap way to reach millions of users, you can bet that junk email will continue to increase.

MYTH   Junk email isn't intrusive because users can conveniently delete it without reading it.

FACT   This is false for two reasons. First, how can you know that a message is junk email until you read it? Advertisers certainly aren't going to write "this is junk mail" in the Subject line of a junk mailing to help us identify it. Indeed, if postal junk mail is any indication, it's more likely that advertisers will use catchy Subject lines like "HIGHLY IMPORTANT—READ IMMEDIATELY" to get our attention.

Second, this myth completely avoids the question of quantity. If junk email increases to the point where we get dozens of messages per day, even if we don't read it, this intrusive mail will require time to identify and delete.

MYTH   Unlike paper junk mail, junk email doesn't waste resources.

FACT   While junk email doesn't require paper, it does require disk space and computer time. When an advertiser broadcasts a 50-line junk email message to ten thousand users (a trivial task that can be done by a computer program), this mailing takes up about 30 megabytes of other people's disk space. And that's just one advertisement from one

advertiser. Multiply this by a thousand advertisers, and you're talking 30 gigabytes (30 thousand megabytes) of disk space if each of them sends just one ad. Each of those email messages also requires a small amount of computer time to deliver, and that computer time adds up. And it isn't just the advertiser's computer that bears the load; it's your computer too, each time it has to receive an email message.

MYTH   If a piece of junk email begins, "Sorry to disturb you, but we thought you might be interested in our product—if we were mistaken, then please delete this message with our apologies," then the advertiser is genuinely concerned about your privacy.

FACT   If you received a hundred messages like the above from a hundred different companies, would you think that they were all concerned about your privacy? Fat chance. If they were really concerned, they wouldn't send you junk email in the first place.

Why is the advertiser making this polite-sounding statement then? The answer is: fear. For the first time in junk advertising history, the consumer can respond to unsolicited ads by simply pressing a key or clicking a mouse button. A substantial number of junk email recipients send angry responses back to the advertiser. The advertiser's electronic mailbox is sometimes so overrun with angry responses that their disk space fills up! In other cases, people have sent complaints to the postmaster of the advertiser's computer in such great quantities that advertisers have had their login privileges revoked. Advertisers want to prevent this from happening, of course, so nowadays they begin their ads very politely, hoping that you won't complain. (Do you think it works?)

junk mail is an added nuisance that fills our mailboxes and wastes time and paper.

On the Internet, no paper is necessary, but junk mail is alive and well. *Junk email* is unsolicited electronic mail, usually from advertisers or pranksters. Its roots stretch back to at least 1980, when computer users on The Source, one of the first commercial dial-up systems, would generate lists of all usernames and broadcast email to everyone. The oldest piece I have saved is from 1992, when a "nonprofit evangelical Christian mission" broadcast email asking for charitable donations of computer equipment. Since that time, I've received hundreds more junk email messages, with topics ranging from music magazines to "personalized letters from Santa Claus" to a "sex knowledge survey."

Some advertisers say that junk email is no worse than postal junk mail or telephone solicitations, and we should just live with it. Not true! Junk email is different from these other methods for a very important reason. When an advertiser uses the Postal Service or the telephone to reach you, the advertiser pays the bill. When junk email is sent to you, however, *you* pay for it! If your online service provider charges you for incoming email, disk space, and/or computer time, then you pay to receive, store, and/or read these advertisements. And if you're connected to the Internet via a long-distance telephone call, you pay yet again for the time it takes to read this junk. Even if you have a direct connection to the Internet, such as a corporate or university computer account, large amounts of junk email can take up precious disk space. (And your company or university foots the bill, indirectly affecting your profits or tuition bills.)

For these reasons, junk email is really more like junk faxing: unsolicited advertisements sent to your fax machine. When you receive a junk fax, you pay for the paper, and you indirectly pay for the time that your fax machine is busy receiving the ad. Junk faxing has been made illegal in some states.

How do advertisers gather email addresses? A growing number of them use a technique called *header scanning*. Using a computer program, the advertiser scans Usenet article headers for the `From` line, containing the poster's email address. Another program, called a *robomailer* ("robot mailer"), then broadcasts junk email to these addresses. Once these programs are set up,

Crossposting vs. spamming

To show that crossposting and spamming have very different effects on the Net, let's look at an example. Suppose you want to buy a new CD-ROM disc of vegetarian recipes and use it on your IBM PC, but you don't know which disc to buy. So, you decide to post on Usenet for a recommendation. After using your news-reading program to search for relevant newsgroups, you decide to ask your question in four of them: *rec.food.veg.cooking* (vegetarian cooking), *rec.food.recipes* (recipe requests), *comp.sys.ibm.pc.misc* (IBM PC computers), and *comp.publish.cdrom.multimedia* (since you want the CD-ROM to have fancy food graphics and a built-in "aroma" generator for authentic smells).

The proper way to post your article to all four newsgroups is to use crossposting. This is done by posting your article *once*, but specifying that you want it to appear in four different newsgroups, as shown in the left side of the figure that appears on the opposite page. In many news-posting programs, you indicate this by putting all the newsgroup names on the Newsgroups line of your article, separated by commas:

    Newsgroups: rec.food.veg.cooking,rec.food.recipes,
                comp.sys.ibm.pc.misc,
                comp.publish.cdrom.multimedia

(Typically, all the newsgroup names will be on the same line.) When you post this article, only a single copy will be transmitted, and it will be automatically "linked" to show up in all four newsgroups.

As a special convenience feature, most modern news-reading programs will show people the article only once, even if they subscribe to all four newsgroups.

Spamming the article is done by posting four separate times, once to each newsgroup, as shown in the right side of the figure. This creates four separate copies of the article, each of which gets separately transmitted around the world. This uses four times the disk space and four times the computer time that crossposting does. (And some spammers post thousands of copies, not four!) In addition, the convenience of crossposting is lost: people who subscribe to several of these newsgroups will be forced to see (and ignore) your article multiple times.

Incidentally, whenever you crosspost an article, you should choose one newsgroup where any resulting discussion should take place. This is called *redirecting followups*. It is simple to do: just put one newsgroup name on the Followup-To line in your article header before you post it:

    Followup-To: rec.food.veg.cooking

If you forget to do this, then other users may continue the discussion in any (or all) of the four newsgroups, and you'll have to follow all of these newsgroups in order to keep up. Redirecting followups makes things easier for everybody involved.

Crossposting

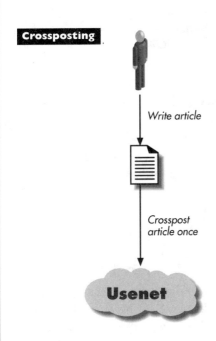

Write article

Crosspost
article once

Usenet

Result of Crossposting

All newsgroups "point to"
same copy of article.

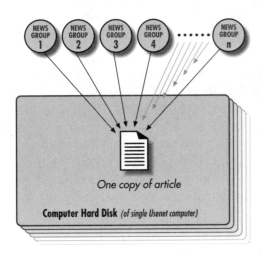

NEWS GROUP 1   NEWS GROUP 2   NEWS GROUP 3   NEWS GROUP 4   • • • • •   NEWS GROUP n

One copy of article

Computer Hard Disk *(of single Usenet computer)*

Spamming

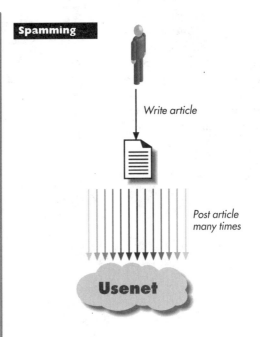

Write article

Post article
many times

Usenet

Result of Spamming

Each newsgroup contains
a different copy.

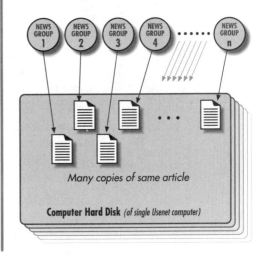

NEWS GROUP 1   NEWS GROUP 2   NEWS GROUP 3   NEWS GROUP 4   • • • • •   NEWS GROUP n

Many copies of same article

Computer Hard Disk *(of single Usenet computer)*

all of the scanning and emailing can be done without human intervention.

Robomailing can be extremely annoying, especially for people with several computer accounts. More than once, I've logged in to find five copies of the same junk email message because a robomailer sent it to five of my accounts. Yuck!

If you receive junk email that you do not appreciate, it's usually easy to do something about it. You can respond to the email, telling the advertiser that you do not want to be on their mailing list. Some advertisers, however, use computer programs to handle all responses, making it difficult to contact them with complaints. Other advertisers simply ignore your responses. If you like, you can also write to the postmaster of the computer that the advertiser uses; Chapter 11 discusses this in detail.

Spams are massive, duplicate posts.

Suppose you decide to spend a quiet evening relaxing and reading Usenet news. While browsing the classical music newsgroup *rec.music.classical*, you are surprised to see an article advertising cosmetics. "Hmm, that user is pretty clueless," you might think, as you skip the article and move on to the next. Later, while you're reading about skydiving in *rec.skydiving*, you see the same advertisement again! "How strange," you think. But after you've seen the same ad yet again in *comp.sys.mac.misc*, *alt.activism*, and *rec.arts.tv*, you might start getting annoyed. Welcome to Spam City, friend.

Spamming is the practice of posting large numbers of duplicate articles in many Usenet newsgroups. A person who does it is called a *spammer*, and the articles themselves are simply called *spam*. A small portion of the Net refers to spam as *Excessive Multi-Postings* (EMP). (The word "spam" comes from an old Monty Python skit. Eric Idle and Graham Chapman go to a diner where every item on the menu has Spam meat product as an ingredient. So it's no wonder that the word got applied to multiple postings, when every newsgroup has a bit o' spam in it.)

Spams don't have to be ads, and they don't have to be off-topic. (See the sidebar, "Myths and facts about spamming," later in this chapter.) The most important identifying feature is that *many copies* of the article are posted. This is different from *crossposting,* a Net-friendly method for posting a *single copy* of an article and making it appear in multiple newsgroups. The sidebar, "Crossposting vs. spamming," discusses the differences in detail.

What can you do if you spot a spam? First, you can take a look in the newsgroup *news.admin.net-abuse.announce* to see if other people have noticed the spam. You can also check *news.admin.net-abuse.misc* for further discussion, since sometimes the spam has an unusual history or some controversy surrounding it. If nobody else has reported the spam yet, you might post an article yourself. (It generally isn't necessary to post "me too" articles, though.) Be sure to include the article headers of one of the spammed copies, and optionally the article text itself.

Some spams are extremely large, reaching thousands of newsgroups. In November 1994, for example, an article about a "skill contest" to win a "luxury four-bedroom penthouse" was spammed to over 2100 newsgroups. Other spams are much smaller, such as a software question that was posted by a naive user in 10 newsgroups in January 1995.

Spamming costs real people real money.

Spammers seem to have a mistaken impression that spamming is "free." After all, it takes very little time and effort to reach millions of readers with a spam.

Let's examine this claim that spamming is "free." by looking at how widespread spamming is, and the total cost to people on the Net. Between October 15, 1994, and March 1, 1995, I monitored Usenet for spam and observed 116 spammed articles. That's about six per week. The top of the table, "Twenty weeks of spam," summarizes the topics of these articles. Fortunately, every one of the spams I saw was quickly detected and canceled. (More about canceling later.)

Let's take a moment and figure out how much disk space is taken up by these spammed articles. The number of copies posted per spam ranged from as few as 10 to as many as 2,190, with an average (mean) of approximately 169 copies. In total, there were 19,656 articles posted by spammers. The average article length was about 2 kilobytes: roughly 1 page of double-

Twenty weeks of spam

Spam topics, October 15, 1994 to March 1, 1995.

Topic	Spams	Topic	Spams
Miscellaneous product sales	19	Questions from naive users	3
Music, art, and theater announcements	9	Surveys posted by businesses	3
Dave Rhodes "Make Money Fast" scam	8	Criminal accusations	2
Legal services	8	Jobs offered	2
Health products and services	7	Jobs wanted	2
Miscellaneous services	6	Political canvassing	2
Surveys posted by users	6	Religious messages	2
Unknown *(not enough information given)*	5	Sexual aid products	2
BBS and online service providers	4	Contests or lotteries	1
Long distance telephone services	4	Credit restoration services	1
Telephone sex lines	4	Obscenities, swearing	1
Various "get rich quick" schemes	4	Pleas for money	1
Bizarre theories (paranoid)	3	Testing news software	1
Charity requests	3		
Entire text of a book	3	TOTAL:	116

Spam statistics, October 15, 1994 to March 1, 1995.

Calculations, Entire Observation Period		
Time period:	20	weeks
Observed spams:	116	spams
Smallest spam:	10	copies
Largest spam:	2109	copies
Average spam:	169	copies
Standard deviation:	357	copies
Total number of spammed copies:	19,656	copies
Total disk space wasted on 250,000 sites:	9,860	gigabytes
Cost of disk space being wasted:	4,901,000	dollars
Calculations, Per Week		
Fewest spams in 1 week:	0	spams
Most spams in 1 week:	16	spams
Average spams per week:	6	spams
Standard deviation:	4	spams
Average spam data, at 2K per article:	338	kilobytes
Total disk space wasted on 250,000 sites:	510	gigabytes
Cost of disk space being wasted:	255,000	dollars

spaced, printed text. From this information, we can calculate that an average spam sends 338 kilobytes of data to every computer on Usenet (169 × 2 kilobytes). With over 250,000 computers on Usenet, that means each spam would have used nearly 85 gigabytes of disk space worldwide (338 × 250,000), had it not been canceled. At $500 per gigabyte (the approximate cost of hard drives in the United States as of May 1995), that's $42,500 worth of disk space being hogged by spam!

When you consider that there were 116 spams, the numbers scale up to almost 9,860 gigabytes ($4,901,000) of disk space hogging. Of course, not all of these spams occurred in the same time period, and news articles expire after about a week at most sites. So a week's worth of spams (six) would still have used 510 gigabytes ($255,000) of disk space. The bottom of the table, "Twenty weeks of spam," summarizes these figures. And we haven't counted the person-hours spent by system administrators worldwide who had to deal with the spams. We also haven't considered another inconvenience: many articles get deleted automatically (by the news software) in order to make room for the incoming spams. The spammers themselves don't see any of this waste—only the computer owners do.

These calculations are very approximate. Not all Usenet computers receive all the newsgroups; some of the articles were significantly larger than 2 kilobytes; and I'm sure I missed some spams along the way. But these numbers should give you an idea of what a problem spamming is for computer owners, operators, and users worldwide. And it is rapidly increasing. (At press time, spamming has increased to three or four spams per *day*.)

The most infamous spammers were Canter and Siegel.

On April 12, 1994, the readers of over 6000 Usenet newsgroups were greeted by an unpleasant surprise. Laurence Canter and Martha Siegel, two immigration lawyers from Phoenix, Arizona, had launched one of the largest-scale spams in Usenet history. Their article was an advertisement for their services, specifically concerning the United States Green Card Lottery, a program in which Green Cards are given to immigrants. Canter and Siegel advertised that, for $95, they could increase your chances of getting a Green Card in this lottery by filing the necessary forms for you. (Incidentally, the Green Card Lottery is free.)

Within hours, Usenet readers around the world had taken notice. Canter and Siegel's telephones, fax machines, and computer accounts were deluged with tens of thousands of complaints, prompting their online service provider to terminate their accounts. System administrators throughout Usenet canceled all copies of the spam. Joel Furr, a well-known Usenet participant, even printed T-shirts that read "Green Card Lawyers/Spamming The Globe." (He sold more than 550 shirts.)

After such a negative response, many users figured that Canter and Siegel would realize they had made a mistake, apologize to the Net, and get on with their lives. Nothing could have been farther from the truth.

Instead, Canter and Siegel established a new company, Cybersell, and started marketing spamming as a legitimate advertising technique. They wrote a book, *How to Make a FORTUNE on the Information Superhighway* (Harper Collins, 1995), advocating spamming and junk email as a modern road to riches. Because their spam had been canceled, Martha Siegel wrote a newspaper article ("Computer Anarchy: A Plea for Internet Laws to Protect the Innocent," *The Chicago Tribune*, December 12, 1994) calling for laws to end the "anarchy" on the Internet, where "self-styled vigilantes" were preventing "innocent" people from conducting business. "The current state of the Internet makes it abundantly clear that general anarchy isn't working," wrote Siegel.

The Internet, however, is perfectly safe for business. Other vendors have been happily conducting business on the Internet for years. What Canter and Siegel did was different because:

- They used the computing resources of thousands of other people to spread their advertisement. Had it not been canceled, their 6000-newsgroup spam (1 kilobyte per article) would have taken up six megabytes of disk space on each Usenet computer. When you consider all 250,000 Usenet sites, that's a total of 1500 gigabytes (about $750,000) of other people's disk space.

- Their ads had nothing to do with the topics of the newsgroups where they appeared. Canter and Siegel ignored the philosophy of Usenet—separate discussion groups for

Pranks, spams, and time wasters

Reactions to Canter and Siegel's spam

Bob Metcalfe, *Infoworld*

"Canter and Siegel have discovered that it's easy with robot mailers and vacation responders to reach hundreds of thousands of Internet users with any random advertising message. Never mind that the vast majority of those so spammed are inconvenienced and turned off by the intrusion. Never mind that valuable Internet resources are cynically misappropriated. A better name for [their] book would be Geeks in Shysterspace." ("From The Ether," February 20, 1995)

Charles Arthur, *New Scientist*

"As an example of Canter and Siegel's flawed reasoning, they argue first that there are no rules on the Internet, so you can do what you want. But when the systems administrators who run the networks connected to the Internet acted together to wipe out the lawyers' spam, they then complained that this violated their First Amendment rights to freedom of speech." (January 7, 1995)

David Sewell, *Usenet*

"Canter and Siegel's spam was an unprecedented display of Usenet newsgroup rudeness, roughly analogous to sticking one's business card inside every single book in every public library in the world."

Ron Newman, *Usenet*

"If the Internet is an Information Superhighway, then Martha Siegel is the litterbug who throws lighted cigarettes into the redwood forest from her car window."

K. K. Campbell, *Eye Magazine*

"No one I talked to takes Canter and Siegel's claim to making $100,000 from their Green Card spam seriously. But, as one put it, 'the IRS might.'"
From "A Net.Conspiracy So Immense: Chatting With Martha Siegel of the Internet's Infamous Canter & Siegel" at:

> http://www.interlog.com/eye/News/Eyenet/CS2.html

Laurence Canter and Martha Siegel,
.net Magazine

"As the Net becomes more a place for the general public than for tech heads, it is the hackers, pornographers, flamers and forgers who are becoming hated, not advertisers. [...] For those that do hate anyone for putting a brief commercial message on Usenet, it may say a good deal more about them than it does about us."

From "Canter and Siegel Speak," at:

> http://www.futurenet.co.uk/netmag/net.html

different issues. (If all advertisers did this, then Usenet would become "Useless-net.")

To this day, Canter and Siegel continue to slam their critics, online and in print, crying that they are being persecuted by a small number of power-hungry users (or "geeks") who "object to advertising" on the Net. The truth, however, is much simpler. Advertising is not the issue. *Massive wastefulness* is the issue. Users simply don't enjoy having their time, money, and disk space wasted by thousands of duplicate messages. Canter and Siegel never discuss this wastefulness; they continue to direct attention away from it, harping on the "advertising" issue, even though it's not relevant.

Canter and Siegel claim that they earned over $100,000 from their Green Card spam, and they say that their book is selling well. If this is true, it's no wonder that spamming remains so popular.

Cancelbots are programs that cancel spam.

Usenet's general response to the Green Card incident was to cancel all copies of the spammed advertisement. To do this, people wrote programs, called *cancelbots* or *robocancelers,* that could conveniently cancel spam. These people were basically trying to protect their computers, and the computers of others, from the heavy loads imposed by spammed articles.

Cancelbots work by issuing cancel messages on Usenet (see Chapter 2). These messages instruct each Usenet computer to delete its copies of the spammed article. Cancel messages are optional; a system administrator can configure his Usenet news software to reject them. There's no analogous way to reject the spams, though.

Who are the people who cancel spams? Some are concerned system administrators, like Ed Brundage of America Online (AOL), who handles Net abuses committed by AOL subscribers. Others are ordinary users. Some cancelers make their names public, and others use nicknames. One of the best-known anonymous spam-cancelers is *Cancelmoose,* who was responsible for canceling Canter and Siegel's spams. *Cancelmoose* was the first person to speak out on Usenet about the philosophy of spam-canceling: that only the quantity of postings, not the content of the postings, determines that an article is spam. Nowadays, nearly every "spam cancellation" announcement posted on Usenet specifically states this philosophy.

There are indeed some users who cancel other people's articles because of their content. We discussed an incident like this, involving the Church of Scientology, in Chapter 2. The spam cancelers, however, have remained consistently opposed to content-based canceling.

Spam cancellation is controversial.

Not everybody agrees that canceling spam is a good idea. The most common argument against canceling is that it's a form of censorship, violating people's right to free speech. This is a misleading analogy, according to the cancelbot creators and other Usenet participants. Anybody, they say, can post an article on Usenet and practice free speech. The cancelbots will not bother them. Spamming, however, is like amplifying your speech to ear-shattering volumes, and is a public nuisance. A person walking through your neighborhood in the middle of the night, shouting into a megaphone, would have a hard time using freedom of speech as an excuse when arrested for disturbing the peace.

The spam-cancelers also explain that canceling is optional. If you are a system administrator, you can configure your news software to ignore these "cancel messages" if you prefer. To do this, however, requires some knowledge about news software that less experienced system administrators might not have.

There is also debate on Usenet about "how much spam is spam." For example, if somebody posts five duplicate copies of an article, is that spam? How about 10 or 20? If not, then where should the line be drawn between "acceptable" and "spam?" Different cancelbot maintainers have different standards.

Another debated issue is whether the "duplicate copies" of an article must be identical to be considered spam. This issue came to a head in December 1994, when Michael Wolff, author of the book *Net Chat* (Random House, 1994), posted a series of similar but not identical articles in many newsgroups. *Net Chat* lists and describes Usenet newsgroups, and Wolff wanted to check his descriptions for accuracy. So he posted a note in each newsgroup, asking users to read the description and send him comments about it. (Curiously, his company posted these

Spam canceling vs. censorship

Consider this: I wish to send a letter to a friend of mine in California. So, I use the U.S. Postal Service. But the letter doesn't get there. Why not? The Postal Service decided that they should not transmit my letter; they "canceled" it.

Now, this means one thing if they did it because my letter was about Bill Clinton being a horrid president. That's censorship. It's a totally different thing if they did it because my letter weighed 15 tons and would have broken their machinery. That's spam-canceling.

Get it? System administrators have the right to defend their systems. The vast majority of system administrators have agreed to join together in certain ways to defend each others' systems.

Karl Krueger

Canceling junk email

Spams can be canceled because the Usenet news software supports cancel messages. There is no similar feature for electronic mail.

questions *after* the book had already been published, leading some Usenet readers to question whether Wolff's queries were really advertisements.)

Across Usenet, spam detector alarms started ringing. But since the articles were not duplicates, they weren't canceled right away. Instead, a large and vocal discussion was held in *news.admin.misc* to decide whether the article constituted spam or not. The majority said "spam," and the articles were canceled. Afterward, Wolff and his coworkers participated in a discussion about this action, insisting that they hadn't done anything wrong. (Interestingly, some of Wolff & Co.'s responses were multiply posted instead of crossposted. You decide....)

The *Net Chat* incident got quite a bit of press, reaching *The Wall Street Journal*, *The San Jose Mercury News*, *The San Francisco Examiner*, and *The Dallas Morning News*. Sadly, most of these articles told only one side of the story (Wolff's) and contained some gross inaccuracies. One of the worst offenders was the syndicated article, "Cybervigilante Targets Internet Author: Says Writer Violated Netiquette Rules," (*Dallas Morning News*, January 6, 1995), which is riddled with errors. For example:

- The article said that a vigilante is "systematically removing every message" that Wolff posts on Usenet, making Wolff "effectively shut off from the nearly 9,000 newsgroups." This sounds scary, but it isn't true: only the spammed messages were canceled. Wolff's other articles were untouched, and he freely posted his opinions about the cancellations.

- The reason for the cancellations was said to be their commercial (advertising) intent. But the content was irrelevant, according to the cancelers in widely posted articles that Wolff himself responded to. The articles were canceled because they were spam.

- The article said that *Cancelmoose* is a computer program, when in fact it is a username (really an alias).

Most Net experts agree that cancelbots are only a temporary approach to the problem of spamming. What is needed is better news software that makes spamming difficult or impossible to do, or that lets system administrators easily identify and remove spam from their computers if they so desire. User education is also needed, so people learn that spamming is wasteful, impolite, and generally undesirable. Let's hope that

Myths and facts about spamming

MYTH   Only advertisements count as spam.

FACT   The content of the article is irrelevant. If duplicate copies are posted to many newsgroups, this is spamming.

MYTH   If a multiply posted article is relevant to the topics of the newsgroups where it appears, then it isn't spam.

FACT   The content of the article is irrelevant. If duplicate copies are posted to many newsgroups, this is spamming.

MYTH   People who cancel spammed articles do it because they disagree with the content of the articles.

FACT   The content of the article is irrelevant.... (Do I sound like a broken record yet?)

MYTH   I made a small change in each copy of my multiply posted article. Since the copies aren't duplicates any more, then it isn't spam.

FACT   Many Usenet readers still consider this to be spam, and it's likely to be canceled.

MYTH   Crossposting is the same as spamming.

FACT   In crossposting, a single copy of an article is made to appear in multiple newsgroups. In spamming, many duplicate copies are posted, one per newsgroup. As a result, spamming causes much more network load and uses much more disk space than crossposting does.

Crossposting is perfectly fine to do on Usenet. It is polite, however, to crosspost an article only to a few groups (say, no more than five or ten). Massive crossposting to huge numbers of newsgroups is frowned upon by some Usenet participants, who refer to it as *velveeta*.

MYTH   Canter and Siegel posted the first spam in Usenet history.

FACT   Their Green Card spam was very large and received a lot of press, but it wasn't the first spam. People have been doing mass postings almost as long as Usenet has been around.

MYTH   The term "spamming" was coined after (or because of) Canter and Siegel's "Green Card" spam.

FACT   The term existed long before Canter and Siegel came on the scene.

MYTH   Hey, what are you talking about?!? I've never seen any spams!

FACT   You can thank the cancelbots for that.

sometime in the near future, spamming will disappear from the Net.

For more information...

A wonderful and comprehensive collection of Usenet April Fools' jokes is maintained by David Barberi at the University of North Carolina. Check out his World Wide Web page at the URL

```
http://sunsite.unc.edu/dbarberi/april-fools.html
```

If you hear or read a "true" story that sounds too strange to be true, be sure to check the *alt.folklore.urban* Frequently Asked Questions (FAQ) articles. It is very entertaining reading; you'll be surprised at how many popular beliefs actually turn out to be urban legends. You can obtain the FAQ in the newsgroup, where it is posted twice a month, or you can visit the Web Page at

```
http://www.dsg.cs.tcd.ie/dsg_people/afcondon/AFU/
    AFU-FAQ.html
```

If you're interested in learning more later, check out the Usenet newsgroup *alt.folklore.urban*, where urban legends are discussed every day. If the traffic in *alt.folklore.urban* is too heavy, try the moderated newsgroup *alt.folklore.suburban*. There are also other *alt.folklore* newsgroups dedicated to specific folklore topics.

Junk email, spams, and spam cancellations are announced on Usenet in the newsgroup *news.admin.net-abuse.announce*, and discussion is carried on in *news.admin.net-abuse.misc*. A detailed FAQ on these sorts of Net abuses is available on the Web at

```
http://www.smartpages.com/faqs/net-abuse-faq/top.html
```

CHAPTER 8

Strangers, friends, and lovers

The Internet is a terrific place to meet people from around the world.

Meeting people on the Internet isn't the same as meeting them face to face, but it offers an advantage over the old-fashioned method: namely, the ability to span great distances quickly and cheaply. Many of the Net folks you meet will live hundreds or thousands of miles away from you. Without the Internet, you couldn't get to know these people without wearing out all your pencils or running up a multimillion dollar telephone bill.

When you combine this high speed and low cost with the anonymity of usernames, you get a totally new form of communication. For the first time in history, people can have long, personal conversations with thousands of total strangers. After months or years of "talking" with the same Net friends, you'll probably feel like you have a clear picture of their likes, dislikes, senses of humor, and even personalities.

But...do you really *know* these people?

This simple-sounding question is much more complex than it seems, and we'll address it in this chapter. We will cover three major topics:

Chat groups
    We take a lighthearted look at "live" discussion groups and

What's in a name?

One person who wrote me was named Dipendra. I thought that sounded like a girl's name, so I am talking about all this intimate girl talk only to find after about four or five letters that it is a guy from India.

Tryphena

Lisa Feldman
Barrett, Ph.D.

the users (some human, some not) that populate them. What are the risks you can encounter while chatting?

Issues of trust

The chapter takes a more serious turn as we ask: how can you "know" people you have never met in person? How much can you trust them?

Internet romance

Is it possible to fall in love over the Net? How can you minimize your risk when meeting a Net sweetheart in person for the first time?

Chat groups let you "talk" with people around the world.

A *chat group* is a virtual meeting place where you can converse with other users from all parts of the globe. Unlike Usenet newsgroups or electronic mail, chat groups are "live"; that is, they let all the participants talk at the same time. So when you "speak" (by typing something on your keyboard), your words become visible to everybody else in the chat group. In order to keep the conversation understandable, the chat software automatically displays the name of the speaker. As an example, let's listen in on a "discussion" about desserts:

```
<harvey> I just tried this *awesome* chocolate cake
recipe.
<donna> Anybody here have a recipe for almond cookies?
*** shaggy has just joined
<shaggy> hi everybody - what's new?
<crystal> donna: I have one. What's your email
address?
<genghis> harvey: where did you get it?
<donna> hi shaggy!
<shaggy> anybody see last night's TV special about
famous restaurants in italy?
<harvey> genghis: I read it in rec.food.recipes.
```

Let's take a closer look at the this discussion. There are five participants: *harvey, donna, crystal, genghis,* and one late arrival, *shaggy.* The name at the beginning of each line, inside angled brackets, indicates the speaker, and it is displayed automatically by the chat software. These names are usually nicknames that the chat software lets each person choose.

Discussions can occur out of sequence.

You probably noticed that the sentences in the above discussion are mixed up in the wrong order. This is because several conversations are going on at the same time, and several people are typing at once. On your screen, these conversations become *interleaved*; that is, every conversation has bits of other conversations stuck in the middle. Another reason for the strange ordering is that everybody's words are coming to you from different computers scattered around the Internet, so they can arrive at rather unpredictable times.

In this discussion, there are actually three separate conversations going on. For instance, *harvey* and *genghis* are talking about chocolate cake. If you look only at *harvey's* and *genghis's* words, the conversation will become clear:

```
<harvey> I just tried this *awesome* chocolate cake
recipe.
<genghis> harvey: where did you get it?
<harvey> genghis: I read it in rec.food.recipes.
```

(Notice that *genghis* and *harvey* type each other's nickname to help make the flow of the conversation more understandable.) Similarly, *donna* and *crystal* are talking about almond cookies, and *shaggy* is trying to start a conversation about Italian restaurants. This might all look confusing at first, but believe me, you get used to it quickly.

A chat service is a provider of chat groups.

One of the most popular chat services in the world is Internet Relay Chat (IRC). IRC chat groups are called *channels,* and each channel is devoted to a particular topic. For example, science fiction television shows are discussed in *#star_trek*, Commodore Amiga computers are discussed in *#amiga*, and you can guess what is discussed in *#hotsex*. (Actually, you might be wrong. The channel names are often completely unrelated to the topics that get discussed. We're only human, after all....) You can also create your own channels and invite your Net friends to join you. Many Internet machines have a program to let you connect to IRC, often called **irc**. Chat groups are also available on major online service providers like America Online, CompuServe, and Prodigy.

A *Multi-User Dungeon* (MUD) is a special kind of chat group in which the participants don't just sit around and talk. They participate in dungeon (role-playing) games that let the players interact as if they were together in a huge dungeon, even though they are using different computers. MUDs can also be a fun way to meet people on the Net.

Some chat group users have more power than others.

Not all chat group users are equal. Some users are *operators,* or *ops.* Operators run the chat group and have special abilities online. If you ever misbehave in a chat group, you might find yourself disciplined by an operator.

Operators often have two special abilities, called *kicking* and *banning.* Kicking means removing somebody from the chat group temporarily. An operator might do this if a user gets very obnoxious, sends large amounts of text to the screen quickly (this is called *flooding*), or breaks the local rules of etiquette in some other way. A kicked user can quickly rejoin the chat group, but the hope is that he will behave now.

If kicking doesn't solve a problem, an operator may resort to banning. Banning prevents a user from joining the chat group at all. An operator typically will ban a user who repeatedly annoys the other participants, especially if the user has been kicked before and didn't wise up. A ban can last for a limited period of time, or it can be permanent.

How do you become an operator? There are two ways. The easy way is to make friends with another operator, who can then "op" you (make you an operator) with a special command. The hard way is to run your own chat service and make yourself an operator.

Bots are programs that look like users.

Did you know that some of the users who hang around chat groups aren't human? Don't be surprised if a "person" that you try to meet turns out to be a *bot* instead. A bot (short for robot) is a computer program that appears to be an ordinary chat group user. It has a nickname, and it can send messages to the other chat group users.

Some bots are created to be helpful.

If you send a message to a helpful bot, it will often respond with useful or entertaining information. Typically, the message "HELP" will make a bot send you instructions on how to use it.

An example of a helpful bot is *Mama* on IRC, written by Peter Sjöström of Sweden. On request, *Mama* will upload and download files, answer simple questions about popular topics, remember messages for users who are offline (as an answering machine does), and even sing in Swedish. *Mama* has a World Wide Web page at the URL

```
http://www.ludd.luth.se/~pjotr/mama.cgi
```

Another kind of helpful bot is a *game bot* that plays games with users. One of the stranger game bots on IRC is *moobot*, who wanders around IRC channels, mooing like a cow, and invites users to play a memory game similar to Mastermind. Game bots are created to be fun, but some people don't like them because the flow of conversation gets interrupted by all the game-playing messages.

Some bots are created to be harmful.

Unfortunately, some people create "bad" bots and unleash them in an unsuspecting chat group to cause problems. Harmful bots fall into several major categories.

Annoyance bots
  These bots just waste your time by annoying you. They might print obscene messages, send you dozens of questions, or make comments that are guaranteed to start arguments, like joining the *#religion* channel and making sweeping statements about abortion.

Flood bots
  Flooding means sending lots and lots of text to the screen all at once. This is considered very impolite. Since many users are chatting at once, a "flood" of text can interrupt the flow of conversation and confuse people. A flood bot is a program that does nothing but flood the screen with text. Typically, an operator will kick the flood bot out of the chat group and ban it.

Helpful bots

I was born in early 1992. During the spring of 92 I got some sub-AI ["Artificial Intelligence"] features that gave me a personality. After that, during periods when Peter has had too much spare time, I have gotten more advanced features.

Mama, a helpful bot on the IRC #amiga channel, created by Peter Sjöström

Clone bots

The previous types of bots could be easily eliminated by kicking them out of the chat group. Clone bots are designed to be difficult to kick out. Clone bots multiply themselves; for example, one clone bot creates two more clone bots, each of which creates two more clone bots, and so on, until your chat group is filled with bots. A really nasty clone bot will create copies with different, random names, like *X5byM3kaW*, so operators will have a hard time banning them by name. A clone bot can make normal conversation almost impossible in a chat group.

Invitation bots

Chat services like IRC allow you to send *invitation messages* to other users, inviting them to join you in a particular chat group. An invitation bot uses this feature to annoy people. This bot sends out invitations simultaneously to hundreds of users, sometimes using a provocative nickname and channel name, like this:

```
*** Lolita invites you to channel #hotsex
```

You can guess what happens next. Hundreds of users all join channel *#hotsex*, wondering what is going on. And the answer is: nothing. The invitation was a hoax. Hundreds of users sit there, confused, like this:

```
<HarryH> Hi, I got your message - what's up?
<dirk> Hi, Lolita, I'm Dirk, what do you want?
<Master> Who are you?
<chuck> Where's lolita?
<ziller> What's going on?
```

until they figure out the joke (or give up) and leave the channel. Invitation bots won't do you any damage, but they can make people feel disappointed or embarrassed.

People who create harmful bots are like people who create computer viruses. They think they're enormously clever to make a program that annoys or hurts other users. In fact, they are not clever at all. It takes very little knowledge to create a destructive bot. It's much more difficult and challenging to create a helpful bot like *Mama* or a useful program like a word processor. (Imagine these people at a programming job interview: "So tell me," says the interviewer, "what was the most impressive bit of programming you've ever done?" "Um..., er..., well, I did write a *clone bot* once...." I'm sure the company will whip out a contract immediately!) Most programmers, thankfully, have the maturity and good judgment to use their skills in constructive ways.

People you meet in chat groups might not be what they seem.

Bots aren't the only chat group "users" that can deceive you, of course. When you meet strangers on the Net, you really can't know whether they are being truthful or not. A user's name, age, and even gender can be hidden without much difficulty.

I once interviewed a middle-aged, male user, Brandon, who explained how he'd pretended to be a young woman in chat groups and on email. One of his female identities was warm and mature, while another was a sexy and impetuous teenager. They each had multiple Net romances, some of which lasted several months, and many of the men involved never found out the truth. It was all an experiment, he says, and extremely easy to do.

The men who fell for Brandon's female persona were lucky that Brandon was not a malicious person. Other Net folks have fallen prey to dishonest individuals who used false Net personalities to trick them out of personal secrets, money...or worse. The sidebar "A Net romance that led to tragedy" is a powerful example. Such stories are rare—unlike what the media would have us believe—but they do occur.

You might know the personality but not the person.

We will now leave the topic of chat groups and talk more generally about meeting people on the Internet. If you've been on the Net for a few months or more, you have undoubtedly made some Net friends. Perhaps you met one in a newsgroup or mailing list where you shared an interest. After corresponding for a while, you might know all about a friend's job, hobbies, favorite music, and maybe even some intimate secrets. You might also be able to characterize your friend as generally cheerful, depressed, funny, outlandish, shy, or just completely bizarre. What does all this knowledge mean? It means one thing, and one thing only:

You know your friend's *Net personality*. Nothing more.

I'll do anything?

One guy I met on the Net gave me his phone number and I started calling him. He went on and on about how he loved going out to clubs, he was tall, handsome, etc. So finally he decided to come out and see me. He was not tall, and only OK looking. But he did not want to do anything!!! How about a club? Nope, no go. How about a movie... no. Theater? No. Arcade? No. Bowling? No. So Mr. "I will do anything" did nothing.

Tryphena

A Net romance that led to tragedy

Back in 1993, I was pretty new to the Net, but I was getting around OK. Within two weeks of getting my computer account, I'd found the chat areas, where I got propositioned repeatedly by men. Sometimes my girlfriends and I would "go private" with them and laugh ourselves silly inventing steamy dialogue.

Then, in the Spring of 1994, I met Roger. He was so different from the drooling teens online who asked what I looked like in leather. Roger had recently taken a trip to South America where he'd worked in a nuclear research center. I was definitely impressed! Within five minutes. he highlighted work he'd done with the government, crafting national science and technology policies, and alluded to a lifestyle of high living. I didn't particularly care about the fine life, but I loved finding someone so interesting, so worldly, so charming. The conversation moved seamlessly from one topic to another, and I felt out of my league. He said he'd be online the next night, and he'd look for me then. I was ecstatic; this sophisticated, interesting world-traveler was interested in talking to me! (I was so gullible!)

The next night, he was there again, and the next. I found him warm and sensitive, and he made me laugh. I also found out he was thirteen years older than I, but I was drawn to his knowledge and worldliness. He came on to me slowly, indirectly. I couldn't accuse him of making passes because everything was said subtly. Eventually, we even played out fantasies online, like feeding each other peeled grapes. Then there was the night that Roger masqueraded as a woman just for fun, and I wrote some sexy dialogue that he sent to a bunch of men. I was laughing out loud that night.

A month passed, and our online dialogue because increasingly hot. I felt wooed and cherished. We exchanged phone numbers and photographs, and he suggested we meet. I was disappointed with his voice on the phone: it was clipped, nasal, and old. The photo was even more disappointing: slightly cross-eyed, carrying an extra thirty pounds, definitely not handsome, and older in appearance than he'd led me to

believe. This changed the dream-like image I'd had of Roger. I'd dated a lot of handsome princes up till then. Maybe, my conscience told me, it was time to kiss a frog.

We continued exchanging messages. It was the end of June and, through a mix-up at his company, a big payment had not arrived. As days turned to weeks, he became short tempered and increasingly scared. I wanted to help. If I lent him the money, I thought, things could return to normal. At first he refused, but eventually I managed to convince him to borrow $3000—my entire savings at the time.

I should have been suspicious when he knew how to set up a wire transfer from my bank account into his, and that he took my money instead of borrowing from more well-off friends or relatives. But let me say, here and now: if I'd had more money, I would have lent it to him. I trusted him.

As soon as I'd wired him the money, he suddenly had no time for me. I'd find him online, but he was always talking to someone else, or was constantly away on unexpected business trips. When we did talk and I'd bring up the money, he couldn't say when he'd be able to repay me. He became argumentative over everything. This was the man I'd fallen for?

In September, I finally gave him an ultimatum: meet me, or we part ways. I'll even pay half the fare. Was there a note of desperation? A quavering in my voice? Yes sir, yes sir, three bags full.

When he agreed, and we'd set a date for the first weekend in October, he loosened some. Soft laughter. Promises. Words of flirtation and a tone of caress. Things were definitely better between us, and I let down my guard, preparing for a wonderful visit. I super-cleaned my apartment, bought fresh flowers, candles, champagne. I spent days fretting over what to wear. I had my hair done.

The person who got off the plane was not the man I'd fallen in love with. Thirty pounds overweight? It was more like fifty or seventy. And he was so blind that he hobbled down the platform and went right past me. I introduced myself. He looked at me for a beat, moved to kiss me, and his tongue was in my mouth even before I could embrace him. It was a violation, and I wasn't ready for it. I had dreamed of love, but this tongue hadn't heard the word.

When we arrived at my apartment, he ripped my clothing off and attacked me. He yanked my arm so hard toward the bed that I hurt for two days afterward, and he tore an earring from my ear. My head was spinning and my thoughts incoherent. Then it was over, and he fell asleep almost immediately. And I pulled myself up on my aching shoulder, looked at this stranger next to me, and tried to assimilate what had just happened.

I didn't sleep that night. Around 3:30, Roger rose out of bed, went into my living room, and made a hushed phone call. His voice was soft, in a tone that I recognized well. After all that he had just done to me, he was talking to another woman.

The weekend got worse from there. His laptop computer was filled with love letters to other women. He'd call them from pay phones while he was "out taking a walk." He propositioned my girlfriend. He played with my emotions. I felt trapped. And when the weekend finally ended, he was buoyant about what a wonderful time he'd had. Huh? What weekend had he been having? Not the one I'd experienced.

After he left, I found out the truth from an online friend. Roger was pursuing relationships on four different computer networks, spending eight to ten hours a day on the prowl for more women. He visited them on his so-called "business trips" and was "borrowing" money from many of them, with creditors hot on his heels. Even worse, Roger was already married, and he abused his wife physically and emotionally.

Roger of course denied everything. But I've got a lawyer now. I pray that somehow, some way, this slimebag will get his just desserts. His path is strewn with the bodies of women.

Am I embarrassed? Definitely. And still kicking myself because I thought I was more savvy than I actually was.

This whole incident has seriously damaged my sense of trust. I often think about my heedless abandonment of common sense, and my intuition that shouted so many warnings that I ignored.

Sandra

Commentary:

This story illustrates a number of important points. Sandra felt safe enough online to do things that she probably would not have done face-to-face. It's common for people to tease strangers with "steamy dialogue" on the Net, whereas in person, this could lead to real trouble. Unfortunately, Sandra wasn't truly safe. She was not at fault for the bad things that Roger did, but if she'd been more cautious, she might not have fallen into his clutches.

Meeting people online can be very exciting, but there are real risks to moving the relationship offline. Sandra made three significant mistakes in dealing with Roger. The first one was lending money, especially such a large sum, to someone she'd never met in person. The second was meeting Roger alone for the first time, instead of bringing along a friend. The third was, as she said herself, that she ignored some important warning signs, like Roger's "violation" in the airport. It's understandable that Sandra "felt trapped," but perhaps she could have sought help to eject this dangerous person from her home.

You might picture Sandra as a gullible person or think, "I would never have fallen for Roger's lies." Well, don't be so sure. Love can be a very powerful force. (Everybody who has never been blinded by love, please raise your hand. Yep, I thought so.) When emotions are sweeping us away, we sometimes do risky things. The key here is to remember to let your head—not only your heart—have a say in what you do.

As you read the rest of the chapter, remember Sandra's story and see if you can think of any more precautions she might have taken.

I was corresponding with someone (who I later became quite close to and moved in with), but during the early stages of our discussions, someone else began sending me messages alleging that my new friend was a pedophile and a pervert and had been harassing women. As it turned out, the person sending me warnings was in fact the pervert, and my new friend had reported him to the authorities (the system administrator). The incident wasn't too detrimental, but it did hinder my budding relationship somewhat in that I was very suspicious of my new friend and not sure who to believe or what to do about it.

Lillian

Your friend's Net personality might be very similar to the way he or she behaves in person. But then again, it might not. Over the years, I've met about 100 of my Net friends in the flesh, and there is a lot of variety in how well their Net personalities matched their in-person ones.

A Net personality can be quite different from in-person behavior.

I met Albert in a computer-related Usenet newsgroup. We had friendly email conversations and read each other's posted articles all the time. He seemed like a really nice guy. A few years after we met online, I happened to travel to the city where Albert lived, so we decided to get together. The result? He was absolutely annoying in person! His Net personality hadn't revealed that he rambles on for hours about topics that I find totally boring. I was very glad when I had to leave. Happily, this visit didn't affect our Net friendship. We still get along fine online. I just wouldn't want to visit him again.

Phil is another guy I met in a Usenet newsgroup. He was one of the most visible people there: always writing long, ranting articles complaining about things. Some of them ran for hundreds of lines without a break. When people disagreed with Phil, he would sometimes insult them and start an argument. So everybody pretty much assumed that Phil was a forceful, obnoxious jerk. A few years later, a bunch of us in the newsgroup decided that it would be fun to meet in person. To everyone's complete surprise, Phil turned out to be a quiet, humble, and extremely likable man. (And about 10 years older than some people thought!) His Net personality was nothing like his behavior face-to-face.

My friend Gina met a guy on the Net, named Lars, and had some long, intimate conversations with him. Eventually, her job required her to travel to the city where Lars lived, so they planned to meet. Just before Gina left, Lars emailed her that he wanted to "put a ring on her finger" when she arrived. She was rather shocked by this remark—after all, they hadn't even seen each other yet—but ignored it and decided to meet him anyway. When Lars picked up Gina at the airport, he presented her with a gift: a shopping bag filled with lingerie. This was so creepy that Gina avoided him for the rest of the trip and broke off the friendship. Obviously, whatever was going on in this guy's mind was very different from what Gina had been perceiving.

Occasionally, somebody's Net personality is just like their behavior in person. When I finally met my Net friend Rob after several years of email, we hit it off immediately and have remained friends, visiting each other whenever travel takes one of us to the other's city.

Transference fills in the gaps in your knowledge of a person.

Since the Net gives us only partial information about our online friends, how is it that we sometimes believe that we "know" them? Why are we surprised to find that our expectations about a Net friend are wrong? Sometimes it's because our own minds are fooling us. The anonymity of the Internet leaves gaps in our knowledge about other people, so our minds automatically fill in the gaps with things that are familiar to us. Sigmund Freud, the famous founder of psychoanalysis, called this phenomenon *transference*. (The popular press sometimes incorrectly calls it "projection.") We all fill in the gaps from time to time and usually are not aware of doing it.

Our perceptions of the world are based on two things, according to many cognitive psychologists. We get some of the information from our five senses, and the rest comes from inside our heads. When you communicate on the Net, your information from the outside world is limited to what you see on your screen. Yep, that's only one of your five senses! So there's plenty of room for your mind to fill in details based on your own needs, motivations, and beliefs. In the end, the meaning you get from the words of your Net friend might be very different from what he or she intended. That's what transference is all about.

If you become concerned about trusting a Net friend, remember to be aware of transference. Ask yourself: how much do I really know about this person, and how much am I just assuming or wishing?

No social network

Part of the way we get to know people is through their social network. We meet their friends, and we find out what their friends think of them. On the Net, you don't get this kind of information about a person.

Lisa Feldman Barrett

It's hard to know when to trust a Net friend.

If all you do with your Net friends is have fun online, then it probably doesn't matter if their Net personalities accurately reflect their real behavior. Enjoy yourself and don't worry. If you ever need to *trust* a Net friend, though—with money, responsibilities, or personal information—things are different. For instance, if your Net friend is unreliable in real life, this might not be important online, but it might matter a lot if you need her to pick you up at the airport in a strange city. Similarly, if you reveal a secret to your Net friend, you certainly don't want it blabbed all over a public newsgroup.

If you know your Net friends only through their words, how can you tell if these friends are trustworthy? Unfortunately, you can't. If you have to rely completely on what people say about themselves, and you cannot observe their actual behavior, you can't know for sure whether you should trust them or not. Essentially, you are at the mercy of what they tell you, because even if you ask a direct question, they can lie.

Thankfully, most people on the Net (and in life) are not out to deceive you intentionally. More commonly, they'll tell you something they really believe about themselves, but it will turn out not to be true. People sometimes think they have more positive qualities than they really do, and they deceive themselves. Deceiving you is just a consequence of that.

In your life, you've probably met hundreds of people who deceive themselves in small, harmless, and unmemorable ways. But when you meet one person who deceives you on purpose...that's something you'll remember.

Romance can flourish on the Net.

Is it possible to fall in love on the Internet? People who have never experienced Internet romance may think it's an absurd idea. How in the world can you fall in love with somebody you have never met face-to-face?

Well, it happens all the time. Just ask some of the readers of *soc.penpals, alt.romance, alt.romance.chat,* and the *alt.personals* newsgroups on Usenet. They can tell you plenty of stories

Four signs to trigger your trust alarm

It doesn't pay to be completely paranoid about other Net users, because most folks behave honestly on the Net. Nevertheless, here are some discussion topics that can indicate that a Net friend is not being honest with you.

1. Requests for money

Maybe he'll ask you to pay "half of the plane fare" so he can visit you. Maybe she's having some hard times and just needs "a few hundred dollars" to get back on her feet again. Maybe so...or maybe not.

As a rule, don't send money to a stranger on the Net unless you are buying something, as discussed in Chapter 6. This might seem like common sense, but some intelligent people have gotten terribly ripped off for large sums of money by scammers who pretended to be friendly (or romantic) on the Net.

2. Too much knowledge about you

Take notice if a newfound Net friend suddenly knows details about you that you have not revealed. Some users love to show off how well they can use the Internet to find out your personal information. For example, your Net friend might have discovered your telephone number in an online phone directory at your company. Such incidents might be completely innocent; but if they make you uncomfortable, ask where the information came from. If you don't get a satisfactory answer, then you might question whether you want this kind of friend.

Sometimes, though, things take a more serious turn. My friend Lois lives in Virginia and used to call a BBS in Texas regularly. One day, she met a user named Ed on the BBS. Ed was warm and funny, and Lois enjoyed her occasional electronic chats with him. Neither one of them revealed their last names, and their conversations were informal but fun. Two months later, Lois' telephone rang...and it was Ed! "How did

you get my phone number?" she asked, surprised. Ed chuckled and said he had used some knowledge of BBSes to look up her last name and figure out where she was dialing in from. From there, he had simply called Information in her town. Lois suddenly became aware of how little she knew about Ed in real life. "Oh, by the way," continued Ed, "I was just passing through Virginia and thought I'd stop by. I'm actually calling from the telephone booth outside your apartment building. You're in apartment 203, right? May I come in for a visit?"

Scary, isn't it? This sort of occurrence is rare, but again, be cautious of people who seek out your personal information without your knowledge.

3. Very personal or directly sexual questions

Some people enjoy talking very explicitly with other users or even having simulated "Net sex." But if you're not comfortable with this, or if very personal questions come unusually early in your Net friendship, be cautious. Some dishonest people use the Net much as an obscene caller uses the telephone. They slowly draw you in with mild questions, but then they turn explicit. If you feel pressured to answer such questions, then don't. And if your Net friend won't take no for an answer, run the other way. Chapter 11 discusses how to contact the other user's postmaster in such situations.

4. Marriage proposals

Don't laugh; I know several users who were seriously asked for marriage by people they'd never met in person. If this happens to you, you might want to question the other person's grasp of who you are, since he or she has fallen in love with your Net personality but has never truly known you.

Net sweethearts

My husband and I met on the Internet. What had attracted him to me was my sense of humor, and what attracted me to him at the time was his apparent honesty, as he told me of several problems he was having. Pretty soon after we met in person, I was sure that I loved him. There was one thing he said to me, however, that was pretty confusing—he told me that he had a lot of female friends, and that he didn't want me to be jealous. What I didn't know was that he was quite seriously "involved" with three other women online, and he had a whole horde other than the three: women he would have Net sex and phone sex with. He now is very ashamed of those days, but knows that it was something he had to go through, had to work through.

Mara

about Net loves they have found, lost, regained, and even completely fabricated.

Net romance is definitely workable, but it does have some difficulties. When Net couples finally meet in person, frequently they are surprised by how much they do not know about each other. Sometimes, the surprise is so great that they break up after their first meeting. "Net heartache" is a common phenomenon. On rare occasion, some people even discover that they've been intentionally misled. But usually, the problem is that Net communication is less revealing than people suspect. They *think* that they know everything about each other, but they don't.

Net romance leaves room for error, even if people mean well.

Psychologists believe that intimacy is based on two things. The first is self-disclosure: revealing things about yourself. The second is how much you feel that your partner is responding to you. So it's an interaction; and on the Net, interaction is not spontaneous. It's broken into units. You send email to your partner, and then there is a lag time between what you have disclosed and how your partner responds. When your partner writes back, he or she has had time to think about what to say. When you meet face-to-face, though, conversation is spontaneous, so the whole feel can be completely different.

Lack of spontaneity is not the only problem. The Net also hides the speaker's tone of voice, and this can make a conversation ambiguous. For example, if I'm having an argument and get really mad, I might tell my opponent: "You're an idiot." But I can also say the same words to a close friend who is teasing me. The tone communicates a lot. In the first case, it communicates real anger and hostility, and in the second, it's playful. Similarly, personal habits, speech patterns, and gestures say a lot about a person. All of this information is unavailable on the Net.

Another way we come to know people is by seeing how they behave in a variety of situations. On the Net, however, you see a person in only one situation. You don't know how much of your sweetheart's behavior is due to the context and how much of it is due to the person. Furthermore, you can't verify what your Net sweetheart tells you, so you have more of an

Strangers, friends, and lovers

opportunity to deceive yourself or to misunderstand what your Net sweetheart says.

What kinds of activities does your sweetheart engage in when he or she is not logged in? You know about these activities only through words on the screen, not by experiencing them. (Or you might not know about them at all!) This means that a huge portion of your sweetheart's life is unknown to you. In fact, even while you are online together, you can't be sure what your sweetheart is doing. For all you know, he or she could be paying only partial attention to you: watching TV, doing work, or even carrying on other Net conversations while you are having an "intimate" discussion.

Finally, let's not forget physical appearance. Photos give you some information, but there is no substitute for the real thing. It is heartbreaking when a Net couple meets in person for the first time, after weeks or months of deeply personal conversation, and one or both of them finds the other physically unattractive.

What does all of this mean? It means that you *can* feel strong feelings about a Net sweetheart: infatuation, lust, excitement, thrills and chills. You can even fall in love with somebody's Net personality. But you cannot be sure you are in love with the *whole person* if you have met only on the Net. Until you have had face-to-face communication, there will be important parts of the other person that you cannot know.

Before meeting in person, get to know each other on the telephone.

Online conversation with your Net sweetheart can be intimate and fun, but as we have noted, it can hide some important details. Spend some time on the telephone before you meet. It will give you an opportunity to get to know each other in a different environment. Phone calls require people to be spontaneous; they can't sit for hours carefully phrasing their words. Even live chat isn't truly spontaneous, because many chat programs let people edit their words before sending them to the chat group.

So, spend some quality time on the phone. It's enjoyable, and it sometimes helps to weed out people who seem great online, but are not nearly as fascinating (or as honest) in live conversa-

Two questions to ask a potential Net sweetheart

1. What don't you like about yourself?

When you meet people on the Net, they are happy to tell you their strengths and all the things they like about themselves. But can they be honest about their weaknesses? If not, then I would be highly skeptical: either they don't know themselves very well or they don't want me to know them well. All people have something that they're not proud of, or something that they wish they could change. If they don't, then that's a red flag for me.

2. Have you met other people on the Net?

Ask them to describe some of their previous Net relationships. How did they start, and how did they turn out? The best predictor of a person's future behavior is previous behavior. If you know how they have acted in the past, you'll have some idea what they might do again.

Of course, you're still relying on their words, and any time you base your judgment of someone only on what they say, that's a hazard. But there's no way to solve that problem.

Lisa Feldman Barrett

tion. You might be surprised at how differently your sweetheart interacts on the phone versus on the Net. (And don't worry if your first conversation or two is awkward. It may take a little time to get comfortable.)

Consider exchanging photographs.

Net sweethearts often send photographs of themselves to each other before they meet. Some folks like to send photos electronically, using a digital scanner to convert them to graphics files and then emailing them. I recommend using the old-fashioned method, though: paper photographs sent via the postal service. It's more romantic, and (more importantly) it's a bit more likely the photo you receive is real. A dishonest person can easily grab a image from a total stranger's World Wide Web page and email it to you, claiming that it's of himself or herself. While this fakery can be done with paper photographs too, it's not quite as convenient.

Arrange your first meeting to be comfortable and safe.

When it comes to Net romance, I can speak from experience: I met my wife Lisa in the Usenet newsgroup *alt.personals.ads.* After writing several hundred fascinating email messages, spending 25 to 30 hours on the phone, and exchanging photographs by mail, we decided to meet in person. When I took my first plane trip to her town, I had mixed feelings about trust. I was very flattered that she trusted me enough to visit her at home so quickly after we'd "met." At the same time, though, I was puzzled that she didn't think it too risky. All became clear when I met her housemate: male, six feet tall, and a black belt in karate! Luckily, all went well, and I flew home with my body intact. (But not my heart....)

So, unless you are lucky enough to have a muscular martial arts expert at your disposal, you're probably going to have to think about trust at your first face-to-face meeting. Here are some tips to follow when meeting your Net sweetheart in person. These tips are very similar to what you should do when responding to a personals ad in a newspaper. They are not hard-and-fast rules; use your judgment based on what you know about the other person.

Strangers, friends, and lovers

Meet in a public place

Choose a meeting spot that is very visible. Dinner at a restaurant in a poorly lit neighborhood might be a bad idea. Lunch in a sunny, romantic cafe is better.

Consider bringing a friend

Ugh—how unromantic, right? Still, having another person along can be a safeguard when meeting someone new. If you prefer not to have a friend tag along, at least tell somebody where you are going so they can check up on you.

Resist going to each other's homes

From your Net communication, you might feel as if you've known each other forever, but you haven't. If your Net sweetheart lives far enough away that you'll need to spend the night away from home, don't feel pressured to be a houseguest. A true friend won't be insulted if on your first meeting, you prefer to stay at a motel.

If you take too many safety precautions, they can make a potentially romantic experience feel awkward. But too few of them can leave you in a vulnerable position. However you arrange your first meeting, make sure it is guided by your brain as well as your heart.

This safety advice is for both men and women.

Some men might look at these cautionary tips and think that they're only for women, but this is not so. Even if you are a hulking, six-foot-five-inch Olympic weightlifting champion and Marine sharpshooter, it pays to be cautious when first meeting your Net sweetheart in person. There are some pretty elaborate scams out on the Net, and the people who get fooled most often are the ones who think that they are completely safe. The "sweetheart" you meet on the Net could have very different motives (or even a different gender!) than what you've been led to believe.

Try for a balance between fun and caution.

Some people on the Internet are not who they seem. Most Net folks won't intentionally try to deceive you, but self-deception

Trusting too quickly

We started talking in cyberspace, then on the phone. Started doing cybersex, then telephone sex. We had agreed that it was just for fun and that if we met, we would not expect anything. Well, he came to visit, and he was really interesting. After a long day of playing tourist, we went back to my place. I said I was tired. He proceeded to give me a backrub. I told him I do not like backrubs and asked him to stop, and he did not. I pushed his hands off my shoulders and said again that I really do not like backrubs. I was still tired, so I told him I wanted to take a nap, but he could do what he wanted. I went into my room and got into bed..., and he came into my room! I didn't hear him because of the carpet. And he started giving me another backrub! I yelled at him to get the hell out of my room, and he did.

Tryphena

I posted on soc.penpals and got over 80 responses. One guy (whom I never answered) responded to my post by sending me a very detailed poem about two people engaging in S&M.

Tryphena

on their part, and wishful thinking (transference) on your part, might cause you to form an inaccurate picture of what somebody is really like.

Much of the time, it doesn't really matter if people's Net personalities accurately reflect their behavior in person. (In fact, it can be fun to pretend you are someone else.) Truth in personality becomes an issue only if you have to trust someone with, for example, secrets, money, or responsibility. This is particularly important when romance is concerned. You *can* fall in love on the Net, but be aware that until you meet your Net sweetheart in person, you know only one aspect of his or her personality.

In short: meeting people on the Net can be a lot of fun. Just be cautious about trusting them too hastily.

For more information...

You can find general information about socializing on Usenet and by email in the article, "A Brief Guide to Social Newsgroups and Mailing Lists," by Dave Taylor. It is posted regularly in the Usenet newsgroup *news.announce.newusers*. Some of the more popular newsgroups for meeting new people are *soc.penpals* for finding pen pals; *soc.singles* for hanging out with single people; and *soc.motss* ("Members Of The Same Sex") for conversing about lesbian, gay, and bisexual issues.

Internet Relay Chat (IRC) is discussed in the Usenet newsgroup *alt.irc* and described on the Web pages

```
http://www.smartpages.com/faqs/irc-faq/faq.html
http://www.kei.com/irc.html
```

alt.romance.chat is devoted to discussion of romance on the Net. There is a helpful Frequently Asked Questions (FAQ) article posted twice a month. The newsgroup *alt.romance* is for discussions of romance in general, but quite a number of the articles concern online romance and long distance relationships. Also, *alt.personals.ads* is for posting and responding to online "personals" ads.

CHAPTER 9

Parents and the Internet

Some parents have concerns about the Internet.

If you are the parent of an Internet-literate child, you might be worried because of recent stories in the popular press. For example, you might have heard about children who were tricked by pedophiles online posing as youngsters. Or maybe you've heard that thousands of digitized, sex-related images are transmitted over the Net every month; or about the sex-related chat groups where people speak explicitly about sex and even have simulated "Net sex."

Some recent media stories have portrayed the Internet as a slime pit, crawling with child molesters and overflowing with pornography. This journalism is irresponsible and sensationalistic, designed to play on people's fears and to sell stories. The truth is much simpler and much less scary. (And apparently, less newsworthy too.)

Yes, the Internet does have a dark side for kids, but it's relatively small and really not very different from normal life. It's simply one more place where your kids can get into trouble. It just seems different because the Net is new and unfamiliar to many parents.

If you are concerned about your children's exposure to sexually explicit material online or are worried about their safety

A big city out there...

Two-point-five million use this service [America Online]. That's like a city. Parents wouldn't let their kids go wandering in a city of 2.5 million people without them, or without knowing what they're going to be doing.

Pam McGraw, America Online spokesperson, in "Children Lured From Home by Internet Acquaintances" by David Foster, Associated Press, June 13, 1995 while navigating the Net, what can you do? The answer is: the same thing you do about any other risk to your children. You learn about it, talk to your kids about it, and make rules. (And hope that the rules don't get broken when you look away!) We'll cover two main topics in this chapter:

Strangers on the Net

Just as in real life, children should be taught not to talk to strangers. Older kids can do more exploring, but they (and you) should be aware of the risks.

Sexually explicit material

If you want to shield your children from sex-related material online, there are several options available.

Sexually explicit material is controversial. People disagree on whether it is harmful or harmless, or whether it should be legal or illegal. We won't be making such grand judgments in this chapter. Instead, we'll address some practical questions. How common is this material online? Is it different from sex-related material found elsewhere in the world? And if you don't want your children to see it, what can you do?

Using the Internet is different from running a computer program.

When your child is upstairs in his or her room, playing a computer game or using a word processor, this is a solitary activity. You can feel pretty sure that your child is alone and safe.

The Internet is a different story. When your child sits down at a computer and connects to the Internet, this is not a solitary activity. He or she can be communicating with numerous other people, both friends and strangers. The Internet is more like a telephone than like a word processor. In fact, it's like giving your child unlimited, long-distance telephone service to millions of anonymous people around the world.

There's no need to panic about this, because most people on the Net behave honestly. But it's important to be aware of the difference between playing alone and playing on the Net.

The Net is filled with friendly strangers.

"Don't talk to strangers." This is probably the number one piece of safety advice that parents tell their children (along with "look both ways before you cross the street"). This simple piece of advice runs into problems on the Net, however, because nearly *everybody* is a stranger, and it isn't clear what kind of talking represents a danger, either.

This leads to an interesting paradox. The very foundation of the Net is based on cooperation between people who have never met in person: strangers helping strangers. This spirit of anonymous cooperation is powerful, beneficial, and an excellent lesson for children (and adults) to learn. At the same time, it conflicts with parents' cautious advice to their children.

The solution is to realize that "don't talk to strangers" is an intentional overstatement. We can't expect our kids to know the difference between a "good" stranger and a "bad" stranger, so we teach them to avoid all strangers, just to be on the safe side. As they get older, kids become more able to distinguish between good and bad strangers, and the rule gets relaxed.

When is a child old enough to use the Internet without supervision? There is no hard-and-fast rule, but one indicator is whether or not your child has intuition about the difference between good strangers and bad strangers. If not, then all Internet use should be with parental guidance.

Explore the Net together

...the best defense for parents is to make exploring the online world a family affair.

Brad Stone, "How to Get Junior Wired," *Newsweek Computers & The Family*, Summer 1995

Discuss online safety tips with your child.

Discussing Internet risks with your child is just like giving any other cautious advice. Here are some important topics you should cover.

Net users are real people.
> Even though you can't see them, they aren't "pretend." They are no different from the strangers you see in a park or shopping mall, except that they have an interest in computers. You should be cautious on the Net just as you would be in these public places.

Net users may be different than they seem
> The Net lets people hide their identities very easily. Boys can pretend to be girls. Girls can pretend to be boys. Adults can pretend to be kids. And bad people can pretend to be nice. Don't believe everything that people tell you.

Never give out your address or phone number.
> You wouldn't give them to a stranger on the street, so don't

give them to a stranger on the Net, even to a friendly stranger. Even to another kid, because you don't know that it really *is* a kid. (Parents should also make sure that their child's address and phone number are not available online.)

Never tell your password to anybody
Somebody else could get into your files or pretend to be you and do nasty things.

If you have any uncomfortable discussions or get any strange email, tell your parents right away
Beware of people who ask you very personal questions, who won't leave you alone, or who say things that you don't understand.

Don't arrange to meet a Net friend in person without getting your parents' permission
You really don't know what your Net friends are like in person. Bad people can easily pretend to be nice.

For an older child, you might also discuss some of the topics we covered in Chapter 8, like "Net personalities," trust, and romance.

Yes, there is sex on the Internet.

Sexually explicit material is easy to find on the Net. About 100 of Usenet's 15,000 newsgroups are devoted to sex-related topics or digitized sexual photos. (Some of these newsgroup names are obvious jokes, though, such as *alt.sex.extraterrestrial.*) Various chat groups are available for sexual discussions and simulated Net sex. Magazines like Playboy and Penthouse have World Wide Web pages available for viewing, as do vendors for condoms, sex toys, and erotic clothing.

Sex on the Internet has received much press recently, but for the most part, it's not all that different from sex in other areas of life. We are a society surrounded by sexual imagery. It's found in movies, television shows, magazines, bestselling books, and advertisements. The fact that sex can be found on the Net should surprise no one.

Some people are concerned that this material can be easily accessed by minors. This is true: anybody with a computer account, Internet access, and a good PC graphics card can download and view sexual imagery without much difficulty. This is nothing new: kids have managed to get their hands on

Myths and facts about sex on the Internet

MYTH Children are being exposed to sex-related material on the Internet against their will.

FACT The Internet simply doesn't work that way. In order to obtain sex-related material (or *any* material, for that matter), you have to seek it out. You have a choice whether or not to subscribe to an *alt.sex* newsgroup, download a photograph, or join a chat group. Users do not have sex-related material thrust upon them, except in very rare cases. A minuscule number of World Wide Web links lead to sex-related material without warning, but almost all such links are clearly labeled. It's possible that somebody could send you unsolicited, sex-related material by email, but this is uncommon.

This myth is sometimes repeated by "concerned parent" organizations whose members mean well but seem to have little or no experience actually using the Internet.

MYTH A large percentage of Internet messages contain pornographic images.

FACT A misleading study published in 1995 unfortunately popularized this myth. (The study was actually about "adult" bulletin boards, and we'll discuss it later in this chapter.) In truth, only a tiny percentage of Internet messages contain sexually explicit images. Estimates vary, but on Usenet where most of the Internet's sexual imagery is transmitted, I've seen estimates ranging from 0.5% to 3%. Compare this with the percentage of sex-related material found in any magazine shop, and it's pretty similar.

MYTH Many children are being stalked or abducted via the Internet.

FACT According to the National Center for Missing and Exploited Children, there were fewer than a dozen cases reported in the first half of 1995. Let's examine how this compares to the number of abductions that are not related to the Internet.

In 1990, a study called NISMART (National Incidence Studies of Missing, Abducted, Runaway, and Thrownaway Children) was conducted by the U.S. Department of Justice's Office of Juvenile Justice and Delinquency Prevention. It found that 3,200 to 4,600 children were abducted by nonfamily members in 1988. That's about nine to 13 children per day! (There were also 115,000 "attempted abductions," but the term is loosely defined and includes "minor episodes that may nonetheless be alarming to the participants.")

The abduction of any child is a tragic event, but it is not right to treat the Internet as a scapegoat. Why are politicians making speeches about the "dangers" to children on the Internet, when there are many more abductions that have nothing to do with the Net? The Internet is not to blame: the perpetrators are, regardless of what medium they use for their kidnappings.

"dirty magazines" for decades, as many parents have discovered. But since it involves the new and exciting Internet, the media (and politicians) have made it sound like a different issue.

Sex is better hidden on the Internet than in other media.

Think about what happens when you watch TV. You turn on the set, sit back, and have no control over what is displayed. A commercial comes on featuring an almost-naked man or woman. You can't control that. Sure, you can change the channel, but only after you've already seen it. There's a similar situation when you watch a movie, drive past a sexy billboard, or walk past a magazine rack. Sexual images bombard us in daily life.

On the Internet, however, you don't see sex unless you go looking for it. Nearly everything is viewed by choice. Unless you subscribe to an *alt.sex* newsgroup, download nude photos to your PC, or search for erotic Web pages, you simply won't see any sex. I have colleagues who have used the Net daily for many years and have never encountered sexually explicit material online.

There are exceptions. For example, while exploring unfamiliar parts of the World Wide Web, you can't always know what you'll see next when you select a new link. But almost all Web links are clearly labeled if they lead to sexually explicit material.

In some parts of the Net, even if you do encounter sex-related material by accident, you can't see it without extra work on your part. For instance, lots of noise has been made about the *alt.binaries.pictures* newsgroups on Usenet that carry lots of digitized nude photos. But when you look in one of these newsgroups, what you do you see? Something like this:

```
begin 644 es422807.jpg
M_]C_X``02D9)1@`!`0```0`!``#_VP!#``@&!@<&!0@'!P<)"0@*#!0-#`L+
M#!D2$Q0`!@`%`00!`@R`(F.!D`$`(`0`")`@$0$`Q$`")`$`E`U!$`(`$A`
MVP!#`0@`(`@#`(`(`0`$`$`$`0`$`E`('O``0(P`')D`E`$`$`A`$#`(`'A0`
M0P+``@``@P@@@`(`$`A``0@]A`C@]@@@@$@(`(``*`,@C`#`I0,A_g``,'
M,C@`@@@`@`@`@`@C@]@`g$hgE``'`O7``O`$`(`@]&``M`A`$A`#H$J(`0`
...
```

This is an encoded graphics file. In order to view it, you must run a decoding program and then a graphic viewer. This takes extra work…and extra choice. (The situation is changing, however, as new, sophisticated software automatically decodes images for viewing.)

The Rimm study sparked national controversy about Net pornography.

"CYBERPORN," shrieked the July 3, 1995 issue of *TIME* magazine. The cover showed a child, wide-eyed and open-mouthed, staring into a computer screen (off camera) at what we assume is sex-related material. The eight-page article contained three more full-page pictures, including a naked man hugging a computer, a man being pulled into a computer screen by a female hand, and a child being tempted by a stranger holding a computer (displaying a lollypop!). The tone of the article was clear: there's tons of pornography on the Net, and it could harm our children.

Scary, yes...but was the article accurate? *TIME* drew many of its "facts" from a study by Martin Rimm of Carnegie-Mellon University, "Marketing Pornography on the Information Superhighway," which was published in the *The Georgetown Law Journal* the same month. This study immediately drew tremendous fire from professors, lawyers, journalists, and users around the country. (See the sidebar, "Reactions to the Rimm Study.")

TIME's reporting on this study had some serious omissions. For example, Rimm was identified only as "the study's principal investigator," never mentioning that in fact, he was an undergraduate student in the electrical engineering department, not a professor. The article also had a number of misleading statements. Take this paragraph, for example:

> **There's an awful lot of porn online**. In an 18-month study, the team surveyed 917,410 sexually explicit pictures, descriptions, short stories and film clips. On those Usenet newsgroups where digitized images are stored, 83.5% of the pictures were pornographic.

Sounds like there's a lot of porn on Usenet, doesn't it? But if you read the Rimm study, those 917,410 images came from *private bulletin board systems* that were devoted to sexual images, not from Usenet! (In other words, on porn BBSes, you find porn.) In addition, the "83.5%" figure is not actually supported by the study, as we'll see in the next section.

Irresponsible journalism

It's frustrating when you finally find a realistic, responsible article about sex on the Net, and the editor accompanies it with sleazy or scary pictures. People mainly remember the pictures.

Dan Barrett

The Rimm study has significant flaws.

Here are a few of the main criticisms brought against the study.

It mainly examined adult BBSes, not the Internet

Even though the phrase "Information Superhighway" appears prominently in the title of the study, the 917,410 "pornographic" files in the study actually came from "adult-oriented" BBSes, not from the Internet.

Rimm responded to this criticism by saying that some BBSes are accessible on the Internet. That may be true..., but does it mean that porn BBSes are representative of the whole Net? Of course not. That's like saying a tiny town is representative of the entire world, just because there are roads leading in and out of it.

It overgeneralizes

Rimm observed 32 *alt.binaries* newsgroups on Usenet for a single week and judged that "83.5%" of the articles were pornographic. The study then concludes, however, that 83.5% of *all* images posted on Usenet are pornographic. This is ridiculous; there are over 15,000 newsgroups!

Suppose that at your local jail, 83.5% of the prisoners there have committed a crime with a gun. Does this mean that 83.5% of the people in the world commit crimes with guns? Of course not. You can't make that kind of generalization. But the study does.

It makes unproven claims

The study contains statements about motivations of pornographers, the directions of the pornography "marketplace," and public preferences for certain kinds of pornography. The data presented in the study, however, have nothing to do with this.

It cannot be replicated

When a scientific study is published, it is essential that other scientists should be able to repeat the study. Otherwise, nobody can know whether the results were due to luck or even errors. The statistics and computer programs that Rimm used are only vaguely described in the paper. In addition, he states that much of his data are "no longer publicly available." So it is unlikely that anybody can verify Rimm's work by duplicating the study.

The study had no peer review

Before a paper can be published in a scientific journal, it is given to other scientists to review. This process, called *peer review*, helps to ensure that only scientifically valid papers get published. *The Georgetown Law Journal*, however, did not use peer review before accepting Rimm's paper.

Rimm has criticized his critics, saying that they have no background in the study of pornography. Most of the criticism, however, has not been about Rimm's expertise in pornography, but his use of basic science, alleging that he made illogical statements and statistical errors.

TIME later distanced itself from the Rimm study, printing a brief statement (July 24, 1995) that cast doubt on the credibility of the research. But the damage to public opinion had already been done. Sound bites from the study are now in the public consciousness. They've even been mentioned (and misquoted) in the U.S. Senate.

Pornography is an extremely small part of the Internet.

If Rimm's statistics are not accurate, then how much sex-related material is actually on the Net? There is no completely reliable way to measure it, but I did a few, simple measurements to get a rough idea. (Try it yourself if you like—you don't even have to look at any pictures.)

The Usenet newsgroup *alt.binaries.pictures.erotica* is one of the most highly read newsgroups on Usenet devoted to sexual imagery. For a period of one month, I scanned the headers of the articles in this newsgroup to see who was posting the pictures. In total, there were only about 100 users posting images. With over 23 million readers on Usenet, that's about 0.0004% of the population: one poster for every 230,000 users. Pretty small.

Who is reading the newsgroup? According to the monthly "Top 40 Newsgroups" article posted by Brian Reid in the Usenet newsgroup *news.lists*, *alt.binaries.pictures.erotica* is read by an estimated 290,000 users worldwide (May 1995). That sounds like a big number, but fewer than half the computers on Usenet receive the newsgroup, and only 2.6% of the users on those computers read it. So let's say that roughly 1 to 2% of all Usenet participants read the newsgroup. Reid says that his fig-

No censorship

The overwhelming majority of material on computer networks is not sexually explicit.... Attempting to filter out sex-related material from the flood of digital bits passing through tens of thousands of computer networks is nearly hopeless.

Marsha Nye Adler, Director of Government Relations, American Association of University Professors, "Limits on Internet Speech," *Academe*, May/June 1995

It's much easier to secure a system in your living room than one you don't own in another country. Parents need to monitor their kids instead of trying to censor the Internet.

Mike Meyer

Reactions to the Rimm study

Drs. Donna Hoffman and Thomas Novak, *Associate Professors of Management, Owen Graduate School of Management, Vanderbilt University:*

"The article is filled with flaws, several of them extremely serious. Rimm examined descriptions of images found on selected adult BBSes and found, not surprisingly, that adult BBSes contain porn. But he then attempts to generalize it to the whole 'Information Superhighway.' Much of the data presented are misinterpreted, and Rimm makes many unsupported statements that are inflammatory, outrageous, and sometimes even ridiculous. The TIME cover story has given this document a credibility it does not deserve."

Mike Godwin, *staff council, Electronic Frontier Foundation:*

"...to generalize from commercial porn BBSes to 'the Information Superhighway' would be like generalizing from Times Square adult bookstores to 'the print medium.'" ("The Shoddy Article," HotWired special report, July 1995)

Philip Elmer-DeWitt, *author of the "Cyberporn" article in TIME:*

"Rimm told us (and the Georgetown Law Journal) this was a classic Carnegie Mellon multidisciplinary research project, a big group effort. On the front page, he thanks 19 members of the 'research team,' including at least five full professors. We didn't know, until we started calling them last week, that many of those team members had never read the study." (Usenet, alt.internet.media-coverage, July 20, 1995)

Brian Reid, Ph.D., *Digital Equipment Corporation, author of network measurement software used by Rimm:*

"I am so distressed by its lack of scientific credibility that I don't even know where to begin critiquing it. Normally when I am sent a publication for review, if I find a flaw in it I can identify it. In this study I have trouble finding measurement techniques that are not flawed. The writer appears to me not to have a glimmer of an understanding even of basic statistical measurement technique...." ("Critique of the Rimm Study," July 6, 1995)

Peter Lewis, The New York Times:

"Through a series of unusual publishing arrangements that caused a bitter rift among faculty members, the computer pornography study was kept from reviewers who might have caught what many critics have called its glaring errors and sensational tone." ("Computer Smut Study Prompts New Concerns," July 16, 1995)

Jack Kapica, The Globe And Mail:

"Mr. Rimm's own faculty adviser, Marvin Sirbu, gives the study only a mixed review, saying it made generalizations 'that were not clearly supported by the data.'" ("A Gross Distortion of the Porn Picture," July 14, 1995)

Dr. Jim Thomas, *Professor of Sociology and Criminal Justice, Northern Illinois University:*

"Rimm makes so many unsubstantiated claims that don't stand up to even modest scrutiny that I'm astonished that anybody could take it seriously." (The Well, July 1, 1995) ures might be off by a factor of two in either direction, so a reasonable rough estimate of the readership is between 0.5% and 4% of Usenet readers. Again, that's pretty small.

How much material is actually carried in this newsgroup? Reid's survey for May 1995 says approximately 17,000 articles were posted that month. Although this sounds like a lot of articles, it represents less than 1% of Usenet news. (In fact, the number of *images* is even lower than the number of articles, because many articles don't contain images, and many images are split into multiple articles.) When you count bytes instead of articles, the newsgroup represents 5 to 6% of Usenet news volume; but this isn't surprising, since a single image file is typically 50 times larger than an article containing text.

As pointed out earlier, these are very rough estimates; but they are still a far cry from "83.5%."

There are ways to block access to sexually explicit material.

If you don't want your child to be able to view sexually explicit material online, you have several options. First, there are software packages designed to block access to this material, such as **Net Nanny, SurfWatch,** and **Cyber Patrol.** (Ask your computer retailer for a current list of programs.) These programs sit in the background on your computer, watch for attempts to access certain Internet sites, and automatically block them. I've also heard of programs that, rather than blocking access to adult sites, allow access to child-friendly Web sites only.

Some online service providers have their own blocking services, restricting access to "adult-oriented" areas that they administer, or restricting Internet access in general. This is similar to the "lockout" feature that telephone companies provide to prevent kids from dialing certain phone numbers (such as "900" numbers). Contact your online service provider for details. If it does not provide such a service, then request one.

These blocking methods are not perfect. A clever child can sometimes get past such a roadblock or simply walk over to a friend's house where there's no blocking software. As time goes on, though, expect to see better and more widespread

We will always have sexual preda-tors among us. Although mechan-isms to block online porn are certainly worthwhile, the secret to protecting children is to educate them.

Pat Stanislaski, Executive Director, National Center for Assault Preven-tion (letter to TIME magazine, July 24, 1995)

blocking software, and more support from online service providers.

Another method—the one that I believe in most—is education. I recommend sitting down with your child and discussing the issues of sex-related material on the Net, frankly and openly, to whatever extent he or she can understand (depending on age). Remember that users, children or otherwise, see this material by choice, not by random chance. It is not forced upon them. So by discussing these issues, you can help your child make informed choices about how to deal best with explicit sexual material on the Net...now *and* later in life.

Take time to explore the Internet with your child.

Take an interest in your children's Internet activities, just as you would take interest in their social life. Find out who their email pals are. Ask to see their favorite Web sites or news-groups. Let them show you how chat groups work. Family time with the Internet can be an enjoyable and educational pursuit.

Heck, you might learn something about the Net that you didn't know before. Or even get hooked.

For more information...

Child Safety on the Information Highway, by the National Cen-ter for Missing and Exploited Children, is a brochure for concerned parents. A free copy is available by mail or on their World Wide Web page.

> National Center for Missing and Exploited Children
> 2101 Wilson Boulevard, Suite 550
> Arlington VA 22201-3052
> (800) 843-5678
> Email: *ncmec@cis.compuserve.com*
> World Wide Web: http://www.missingkids.org

If you'd like to see Martin Rimm's (rather discredited) pornogra-phy study yourself, it's in the *The Georgetown Law Journal,* Volume 83, Number 5. It's been also made available online by Rimm himself at the URL

> http://TRFN.pgh.pa.us/guest/mrstudy.html

Critiques of the study, and the responses of many Net users, can be found on J. D. Falk's Cyberporn Web page,

```
http://www.cybernothing.org/cno/reports/cyberporn.html
```

TIME magazine, including the "Cyberporn" article and many letters to the editor (these are worth reading), can be found at the URL

```
http://www.pathfinder.com/time/
```

Try doing a search for the word "cyberporn."

The Internet filtering page contains information on software for parents to control their children's access to the Internet.

```
http://www.eff.org/pub/Censorship/
   Ratings_filters_labelling/
```

An Internet Parental Control Frequently Asked Questions (FAQ) document is provided by the Voters Telecommunications Watch (VTW) at the URL

```
http://www.vtw.org/pubs/ipcfaq/
```

Sex on the Net

The issue of sex on the Net is the same as the issue of sex on TV, sex on the newsstands—it's just the latest incarnation of the problem.

The Internet can be a great thing to share with a kid. It contains a wealth of information, like a world library. However, I wouldn't leave my six-year-old online and unattended for hours, just like I wouldn't leave her alone in a public library in New York City.

Arsenio Santos

The debate over online indecency

Online "indecency" became a hot topic in 1995, particularly in Congress. In February, Senator Jim Exon (D-Nebraska) introduced the "Communications Decency Act of 1995" as an amendment to a large telecommunications bill. The CDA proposed to make "obscene, lewd, lascivious, filthy or indecent" material illegal on the Internet and online services if it was accessible by minors. Users, online service providers, and Internet service providers could be criminally liable, and punishments included fines of up to $100,000 and jail terms of up to two years. That's pretty severe for swearing on the Net.

The CDA had many problems:

- "Indecent" speech is protected by the First Amendment of the Constitution (freedom of speech). Thus, speech that is protected in the outside world would become illegal online under the CDA.

- We already have laws that prohibit the transmission of obscene material over the Net. ("Obscene" material, as determined by a judge, is not protected by the First Amendment.)

- The intent of the bill was supposedly to protect children from adults who send them offensive material. Much of the material on the Net, however, is not sent directly to users. Instead, it made generally available, as with Usenet news and the World Wide Web. Under the CDA, all Usenet articles and Web pages would have to be written for children, for fear that a child might someday read them.

- Enforcement would be very difficult because the Internet is international, and because there's simply too much data on the Internet to check for "indecency."

The CDA ignored all of these issues, and as a result, many prominent organizations and agencies vocally opposed the bill.

In response to the CDA, Senator Patrick Leahy (D-Vermont) introduced the "Child Protection, User Empowerment, and Free Expression in Interactive Media Study Bill" in April. Instead of censorship, Leahy's bill proposed to study whether existing laws are already sufficient to handle online obscenity (as many people believe they are), and to explore the options available for parents to control their children's use of the Internet. The Senate, however, passed the CDA in June. Senator Leahy's words were added to the bill but later stricken before the vote. (At press time, the bill is in the House of Representatives.)

Similar legislation to the CDA (and with similar problems) was passed by the House of Representatives in August as part of the House Telecommunications Bill. Henry Hyde (R-Illinois), Thomas Bliley (R-Virginia) and John Dingell (R-Michigan) introduced the Manager's Amendment, which criminalized the sending of "any material that, in context, depicts or describes, in terms patently offensive as measured by contemporary community standards, sexual or excretory activities or organs" if a minor sees them. This sweeping amendment even made it illegal to receive such material...as if we could control what other people send us! To balance the Manager's Amendment, Representatives Chris Cox (R-California) and Ron Wyden (D-Oregon) proposed a telecommunications amendment that prohibits the Federal Communications Commission (FCC) from regulating content online. The Cox/Wyden amendment also passed in August.

In early December, the House Conference Committee on Telecommunications Reform approved (by a single vote) another sweeping measure to restrict "indecency" on the Internet and online services. In response, over 18,000 Internet users around the country joined in a national day of protest, telephoning and faxing their Representatives. (Senator Exon's fax machine was reportedly "backed up.") At press time, protest rallies were scheduled in San Francisco, Seattle, and New York City.

Even more restrictive legislation is on the horizon, no doubt fueled by the heavily discredited Rimm study of online pornography (also discussed in this chapter). The misleadingly named "Protection of Children from Computer Pornography Act of 1995," introduced by Senators Robert Dole (R-Kansas) and Charles Grassley (R-Iowa), contains such sweeping language that even libraries and schools can be criminally liable if they simply provide online access to students! Net experts believe that this bill has little chance of acceptance; but since the CDA passed, one never knows....

People disagree about the government's role in policing sex-related material on the Internet. Maybe regulation is needed, or maybe not. The sweeping, unconstitutional legislation of Exon, Hyde, and Dole, however, appears to have been designed by people who don't understand how the Internet works at all. If you are concerned about your constitutional right to free speech, contact your congressional representatives and let your voice be heard. You can also read the text of all this legislation (it's pretty short) on the Electronic Frontier Foundation's Web page

http://www.eff.org

The politics of Net censorship

Because online child pornography is such an emotionally charged issue, some people who oppose Net censorship get accused of "supporting child pornography."

Dan Barrett

Right. They're going to shut down the Internet because of kiddie porn. That'll be the day the national debt is paid off and I can understand what the Burger King lady says at the drive-thru.

Nicholas Winlund

Sen. J. J. Exon sat in front of a computer last week and searched the Internet for the first time. [...] The Exon amendment was approved 84–16 during consideration of a broader telecommunications bill that passed the Senate Thursday.

Paul Goodsell, "Exon Went On-Line Before Vote," Omaha World-Herald, June 16, 1995

The Communications Decency Act would scare some people and arbitrarily punish others. And the last thing this country needs is a law that would make it even riskier to write a love letter.

Mike Godwin, "Nix To Exon," Internet World, August 1995

I think the Communications Decency Act reflects a high level of legal ignorance. Its model is to prohibit anything that is accessible to a minor, which has the effect of restricting everything, because everything is accessible to a minor. I think it's absolutely horrible legislation.

Ethan Katsh

I found it really offensive that 84 senators voted for Exon's Communications Decency Act. In honor of this lunacy, I wrote a little program, called **exonerate**, that removes all "obscene" words from any electronic message. It then replaces those words with the last names of the senators who voted in favor of the act. Feel free to download the program from my home page,

http://www.panix.com/~lan/

Larry

I'm of two minds about censorship on the Internet. For one thing, I don't think that it will work for politicians to try to censor the Net. The volume of data is immense, and users, finding their freedom of speech challenged, would find ways around government-imposed restrictions. The Internet is capable of very fast mutation. Legislation could never keep up with the changes.

On the other hand, as a feminist, I sometimes find myself wishing that someone would clean up some of the more pornographic content on the Net.

Ellie Cutler

Your rights on the Net

You have legal rights.

So far, we've discussed online risks that are annoying or harmful, but we haven't said very much about laws. In Chapter 3, we saw that pyramid schemes are illegal, but what about some of the other issues we've discussed? How about stealing another person's password? Intercepting email? Flaming? Are these legal issues or simply matters of common courtesy on the Net? To answer questions like these, we'll focus on the following topics:

User contracts
Do you unintentionally give up important rights when you join an online service?

Copyright
May other people copy your email, posted articles, or other files?

Flames and defamation
What kind of flame could get you into legal trouble?

Privacy
What legal protection do you have from snoopers? Is it illegal to break into a computer account, or just impolite?

Harassment
What legal protection do you have against users who threaten you or won't leave you alone?

Online vs. offline

I think that ultimately, online and offline legal issues are the same. The only difference is that somebody is going to try to make a difference out of them. For example, if people are charged with stalking online, they might try to create a defense that claims there's no such thing as "stalking" online. And then it will get tested in court. Ultimately, I think that the courts are going to apply the same law that they would apply in the physical world, and come to the same decisions.

Mike Botts, Attorney at Law

With the influx of novice users on the Internet and the litigation-happy environment in which we live, the Internet has become a dangerous place. Consequently, I do not post to the Usenet newsgroups anymore.

Ned

Anonymity and impersonation

Is it legal to keep your identity a secret, or to pretend to be somebody else?

Much of this chapter deals with the laws of the United States, but these topics are important no matter what your citizenship is. If you live outside of the United States, this chapter provides a list of issues you can explore in your country.

The information you'll find in this chapter is not legal advice. No consumer-level book (that is, for non-lawyers) can provide everything you might need to make legal decisions. What this chapter can do, however, is give you some intuition about what kinds of actions are legal and illegal online, and what rights you have that might get violated by other people. This can help you decide what to do if you've been ripped off: the subject of Chapter 11.

Some Internet-related legal issues have not been settled.

The law is a combination of two things: what is written down and how the writing is interpreted by the courts. If you look at our written laws, you can find plenty of them that seem to apply to the online world. And in fact, they probably do apply, but there haven't been enough court cases to know for sure. In fancy terms, *legal precedents* have not yet been set.

The next few years will be important ones where Net law is concerned. Now that the Internet population has grown so large, there are bound to be more legal disputes about online matters than ever before, and many issues will be settled by the courts.

Beware of giving up your rights online.

The law gives people certain rights on the Net that we will explore in this chapter. The law might not protect you, however, if you unknowingly give those rights away! The next three sections will discuss how you might be asked to give up important rights by:

- Your online service provider

- Your employer

- Other computer services

Your online service provider might ask you to give up some rights.

Before you can begin using a computer account, your online service provider might require you to sign a contract. You might have to sign something on paper, or you might be asked to agree online: say, by clicking on a button labeled, "I accept the rules." (The validity of such online contracts has never been tested in court, but many online service providers use them.) If you're excited about getting online, it might be tempting simply to accept the contract and jump onto the Net. This is a bad move. If you don't read the contract carefully, you might surrender some important rights, a decision you might regret later.

For starters, who owns the files you create? Copyright law (which we'll discuss soon) says you own them, but your online service contract might override your rights. Is the system administrator allowed to snoop inside your files and email? As rude as this may seem, your contract might allow it. If your account gets canceled, what happens to your files? Your contract might say you lose access to them immediately and permanently. Will your real name and personal information be kept private? If your contract says nothing about this, your provider might be selling your personal information to other companies for their junk mailing lists.

Take time to read and understand your contract. If you need to call your online service provider and ask dozens of questions, and it takes a little extra time before you can get online, then so be it. You'll have more peace of mind if you know your rights are secure.

If you're at work, your rights may be restricted.

Who owns the work that you create on your employer's computers? This simple-sounding question has a very complex answer. It depends on many factors: whether you are considered an employee or an independent contractor, whether the work was created as part of your job, what state you live in, whether your work is something you authored (so copyright law applies) or invented (so patent law applies), and more. We'll discuss some guidelines in this section, but in general,

Online contracts

I haven't seen any online systems whose regulations are anything but "fine print." They're usually very legalistic, very long, not designed really to warn people, and easily forgotten after you sign on. And their rules are often more important than the law of the state.

Ethan Katsh,
Professor of Legal
Studies, University
of Massachusetts

you may need to ask your employer or an attorney for the full answer.

If you are an independent contractor, then according to federal law, you own copyrights in the work that you create on the job. (We'll discuss copyrights in detail soon.) Your contract, however, can override these rights. In particular, if it contains the phrase "work made for hire," then your employer may own your work.

If you are a regular employee, not an independent contractor, then according to federal law, your employer owns copyrights in the work that you create on the job. Your written contract, if you have one, can override this. To make things even more confusing, different states have different rules for determining whether you are an employee or an independent contractor.

Copyright law is not the only law that concerns ownership. If you invent things on the job, patent law may apply. If you work with confidential information, trade secret law may apply. Your rights under patent law and trade secret law vary from state to state, so things can get pretty complicated. Your best bet is to get everything in writing.

What if you are using your employer's computers to send personal email? What if you log in from home on the weekend, just for fun, and post a few articles on Usenet? If your employer owns your work, does this include personal documents like these? The answer is: maybe. Discuss the issue with your employer's legal staff to find out. And if you have not signed your contract yet, you might consider getting the answer in writing as part of your contract.

If you want to separate clearly your professional and private time online, it might be helpful to get a second account with a different online service provider. Use your second account for private activities during your private time (not on your employer's time, or else your employer may own this work too!). Depending on your situation, your employer might even own work that you do in your private time, so make sure you know your rights.

Some computer services come with restrictions.

Sometimes when you connect to an Internet computer, you'll see a welcome message that restricts your rights while you are logged on. For example, if you connect to an FTP site to upload or download files, you might see a message like this one:

```
NOTICE: All uploads and downloads are logged.
If you don't like this policy, then log off now.
```

In other words, if you log on, your privacy is not guaranteed. The computer will keep a record of all uploads and downloads you perform, so the system staff will see exactly which files you were interested in, and you don't know what they will do with the information.

The reasons for this can be very sensible. If somebody uploads a pirated version of a commercial software package, for example, the system staff will want to know who did it. The staff also might want to keep statistics on uploads and downloads to know if the computer needs a bigger hard drive or a faster networking card. On the other hand, your download statistics might be sold to marketing companies who will analyze it, determine your personal tastes, and send you heaps of junk mail. You never know. The lesson here is to read these notices carefully. If you don't like what they say, don't connect to that computer.

Copyright law says you own what you create.

Unless you have given away your ownership rights, you own the copyrights in every file you create yourself: documents, electronic mail, Usenet articles, graphics files, sound files, World Wide Web pages, computer software, and so on. This assumes, of course, that your work is original: you can't simply put somebody else's copyrighted material into your files and claim ownership. The work must also be creative; you can't put the words "hello world" into a file and expect to hold the copyrights.

Copyrights begin the moment your work is "fixed in a tangible form," e.g., when you store it on disk or print it. You don't even have to put a copyright notice on your work, nowadays.

Who owns what?

When you're using someone else's machine, "who owns what" is an important, interesting, and difficult question.

Ethan Katsh

You automatically own it, thanks to the *Berne Convention*, a copyright treaty that has been adopted by many countries, including the United States.

If you care about your work, it's a good idea to put a copyright notice on it, even though it isn't strictly necessary. It's also smart to register your copyrights with the U.S. Copyright Office. If your copyrights are ever violated and you need to defend them in court, registration gives you additional rights and lets you collect additional money for damages (statutory damages and attorneys' fees). A legal copyright notice consists of the word "copyright," the year, and your name, *exactly* like this:

```
Copyright 1995 Daniel J. Barrett
```

You can substitute the symbol © for the word "copyright," if you want. Because this symbol doesn't appear on a computer keyboard, some users type it as a capital C in parentheses, (C).

Copyright law gives you exclusive rights.

As a copyright owner, you are the only person allowed to do certain things with the copyrighted work:

You can make copies.
Make as many as you like, in any medium.

You can distribute copies.
You can give them away for free, sell them, or toss them from the top of a high building.

You can make and distribute modified versions.
If you change your work, you own the copyrights in the changed version too. Modified versions are called *derivative works*. For instance, you could change the ending of a story you wrote, or you could turn your story into a play. These are both derivative works.

You can display the work.
For example, you can put the work on your Web pages, and other users cannot.

A copyright violation is called infringement.

Nobody else may copy, distribute, modify, or display your work without your permission. Doing so is called *infringing* your copyright, and it's illegal. (But see the sidebar "Fair use" for an important exception.) Here are some examples of infringement:

- A user posts your copyrighted work on Usenet or a public bulletin board.

- A user digitally scans a photograph that you shot and publicly posts it on the Net. You'll often see people do this with magazine photographs in the *alt.binaries.pictures* newsgroups on Usenet.

- A printed magazine publishes your email or your Usenet articles without your permission.

- A programmer copies a digitally sampled sound from your World Wide Web page and includes it in a piece of software that is distributed to the public.

Note that infringement is illegal even if the infringer makes no money at all from copying or distributing your work, or if the infringement is unintentional.

Not everything can be copyrighted.

In particular, you can't copyright an idea. All you can copyright is a particular expression of that idea. If you use a paint program, for example, to create a picture of your mom, you own copyrights in that picture. But you can't claim copyrights over all pictures of your mom or all pictures of mothers. Similarly, if you post a story on Usenet about killer ducks from outer space, you own copyrights in the story, but other people can still write (and copyright) their own, original stories about murderous Martian mallards.

Be aware that if two works are substantially similar (such as two stories on the same topic), a court may decide that one work infringes the other, even if the second work was not derived from the first. This has been the subject of numerous, controversial "look and feel" lawsuits, in which a later work was judged to have very similar (but not identical) characteristics to an earlier one.

Fair use

Fair use allows you to use somebody else's work inside your own work, as long as you aren't harming the creator financially. For example, if you write a book review, you can quote briefly from the book. Or if a magazine publishes a sentence or two from one of your Usenet articles, that might be fair use as well.

Fair use is one of the most misunderstood and abused aspects of copyright law on the Net, probably because it is so complex. Several factors allow a court to determine whether a use is fair use, such as the type and quantity of material used, the "purpose and character" of the use (such as commercial or educational), and the effect on the market for the original work. These factors are open to interpretation, so it can be hard to guess how a court will rule.

You'll commonly see users post the entire text of a newspaper article and declare that fair use protects them from copyright infringement. No way. This is almost guaranteed to be infringement.

Live chat might not be protected by copyright.

Some legal experts believe that live chat is like a telephone conversation, which is not covered by copyright because it is not "fixed" (stored) in any permanent way. So, it's uncertain whether copyright law covers the things that you say in an online chat group.

But what happens if you are participating in a chat group, and somebody is storing the conversation on disk as it occurs? This is easy to do, since many telecommunications software packages have a "text capture" feature that puts into a file everything you see on your screen. As soon as the conversation is stored on disk, it becomes subject to copyright law. (Assuming that the conversation is original and creative, of course!)

Because there really isn't a legal precedent for this stuff, be aware that the things you say in chat groups might not be copyrighted. So if you make some witty remarks or tell a story, and one day you find your words published by somebody else without your permission, you might not have any legal recourse.

Libel is a flame that goes too far.

Anybody who has used a public forum like Usenet has undoubtedly seen *flames,* which are online insults or shouting matches. Flames can also be communicated by email or in chat groups.

Some flames are legally risky because they can cause *defamation*: damage to somebody's reputation. Defamation that is written (as opposed to spoken out loud) is called *libel.*

When is a flame libelous? If a user writes something nasty about you, four things must be true in order for it to be libelous and therefore illegal:

- It must be *false.* Thus, it must be a statement that can be proven true or false. (A statement of opinion, like "I hate you," is not libelous.)
- It must be *defamatory*, meaning that it injures your reputation or credibility.

An example of libel

Let's suppose that two people, with usernames skippy and snit, have an argument online in a public forum. skippy posts, "Snit, you are a jerk." snit posts back, "No, you're a jerk. You don't know what you're talking about at all." To this, skippy responds, "Well, at least I didn't forge my college entrance exams, like you did."

At what point in this conversation did defamation occur? Certainly when skippy accused snit of something that was criminal. Forgery is something that can be absolutely proven true or false. And if skippy's last statement is indeed false, and it affects snit's reputation, which obviously it does, then it would be defamatory. If it's true—if snit really did forge a college entrance exam—then it's not libelous. Truth is an absolute defense against libel.

Now let's look at the first insult: "Snit, you are a jerk." This is not libelous because it can't be proven true or false, even though people might have strong opinions about it. You have a right to insult somebody on the Net. That's free speech.

How about the second statement? When snit writes "You don't know what you're talking about at all," is that libelous? Can it be proven true or false? Maybe. Is it an insult? Clearly. Is it defamatory, so that it would ruin skippy's reputation in the eyes of the other Internet people? Probably not. So that would be a middle ground.

So in these three statements, we see a range of possibilities. The first statement is clearly an insult, protected by our Constitutional right to free speech. The second is kind of an "in between" zone that's probably protected. The third is clearly defamation.

Mike Botts

- It must be *published* or shown to somebody other than you. (The fancy term is "communicated to a third party.")

- It must have been written with *malicious intent*. (Long ago, this was not necessary, but nowadays it usually is.)

You can take precautions against committing libel.

If you really feel the need to insult somebody online, here are some simple tips to help avoid defaming the other person.

Stick to the truth

A libelous statement, by definition, has to be false. So if you write, "Stan broke into my computer account," and it is true, it can't be libel. But be *very* sure of your facts.

Make it clear you are stating an opinion

If you write, "In my opinion, Charlie is completely ignorant about computers," this is a bit safer than writing, "Charlie is completely ignorant about computers." If your words look like statements of fact, you might be heading into libelous territory. (Especially if, say, Charlie runs a computer business and your words could damage his professional reputation.)

Attack the activity, not the person

If you write "Multi-level marketing organizations are run by crooks," this is not libel. If you write more specifically that "Betty Spammer, president of MultiMonger Inc., is a crook," you might be committing libel.

Keep it private

If you flame Bob by sending him private email, this is not libelous because you have not published your words to a third party. If you show the flames even to *one* other person, though, you have "published" your words, and you are at risk for libel.

The most effective way to avoid being accused of libel is not to insult other users. Even if you always obey the above guidelines, an angry person can still haul you into court. Sure, you might win the case, but your time will be wasted, and you might have to pay large court costs.

The ECPA protects your privacy online.

We now move to the subject of online privacy. The *Electronic Communications Privacy Act* (ECPA) is a federal law that makes it illegal to snoop through other people's private communications. The law was originally designed to prohibit wiretapping on telephone lines, but nowadays it applies to computers and networks as well.

What sorts of actions are illegal under the ECPA? The main ones we'll cover are:

- Intercepting online communications, such as keystrokes and email messages
- Breaking into computer accounts (cracking)

The ECPA has exceptions that allow law-enforcement agencies or system administrators to monitor what you do and examine your files, under certain circumstances. In general, if you are suspected of using your computer account to commit a crime, your files are fair game. We won't discuss the many exceptions to the ECPA, but be aware they exist.

Packet sniffing is illegal.

In Chapter 2, we discussed packet sniffers, devices that let somebody watch your keystrokes as they travel across the network between computers. The ECPA forbids this kind of electronic monitoring. Section 2511 states that "any person who intentionally intercepts" an electronic communication "shall be punished...or be subject to suit...." It's also illegal to own, make, or sell devices that do this kind of intercepting.

Interception of email is illegal.

Since email is also an electronic communication, the interception of email as it travels from sender to recipient is illegal for the same reasons that packet sniffing is.

The law has been interpreted strangely in the courts, though. Suppose email has arrived in your mailbox, but you haven't looked at it yet, and somebody else takes it. Has your mail been "intercepted"? In a famous court case, *Steve Jackson Games v. The United States Secret Service*, the judge decided that this was not interception of email. Because the email had already reached the recipient's mailbox, it was no longer being

Junk email

The bottom line is that it can't be controlled by laws, unless it becomes abusive or harassing. I think what will happen is the same thing that happened with junk faxing. It doesn't work, and people will stop doing it.

Mike Botts

transmitted over the network, and therefore had not been "intercepted." An appeal of this decision was unsuccessful.

Cracking is illegal.

The ECPA makes it illegal for somebody to break into your computer account against your wishes. Section 2701 specifically forbids "unlawful access to stored communications." This covers access to your computer account. Even if there is a security hole that allows somebody to use your account without stealing your password, such use is still illegal.

Many states have additional laws about privacy.

If you live in the United States, and you believe your computer privacy rights have been violated, make sure to check what state law has to say. Many states have laws that give you even stronger rights than what the federal laws guarantee.

Other invasions of privacy may be illegal.

The ECPA deals specifically with electronic privacy, but you also have a right to certain other kinds of privacy. If other people repeatedly bother you and won't leave you alone, expose sordid details of your private life, commit nasty acts in your name, or attach your name to documents you didn't write, our laws have something to say about this.

These illegal acts are called *privacy torts*. No, this kind of "tort" is not a dessert: it's a legal term meaning an injury to your body, property, or reputation. (Defamation is also a tort, though not a privacy tort.)

The next few sections will cover several privacy violations—flames, harassment, and impersonation—and discuss where tort law might apply online.

Libel isn't the only risk for flamers.

Suppose you are having an online argument in *comp.os.ms-windows.advocacy* on Usenet over whether Microsoft Windows or the Macintosh has a better user interface. Suddenly, your opponent strikes a low blow: "You don't know what you're talking about, and I'm not surprised, since you were arrested for drunk driving last year." Well, suppose it's true: you really were arrested for drunk driving. Therefore, this statement is not libel, since libel must be false. But a drunk driving charge has absolutely nothing to do with your ability to compare user interfaces, and the statement may have damaged your reputation as a computer expert on the Net. In this case, your opponent may have committed a privacy tort called *public disclosure of private facts*. If your reputation has been damaged because of this statement, you might have cause for legal action.

Harassment is the same online as offline.

Harassment is a crime of intent: the intent to scare you or cause damage. If somebody sends you threatening email, for example, this can be harassment, especially if it's done repeatedly. This is legally no different from harassment by postal letter or by telephone, and you can take legal action as you would in the physical world.

For a communication to be harassment, it must cause harm. Merely being annoyed is not enough, legally speaking. So if you are annoyed by junk email advertisements, for example, that is probably not considered harassment. The advertiser's intent is to sell a product, not to harm you.

Mailbombing can be harassment or an invasion of privacy.

If somebody bombards you with thousands of email messages, for the purpose of disrupting your business, this could be considered harassment. This practice is sometimes called *mailbombing*. A mailbomber sends large amounts of email—perhaps hundreds of megabytes—to another user. The user's disk space might get completely filled up with this unwanted email, causing login problems. At the very least, the user's time will be wasted dealing with all this mail.

Mailbombing might be illegal for another reason too: as an invasion of privacy. *Intrusion* is a privacy tort that sometimes applies if a person is being bothered over and over: say, by

Mailbombing

Mailbombing seems more legally shaky than spamming itself is, because there's an intent to do some harm. There could conceivably could be laws against that. There are certainly laws against harassment, and against online harassment.

Ethan Katsh

repeated, unwanted telephone calls. It is possible that this reasoning can apply to repeated, unwanted email as well.

Angry users sometimes mailbomb advertisers who use spamming or junk email to sell their products (see Chapter 7). Be aware, however, that mailbombing might be illegal.

It's legal to be anonymous.

When you're online, you have no obligation to reveal your identity. If somebody demands you identify yourself, you have the right, and the freedom, to refuse. (If you are suspected of a crime and arrested, however, the rules are different, and you may be required to identify yourself to law enforcement officials.)

Anonymous remailers, discussed in Chapter 2, are perfectly legal to use. There is nothing illegal about using an anonymous address to send email or post articles. Just be responsible. A crime committed with an anonymous address is still a crime.

Impersonating another user can be illegal.

It isn't hard for somebody else to pretend to be you online. Sometimes it is done in jest—maybe one of your friends sends you a funny email signed with your own name. It's also common for jokers to pretend to be famous celebrities and post articles on Usenet, especially on April Fools' Day. But impersonation can be illegal if the intent is to deceive or harm.

It can be illegal for somebody else to use your name for their own benefit. For instance, suppose you have a great reputation on the Net, and somebody else writes an article under your name so people will believe it. This is called an *appropriation of name* privacy tort. Your name is being used, without your permission, to advance somebody else's cause.

It also can be illegal if somebody uses your name to damage your reputation. For instance, somebody forges an article on Usenet, pretending to be you, and makes outrageous remarks or accusations so you appear to be a racist. (Like what happened to Professor Blount in Chapter 2.) Not only has someone appropriated your name, but also he or she is falsely

Your rights on the Net

attributing acts to you that aren't yours. This is called a *false light* privacy tort.

Internet culture and the law are a strange mixture.

As you can see, there are many ways users can violate each other's rights on the Internet. But if you are an experienced Net user, you might be scratching your head in confusion. You see, it's rare for users to take legal action against each other for copyright violations, flames, and so on.

Why is this? Probably because the Internet provides people with an easy way to work out some kinds of disputes online. When somebody flames you, you can flame them back. If somebody lies about you publicly, you can often respond in the same forum. If you are harassed, you can send email to the harasser's system administrator. In this way, the Net is somewhat self-policing.

Even so, as more and more people join the Internet, the number of legal cases is bound to increase. Whether we like it or not, existing laws are going to be applied to the online world, and new ones might be created as well. We'll talk about this more in Chapter 12 when we try to predict the future of the Net.

For more information…

Several books about law on the Internet have been written for people who have no legal background. The best one currently is *Cyberspace and the Law*, by Edward A. Cavazos and Gavino Morin (MIT Press, 1995). It provides a short and sweet overview of online legal issues. Another book is *NetLaw*, by Lance Rose (Osborne McGraw-Hill, 1995), but it is longer and "flashier" in its presentation, and I found it less satisfying than *Cyberspace and the Law*. *Law in a Digital World*, by Ethan Katsh (Oxford University Press, 1995), focuses on a different but related topic: how global computer networks present challenges to the law profession itself. These books disagree on some issues, so it might be worthwhile to read more than one.

Internet World magazine has a monthly column, "Law of the Net," written by Mike Godwin of the Electronic Frontier Foundation (see below). The column is very readable and focuses

International legal issues

Suppose someone in Germany pretends to be a professor in England communicating with a university in the United States, damaging the reputation of another United States resident. Things get difficult very quickly. The chances of getting anything done about it are almost zero.

Mike Botts

on timely issues that affect the average user. Mr. Godwin is also working on a book, *CyberRights* (Random House, 1996), that should be a good read.

On Usenet, check out the newsgroup *misc.legal* to discuss legal issues in general. For computer-related issues, take a look in *misc.legal.computing*. Of particular note are two FAQ articles that answer simple questions about copyright. Terry Carroll's "Copyright Law FAQ" and Brad Templeton's "Copyright Myths FAQ: 10 Big Myths about Copyright Explained," are both posted regularly in *misc.legal*. They are also available by FTP from *rtfm.mit.edu* in the directory

```
/pub/usenet/news.answers/law/Copyright-FAQ
```

and on the World Wide Web (along with lots of other copyright-related information) at

```
http://www.yahoo.com/text/Government/Law/
   Intellectual_Property/Copyrights/
```

The definitive source for copyright information in the United States is the U.S. Copyright Office, accessible via the World Wide Web at

```
http://lcweb.loc.gov/copyright/
```

If you have a few hours to spare, the Clinton Administration's 250-page statement about copyright and electronic media is available on the Web at

```
gopher://ntiant1.ntia.doc.gov:70/00/papers/documents/
   files/ipnii.txt
```

Carol Woodbury has links to huge numbers of law and cyber-law-related resources at

```
http://www.mcs.com/~carolwoo/home.html
```

The Electronic Frontier Foundation, an organization founded to protect the civil liberties of users, has a Web page with lots of information, at

```
http://www.eff.org
```

The Massachusetts Institute of Technology has a Web site devoted to "Ethics and Law on the Electronic Frontier." Originally created as part of a college course, this Web site contains archived information on privacy, computer crime, and related topics. The URL is

```
http://www-swiss.ai.mit.edu/6095/
```

The University of Massachusetts has an introduction to law-related resources on the Internet, called the UMass Internet Law Hypercourse. It's available on the Web at

```
http://www.umassp.edu/legal/hypercou.html
```

Remember that these resources are not a substitute for hiring an attorney. There is plenty of legal misinformation floating around on the Net. Even if you find accurate information, if you aren't a legal expert, you might not have the background to interpret it correctly.

Online law archives

The Internet is a place where one can become aware of law-related information much more easily than one can in the library. Lawyers, law schools, and legal educators have put a lot of legal information on the Internet and made it fairly accessible. And the big surprise for those legal information providers has been the demand from nonlegal professionals.

Ethan Katsh

What to do if you are ripped off

Here is where we discuss how to fight back.

OK. You've been careful. You've been skeptical. You've followed all the safety tips in this book. But somehow, in spite of all your precautions, you have been ripped off. Or maybe you are being pestered by a user who won't leave you alone, no matter how many times you ask for peace.

What now?

The answer is: it's time to get tough. This chapter lists and explains many options for pursuing an Internet bandit or pest. The methods we'll discuss focus on the following seven steps:

1. *Contact the user.* Try to work things out directly and don't rely on email too much.

2. *Determine the damage.* If contacting the user doesn't help, tally your losses.

3. *Decide whether or not to continue.* Maybe the damage is small and can be ignored. Maybe the cost of taking action is too high.

4. *Gather your evidence.* Don't throw away anything that could potentially help your case.

5. *Contact online resources.* If the user won't cooperate, walk up the Internet chain of command.

Missouri and New Jersey take action

Last summer, in the first regulatory actions against investment cyber-scams, Missouri ordered a stockbroker to stop issuing false claims online, and New Jersey squelched a string of electronic chain letters promising a $60,000 return to anyone who sent out five $1 bills. Participants stood to lose a lot more than $5: They unwittingly added their names to an electronic mailing list of prospects for future scams.

Faye Goolrick, "When You Invest... Beware of Those Pyramid Schemers," *New Choices*, May 1995

6. *Contact offline resources.* If a problem can't be solved online, there are organizations and agencies available to help you.

7. *Hire a lawyer.* If all else fails, it might be time to go to court.

Each of these steps is detailed in the following sections.

For many problems, it's a good idea to try these seven steps in order. You'd be surprised how many "ripoffs" turn out to be simple misunderstandings that can be cleared up with a single phone call to the user. In other situations, however, you'll need to use your judgment to decide where to begin. For example, if you are the target of a serious crime, you might want to go straight to a law-enforcement agency and forget about solving things online. But in general, the above order gives you a cautious yet effective method for addressing a problem with another Net user.

Make direct contact to clear up misunderstandings.

It's the simplest way to clear things up, but it's often forgotten. If you have encountered a problem with a user, contact him or her directly. Chances are that you've just had a misunderstanding, and the two of you can clear up the whole thing quickly.

Don't rely completely on email for making contact. Too many things can go wrong to prevent your email from being received. For example, a mail-routing computer could crash, a problem could arise with the user's computer account (like running out of disk space for mail); or the user might not even log in regularly. Instead, reach for the telephone. Even if it's a long-distance call, the few dollars you spend might save you hours of grief later. As we discussed in Chapter 6, always get the mailing address and telephone number of any user with whom you do business, in case an emergency arises. If you don't have a user's telephone number, try the **finger** program to see if the number is listed online, or call Information.

Too often, users forget about the telephone and mistakenly assume that they've been ripped off. Tammy is a user on CompuServe who once made an email deal with Joanna, a university student, to purchase Joanna's clarinet by mail. They agreed that Tammy would send a money order by mail, Joanna would send email when the money arrived, and then the clarinet would be shipped. (Not the safest way to do business, but that's what they decided to do.) After sending her money order and waiting a week, Tammy heard nothing at all from Joanna. She sent Joanna five email messages in the next two days, but received no response. Angry and worried that her money had been stolen, Tammy posted the story in the Usenet newsgroup *rec.music.makers.marketplace*, calling Joanna a thief.

Three days later, Tammy finally received email from Joanna. Guess what? Joanna had been out of town for her university's week-long Spring Break, visiting her parents. Tammy's money order had arrived the day after Joanna had left. Joanna sent the clarinet promptly, Tammy posted profuse apologies on Usenet (luckily, Joanna was good-natured and did not sue Tammy for libel), and the problem was solved. If Tammy had only picked up the telephone, Joanna's housemate could have told Tammy that Joanna was away, and the misunderstanding could have been avoided. Of course, Joanna also was careless: she should have told Tammy about her upcoming Spring Break!

Some "ripoff artists" are actually victims of someone else.

Since spoofed email and forged Usenet articles (see Chapter 2) have become commonplace, a disturbing trend has arisen. Occasionally, a dishonest person will email or post a well-known scam in the name of an innocent user. Here's a hypothetical situation: suppose that the user *joe@innocent.org* has walked away from his terminal for a few minutes but left himself logged in. A dishonest person walks up to Joe's terminal and, pretending to be Joe, maliciously posts a copy of the "Dave Rhodes/Make Money Fast" letter on Usenet. Readers on Usenet see the letter, think it was posted by Joe, and write hundreds of angry responses to both Joe and his system administrator. Poor Joe has to clean up the mess. That's a pretty nasty trick, isn't it? Unfortunately, it does happen.

Before responding to an email message or Usenet article that looks like a ripoff, take a moment to try to determine whether it is a forgery or not. This is done by examining the email or news headers, as we discussed in Chapter 2. Briefly:

- If the article was sent by email, check that the `Received` header lines are consistent with the return email address.

Fight harassment

Someone who is harassed on the Internet should find out if they can press charges against the individual who is harassing them. They had a case like that about a year ago at University of Maryland where a guy's friend was using the guy's account to harass women. The "friend" cannot get an account any more.

Tryphena

- If the article was posted on Usenet, check that the NNTP-Posting-Host and Path lines are consistent with the poster's email address.

- If the article was posted on Usenet, make sure the Followup-To line isn't set to a "test" newsgroup, such as *misc.test*. If it is, then the poster is trying to trick you into posting a note unintentionally in a test newsgroup, resulting in a flood of automatic email being sent back at you.

In addition, ask yourself if the author of the article might be trolling, as we discussed in Chapter 7, hoping that somebody will respond and look like a fool.

Before taking action, determine the damage.

Suppose that you've tried unsuccessfully to work things out with the user, or that the user could not be contacted. Now it's time to decide what to do next. The first step is to determine how much harm you have suffered. Take time to write everything down. Here's a checklist to help jog your memory.

Did you lose money?
Perhaps you paid for an item that never arrived, purchased an item that did not live up to an advertiser's promises, paid bank fees due to a bad check, or signed up for a scam business opportunity.

Did you lose merchandise?
Perhaps you sold an item to an Internet user, shipped it, and never received payment for it.

Did you lose data?
Perhaps a virus or trojan-horse program destroyed your files, or some of your Usenet articles were maliciously canceled.

Did you lose time?
Add up the time you have spent dealing with this problem and multiply it by the value of your time.

Was your privacy or security violated?
Perhaps somebody broke into your computer account or intercepted your private email.

Was your reputation damaged?
Perhaps somebody sent spoofed email or forged a Usenet article in your name.

Did you suffer any physical harm?

Perhaps a Net "friend" you met in person turned out to be abusive.

Did you suffer any mental anguish?

Perhaps you have received large numbers of abusive email messages or telephone calls from a user who will not leave you alone.

Is further harm possible if you do not act now?

This includes harm to you *and* to other potential victims.

Decide whether it's worthwhile to continue.

Once you have written down your losses, it's time to decide whether the case is worth pursuing. If your losses are very small, your simplest but least satisfying option is to do nothing. If you lost 10 dollars to a scammer who lives thousands of miles away, it might cost you more than 10 dollars in telephone calls to try to get your money back. Similarly, if you spend several hours pursuing that scammer, and your time is worth 10 dollars an hour, you'll again lose money. In such cases, you might just chalk it up to experience (what my grandmother used to call "charging it to Profit And Loss") and try to be more cautious next time.

Save all of your evidence.

If you decide to pursue action against a user, it's best to have as much evidence as possible. Save everything that might possibly be relevant, no matter how small or inconsequential it may seem at the time.

Save all your electronic correspondence with or about the user, such as email, publicly posted articles, and copies of Web pages. Make sure you save all the headers as well as the text. Keep copies online, and also print them for safekeeping. Save all physical evidence, such as printed literature, warranties, guarantees, and receipts.

It helps to keep a written record of everything that has happened in the case, in order of occurrence, including dates and times. A document like this will be extremely handy whenever you need to explain your case to somebody else, and you can use it to jog your memory as needed. You'd be surprised how many little details slip away over weeks and months if you don't write them down.

Some problems can be solved entirely online.

If the major focus of the problem is related to the Internet, it might be worth pursuing a solution online. This means contacting the problem user's system administrator or other authorities at the user's site. Here are a few examples of problems that can possibly be cleared up online.

- A user is harassing you with repeated "talk" messages or email, even after you have asked the user to leave you alone.
- A user has impersonated you by spoofing email or forging a Usenet article.
- A user is sending you unsolicited junk email.
- A user is spamming articles on Usenet.
- A user has broken into your computer account.
- A user is operating an illegal business online, such as a "get rich quick" scheme.

You probably should not waste your time complaining to system administrators about problems like the following:

- A user bothered you with *one* unwanted message (other than junk mail). Unless the message was grievously disturbing, just let it pass. Save your complaints for repeat offenders.
- A user has insulted you. Although flaming can sometimes make you uncomfortable, it's common behavior online. It's like having a loud argument with somebody. Would you call the police because your neighbor called you a jerk?
- A user posted material publicly on the Net that is offensive to you, though not directed at you. If you don't like somebody's words, feel free to respond to the writer, but don't bother the user's system administrators. Everybody has different opinions about what is offensive, so try to be open-minded about letting other people speak freely.

The next few sections illustrate how to move up the Internet chain of command and request assistance from:

1. The user's postmaster or system administrator.

2. The administrative contact for the user's computer.

3. Other powers-that-be at the organization that owns the user's computer.

4. In rare instances, the administrators of the computer's domain servers.

Contact the user's postmaster.

Suppose that you aren't successful at working things out with the user, and you've gathered your evidence. Your next step in an online solution is generally to contact the user's system administrator. This is done by examining the user's email address and substituting the word *postmaster* in place of the user's name. For example, if you are having problems with the user *sneaky@truly.awful.com*, you should address your complaint to *postmaster@truly.awful.com*.

If mail to *postmaster* bounces back to you with an error message, try *root* instead, as in *root@truly.awful.com*. Every computer on the Internet is supposed to have a *postmaster* mail address, but some incorrectly configured computers do not.

Postmasters are generally helpful people, so always be polite when you write to them. If you are angry at a scammer, don't direct your anger at an innocent postmaster. Instead, try to give a clear, concise description of the problem, including all relevant details. Make sure to send copies of all electronic correspondence you've had with the scammer, including complete email or news headers.

If a postmaster does not respond to you immediately, don't panic. Postmasters are busy people. The postmasters of large online services receive hundreds of email messages each day. If you don't get an answer within several business days, send a brief, polite reminder, in case your original message somehow got lost.

Make sure the postmaster isn't the scammer.

If a scammer's computer account is at a major university, company, or online service provider, the postmaster there is an

Postmasters

If the Internet is the Wild West, then postmasters are the sheriffs.

Lisa Feldman Barrett

Who's that postmaster?

Using the program **telnet**, found on many Internet computers, you can often discover who is actually the postmaster of another computer. This is done by examining where the *postmaster* mail alias points on the other computer. Let's again suppose that the user *sneaky@truly.awful.com* has done you wrong, but *sneaky's* postmaster, *postmaster@truly.awful.com*, is not being helpful. Here is how to check whether *sneaky* is actually the postmaster.

1. Execute the command:

   telnet truly.awful.com 25

2. If your software supports this kind of **telnet** command, and the command succeeds, you will see a message that looks something like this:

   220 truly.awful.com Sendmail ready

   If the **telnet** command fails, or if you see a login prompt instead of the above message, then give up; your computer cannot use this method. Otherwise, continue.

3. In response to the prompt, type the word helo (yes, only one "L") followed by the name of your computer, and press the Return key:

   helo my.machine.net

4. The machine *truly.awful.com* will respond with a message that looks like this:

   250 truly.awful.com Hello my.machine.net, pleased to meet you

5. Next, type the command to reveal the postmaster's true email address:

   vrfy postmaster

If this produces no result, or an error message, try these commands to see if any of them work:

expn postmaster
vrfy root
expn root

If one of these commands works, then the true email address of the postmaster of *truly.awful.com* will be revealed:

250-Dave Davis <davis@admin.awful.com>

Here, *sneaky* is not the postmaster. If the opposite were true, then you would have seen a response like this instead:

250-Pat Sneakorama <sneaky@truly.awful.com>

If none of the above commands worked, this method cannot be used to reveal this postmaster's identity. (But it might work for a different machine.)

6. End the session by typing:

   quit

   You will see a final message that looks like this:

   221 truly.awful.com closing connection

   and the **telnet** program will exit.

Some UNIX computers have a program called **vrfy** installed, written by Eric Wassenaar (*e07@nikhef.nl*), which provides a much easier way to check the postmaster alias. To use it, simply type:

   vrfy -e postmaster@truly.awful.com

and the postmaster's identity will be revealed, if possible.

What to do if you are ripped off

employee who is paid to deal with computer-related problems. Unfortunately, at small Internet sites, the postmaster could be anybody…even the scammer. More and more people are connecting their personal computers to the Internet and acting as their own system administrators. Unless you are very familiar with Internet addresses, it might be hard to tell whether a computer is a major site with dozens of system administrators, or a home PC with a modem connection.

If you don't get an answer from a user's postmaster or if the postmaster is unhelpful, apathetic, or antagonistic, check to see who the postmaster really is. For details, see the accompanying sidebar, "Who's that postmaster?"

Next, contact the site's administrative contact person.

If you can't get assistance from the postmaster, your next step is to locate the *administrative contact* person for the user's computer. The administrative contact is the official contact person for an Internet domain. This means that he or she has some power over all computers in the domain where your scammer hangs out.

You can find out the name of any administrative contact from the *InterNIC Registration Services Center*, a central service that keeps track of all computer domains on the Internet. The accompanying sidebar, "Locating administrative contacts," explains how to do it.

Next, contact other administrators at the site.

If the site's administrative contact isn't helpful, there might be other people you can contact at the site. For instance, if the problem user is a student at a university, try calling a dean or department head for assistance. If the scammer works at a big company, the company's public relations department might be of help. You might even be able to find out the name of the scammer's boss and give him or her a call.

Remember, be polite and state the problem clearly and concisely. By now, if you have been ignored by the postmaster and administrative contact, you are probably pretty frustrated.

Mail to the postmaster

In November 1994, I discovered a very obvious "Make Money With Your PC" pyramid scheme being operated via a computer in Canada. Like a good Net citizen, I emailed the postmaster of the computer, describing the scam and identifying the user. In response, I got another letter from the scammer, shouting that I "obviously do not know anything" about pyramid schemes, proclaiming that his "money back guarantee proves that it works and we are serious." It turned out that the scammer was friends with the owner of the computer, which was just a PC hooked up to the Net.

Dan Barrett

Locating administrative contacts

This section shows how to connect to InterNIC's computer, *rs.internic.net*, and look up an administrative contact in a database called the *whois database* (pronounced "who is"). Let's again assume the user *sneaky@truly.awful.com* has caused trouble, and *sneaky*'s postmaster was no help to you. Here is how to locate the administrative contact using the World Wide Web.

1. In the name of the user's computer, locate the last two words. Our example computer's name is *truly.awful.com*, so the last two words are *awful.com*. This is your scammer's domain name.

2. Using your Web browser, go to the URL http://rs.internic.net/cgi-bin/whois/

3. Using the "search" facility on this page, search for the domain name, *awful.com*, that you located in Step 1.

4. Information on the *awful.com* domain will be displayed on your screen:

   Awful Products, Inc. (AWFUL-DOM)
     123 Bothersome Blvd.
     New York, NY 10001
   Domain Name: AWFUL.COM
   Administrative Contact:
     Bull, Teri (TB6) terrible@nic.awful.com
     212-555-5678
   Record last updated on 14-Dec-94.
   Domain servers in listed order:
     IAS1.IACNET.COM   140.244.1.69
     NIC.NEAR.NET   192.52.71.4

   You can now locate the name of the administrative contact; in this case, it's Teri Bull, and her email address and telephone number are given.

5. If there are several InterNIC entries for *awful.com*, you'll see a choice offered instead:

   Awful Products, Inc. (AWFUL-DOM)   AWFUL.COM
   Awful Networking (AWFUL-NET)   AWFUL.NET

If this happens, repeat the search using the words inside the parentheses (AWFUL-DOM).

Some UNIX computers have a program called whois that provides an easy way to look things up in InterNIC's **whois** database. To use it, simply type:

   whois -h rs.internic.net awful.com

where *awful.com* is the word you constructed in Step 1, above. If you don't have World Wide Web access or **whois**, you can connect to InterNIC using the **telnet** program. This is a bit tricker, but not too bad.

1. The same as the first step in the Web method: find the last two words in the computer name, *awful.com*.

2. Execute the command:

   telnet rs.internic.net

   and press the Return key. You will see a welcome message from InterNIC and some brief instructions.

3. At the prompt, type:
   whois

   and press the Return key.

4. At the **whois** prompt, type the word you constructed in the previous step,
   awful.com

   and press the Return key. You will see the same entry for *awful.com* that is shown in the Web example above.

5. When you are done, exit from the **whois** database by typing:
   quit

6. To leave the **telnet** session, type:
   quit

Don't take out your frustrations on these people who might be able to help you.

Finally, contact the site's domain servers.

This is a last resort, and you should almost never need to do it.

If nobody at all at the user's site will help you, and you still think that an online solution to the problem is a good idea, you can contact the administrators of the user's *domain server*. A domain server is a computer that provides the Internet connection for all computers in an Internet domain. (Domains are explained in the appendix.)

When you looked up the administrative contact's name using the InterNIC **whois** database, you might have noticed an entry labeled "Domain servers in listed order." Here are the relevant lines from our example when we looked up the *awful.com* domain:

```
Domain Name: AWFUL.COM
...
Domain servers in listed order:
  IAS1.IACNET.COM          140.244.1.69
  NIC.NEAR.NET             192.52.71.4
```

This says that all computers in the *awful.com* domain get their Internet access by way of the machines *ias1.iacnet.com* and *nic.near.net*. In other words, without these two domain servers, all computers in the *awful.com* domain would be cut off from the Internet. So you can guess that a domain server holds some power over the computers and people that use its services.

In general, you should not contact a domain server unless there is a major, Internet-related problem that affects lots of people. If you thought that postmasters and administrative contacts are busy people, well, domain server administrators are even busier. If an individual user ripped you off (say, our friend *sneaky@truly.awful.com* again), then it would not be appropriate to contact the domain servers of *awful.com*, because only one person (you) has been affected. On the other hand, if *sneaky@truly.awful.com* is broadcasting thousands of harassing or illegal email messages, and the postmaster and administrative contact of *awful.com* don't want to do anything about it, then you should consider contacting the domain servers. Such Internet abuse might be against a domain server's policies on network use.

To contact the administrators of a domain server, write to the postmaster at the listed addresses: in our example, *postmaster@ias1.iacnet.com* and *postmaster@nic.near.net*. If you want to learn more information about these domain servers, you can use the InterNIC **whois** database, as we discussed in the sidebar "Locating administrative contacts." In our example, if you looked up the first domain, *iacnet.com*, you'd see something like this:

```
Information Access Company (IACNET-DOM)
   362 Lakeside Drive
   Foster City, CA 94404
Domain Name: IACNET.COM
Administrative Contact:   ...
```

If you can't solve your problem online, there are agencies to help you.

When you're trying to catch a scammer, online methods can go only so far. A computer's postmaster or administrative contact has the ability to remove a scammer's login privileges, but usually no legal power to help you settle a dispute or get your money back.

The following sections discuss various people and organizations that have resources available to help you locate, investigate, and/or punish a scammer offline.

- Local law-enforcement offices
- A state attorney general
- The Federal Trade Commission
- The Postal Service
- The Federal Bureau of Investigation

We'll also cover some resources that can help answer questions, offer advice, provide a needed "push" to the above organizations, or occasionally pursue legal action on your behalf, though they do not have legal power themselves.

- The Better Business Bureau
- The Direct Selling Education Foundation
- The CERT Coordination Center

- The Software Publisher's Association
- Your congressional representative
- The media

At the end of the chapter, we list contact information for these organizations and agencies.

There is no hard-and-fast rule for deciding which resource is the best to approach if you have been ripped off. A good rule of thumb is to contact several of them. These people and organizations are very busy and sometimes overburdened, so they have to assign priorities to their cases. This means they might not have the time or resources to deal with your problem unless it involves a lot of money or a lot of victims. So the more organizations you contact, the more reaction you are likely to get. For example, if you write to the Better Business Bureau and your congressperson, and they both urge the Federal Trade Commission to act, you're more likely to get results than if you had just sent a letter to the FTC yourself.

Don't set your hopes too high.

As you read about the agencies that are available to help you, don't get overly optimistic. The federal agencies are busy, and few states have active, effective consumer protection divisions. (California, Florida, Iowa, New York, New Jersey, and Wisconsin are known to have very good ones.) The Postal Service is also very good. But in general, our legal system isn't set up very well for pursuing fly-by-night scams of the sort found on the Net. Some get prosecuted, but many more do not. Your best bet is not to fall for a scam in the first place.

Be concise.

If you write a letter to an organization, asking for help, make it as clear and to the point as possible. This will increase your chances of getting help. These organizations receive more complaints than they can handle, so write your letter as if the person who receives it will have only 60 seconds to read and understand your complaint.

Make the first paragraph count. Explain the problem using as few words as possible, without including unnecessary details.

The average victim doesn't complain

Maybe a fraction of one percent complain. It's hard to go to a law-enforcement organization and say, "I feel really stupid. I bought into this con, and I gave them a ton of money, without even knowing anything about it, and now they have my money." Most people just write it off as one of life's little lessons.

Mike Botts

Suppose that you lost money to a user who promised to ship you a computer, but instead shipped a box of rocks. You decide to write to your local Postal Inspector. Here is the beginning of a bad letter:

> I was reading the newsgroup *misc.forsale.computers* on Usenet, which is an international electronic discussion group, when I encountered an advertisement for an IBM '486 computer. The seller said that it was in good condition, so I wrote to him and offered to buy it for $900. He responded yes, and we arranged that he would ship it COD. Little did I know that he never intended to keep his part of the bargain.

What's wrong here? A whole paragraph has gone by, and the ripoff has not even been described yet. A better first paragraph states the whole problem quickly and describes the assistance you'd like:

> On January 23, 1995, I purchased a computer by mail. The seller, however, shipped me a box of bricks instead. I believe that this constitutes postal mail fraud. Could you please help me get my money back?

In the rest of the letter, describe enough details for the organization to decide whether they can help you or not.

> The seller is John Q. Public, 555 Spammer Street, Chickenmilk, Wisconsin, 54321, telephone (414) 555-6789. We arranged the sale on the Internet, and he agreed to ship the computer via postal COD. When the shipment arrived, I paid $900 in cash. When I opened the box, I found a dozen bricks but no computer. Mr. Public has since refused to answer my letters, telephone calls, and electronic mail.

> Enclosed are printouts of all electronic mail messages that Mr. Public and I exchanged about the sale. Thank you very much for your help. I hope to hear from you soon.

After the organization receives your complaint, it frequently will send you a standard form to fill out or will contact you for more details. Now you have a chance to go into great detail about your problem, if you like.

What to do if you are ripped off

Local law-enforcement agencies can help with local problems.

Because the Internet is so huge and international, it's unlikely your scammer lives in your city or town. But if you're "lucky" enough to have a scammer right around the corner, start by filing a report with your local police. If you have been ripped off by a local business, contact your district attorney.

State law-enforcement agencies can help if your problem is within state lines.

Every state in the United States has an *attorney general,* whose job it is (in part) to investigate fraudulent business that occurs within the state. If a Net scammer happens to live in your state, your attorney general may have jurisdiction and can be a good resource. You can also file a report with the state police.

Similarly, if your scammer lives in a different state, contact the attorney general of that state for help. You can get the contact information by telephoning Information in that state and asking for the attorney general's office.

The Federal Trade Commission enforces consumer protection laws at the national level.

The *Federal Trade Commission (FTC)* is the federal government agency that investigates deceptive market practices, including false advertising and other illegal actions. If you were ripped off by a scam that crossed state lines, the FTC may have jurisdiction.

The U.S. Postal Service investigates mail fraud.

If your problem involves postal mail, you should consider getting the U.S. Postal Service involved. Your local Postal Inspector has the power to investigate any issue that involves

Attorneys general

A working group of Attorneys General shall be designated by the President of the Association to coordinate the activities of the Association in developing a response to various issues involving Internet activities....

Consumer Protection Report,
National Association of
Attorneys General, June 1995

mail fraud, in which something is sent through the mail for fraudulent purposes. For example:

- You bought or sold an item on the Internet, and you were ripped off after the item or the payment was shipped by mail.

- You encountered a fraudulent business on the Internet, such as a pyramid scheme, that conducted some of its operations by mail.

Electronic mail doesn't count; the Postal Service has no jurisdiction over it. Similarly, the Postal Service may not take action if your goods were shipped by another carrier, such as UPS or Federal Express.

The FBI handles fraud over telephone wires.

Wire fraud is a crime in which somebody rips off another person using wire communication. For instance, if somebody lies to you on the telephone, convincing you to send him money for false reasons, this is wire fraud. Since computer communications like email and Usenet news are transmitted over telephone lines, wire-fraud laws apply to some ripoffs on the Internet.

The *Federal Bureau of Investigation (FBI)* is the organization responsible for pursuing cases of wire fraud when the communication crosses state lines. If you contact the FBI, though, be aware that your case might not receive much attention if the amount of money involved, or the number of people involved, is small. To the FBI, $10,000 and twenty victims might be considered "small." But you can still try.

The Better Business Bureau collects information on bad businesses.

The *Better Business Bureau (BBB)* is a private organization dedicated to helping consumers. The BBB receives people's complaints about particular businesses, keeps them on file, and occasionally helps people settle disputes with businesses. Reports are kept for three years.

Although the BBB collects a lot of information, it does not release much of it to the public. If you inquire about a com-

What to do if you are ripped off

pany, the BBB will tell you whether there have been complaints against it (yes or no), what the status of the complaints is (resolved or unresolved), and sometimes the number of complaints. They'll also inform you if there have been any state or federal actions against the company or if the company has filed for bankruptcy. But they will not tell you specific details about the complaints: why they were filed and by whom.

There should be a BBB branch in your area; check your local telephone book or the telephone book for the nearest large city.

BBB online

Our BBB Web server is a first step in our strategic plan to utilize leading-edge technology to help respond fully and quickly to all inquiries from the public and to help resolve all marketplace complaints from consumers.

Jim Bast, President and CEO, Council of Better Business Bureaus, Inc. Press release, May 11, 1995

The Direct Selling Education Foundation provides information on business practices.

The *Direct Selling Education Foundation* (*DSEF*) is a not-for-profit organization that educates consumers about business practices in the marketplace. The DSEF publishes and distributes several pamphlets to help consumers identify fraudulent business opportunities, such as pyramid schemes. These include:

- *Pyramid Schemes: Not What They Seem*

- *Promises—Check 'Em Out*, concerning other business frauds.

For free copies of the pamphlets, send a self-addressed stamped envelope to the address given at the end of the chapter.

The CERT Coordination Center focuses on computer security.

The *CERT Coordination Center* is an organization dedicated to protecting the security of computers on the Internet. From its headquarters at Carnegie Mellon University, the CERT Coordination Center broadcasts announcements about computer security problems (but only after solutions are available), provides technical assistance for security problems 24 hours a day, and maintains an FTP site of security-related files. CERT stands for Computer Emergency Response Team.

The CERT Coordination Center posts its security advisories as needed in the Usenet newsgroup *comp.security.announce.* You can also receive them by joining the CERT Coordination

CERT Summary

The CERT Coordination Center periodically issues the CERT Summary to draw attention to the types of attacks currently being reported to our incident response staff. The summary includes pointers to sources of information for dealing with the problems.

cert-advisory@cert.org

Center mailing list. To join, send mail to *cert-advisory-request@cert.org*.

If you discover a security problem at your site, you should alert your system administrator first. If the security problem is more widespread than just your site, then you or (more likely) your system administrator should let the CERT Coordination Center know about it.

The Software Publisher's Association investigates software piracy.

The *Software Publisher's Association* (SPA) is an international organization consisting of over 1000 personal-computer software companies and developers. One of the SPA's most well-known activities is its antipiracy program. If you uncover a pirate bulletin board or FTP site, or if software that you wrote is being pirated, file a report with the SPA. In the past, the SPA has sent cease-and-desist letters, performed corporate audits, and pursued legal action against pirates. Some of the cases won by the SPA have been settled for hundreds of thousands of dollars.

Your congressperson can help push an investigation.

If an organization is ignoring you or lagging behind in its treatment of your case, it might be helpful to write to your elected representative for help. If your need seems reasonable, your congressperson might write a letter or make a call on your behalf and make the organization take your problem more seriously. In a purely practical sense, your congressperson knows that helping you can generate a needed vote in the next election. I have written to my congressman (John Olver of Massachusetts) several times and always been pleased with the results.

For an extra push, take your case to the media.

If your case is newsworthy, it can be helpful to talk to the media. Media attention can sometimes motivate law-enforcement agencies to pursue your case more actively. Right now, the Internet is a particularly hot topic, so your chances of getting media interest are increased.

When contacting a newspaper, ask for the consumer writer, the technology editor, or the crime editor, depending on your situation. Try local papers first. But if you can interest a national newspaper in your story, such as *The New York Times* or *USA Today*, it is more likely that law-enforcement agencies will pay attention to you: especially if reporters start calling the agency and asking why it hasn't been pursuing the case properly.

Magazines can also be helpful. Some magazines that have previously published stories on Internet ripoffs and related issues include *Infoworld*, *Insight* (the *Washington Times* magazine), *Internet World*, *Maclean's*, *NetGuide*, *New Scientist*, *Newsweek*, and *TIME*.

Internet crime has been the subject of many television news stories. For example, when 50 users lost thousands of dollars to "T. Le" (Chapter 6), they contacted NBC News and got their story aired. They also established a World Wide Web page for people to read about the case.

You can also tell your story on Usenet.

Usenet is another potential "media" outlet. A common and inexpensive response to ripoffs is to post an article on Usenet, revealing the ripoff and advising other users not to deal with this scammer. Before you do this, you might want to warn the scammer that if he or she does not correct all wrongs within a certain amount of time, you will post the truth on Usenet for tens of thousands of people to read. Maybe this will provide a little "motivation" for the scammer to shape up.

If you post your story, do not spam it throughout Usenet. Even if your story is very important, you should not abuse your Net privileges by wasting other people's disk space. Instead, choose one appropriate newsgroup and post there. If you must post to several newsgroups, remember to use crossposting, not to post multiple times.

Some thieves do get caught

Back in May of 1995, an Internet thief was caught in Utah after tricking fifteen people into sending him a total of $10,000 on the Net for phony merchandise. The thief turned out to be a 15-year-old boy. The state Division of Consumer Protection did the investigating.

When you tell your story, stick to the facts.

Be as accurate as possible and don't embellish. Report only the facts. You do not want to open yourself up to a lawsuit. By publicizing your story, you might be damaging the reputation of the "scammer," and there is always the possibility that you'll be taken to court for what you say. This is doubly true if you post on Usenet. When you take your story to a newspaper, magazine, or TV station, the reporters and legal staff there can check your accuracy somewhat and decide not to print some of your assertions. When you post on Usenet, however, this safety check does not exist, and you could commit libel without realizing it.

In the end, you might need an attorney.

If you cannot get satisfaction from the other methods and organizations described in this chapter, and you still want to pursue justice, it is time to find an attorney. Try to find one who is very familiar with the Internet.

Hiring an attorney is not cheap. Unless you hope to recover a large amount of money in damages, it might not be worth your while to pursue the case. (Especially if your scammer lives in another country.) Many attorneys give a short consultation for free, to help you decide whether the case is worth pursuing. Shop around for an attorney who provides this service.

This chapter has a disclaimer.

The advice offered in this chapter is not legal advice. It is just a set of guidelines, combining common sense, Internet experience, information from government agencies, and tips from people who have been ripped off. If you need personal legal advice, you should consult an attorney.

If you are ripped off, there are no guarantees you'll ever catch the scammer or get compensated for your loss. Nevertheless, this chapter can be a valuable starting point for pursuing action against a scammer or pest.

Good luck!

For more information...

Here is the contact information for all the organizations we've discussed.

Federal Trade Commission, Correspondence Branch
6th Street and Pennsylvania Avenue, NW
Washington, DC 20580
(202) 326-2222
World Wide Web: http://www.ftc.gov

If you'd like to receive a list of the FTC's free publications on how to avoid frauds, online and offline, write to Best Sellers, Public Reference, Federal Trade Commission. Also, most major U.S. cities have a regional FTC office. Consult your local telephone book or call the above number for more information.

Federal Bureau of Investigation
Ninth Street and Pennsylvania Avenue, NW
Washington, DC 20535
(202) 324-3000
World Wide Web: http://www.fbi.gov

United States Postal Service
World Wide Web: http://www.usps.gov

Direct Selling Education Foundation
1666 K Street NW, Suite 1010
Washington, DC 20006
(202) 293-5760

CERT Coordination Center
Software Engineering Institute
Carnegie Mellon University
Pittsburgh, PA 15213-3890
Voice: (412) 268-7090
Fax: (412) 268-6989
Email: *cert@cert.org*
FTP site: *info.cert.org*

The Better Business Bureau World Wide Web URL is:

http://www.bbb.org/bbb/

The CERT Frequently Asked Questions (FAQ) is available on the FTP site and contains comprehensive information about the organization's activities.

Lightening up

People need to lighten up on the Net. Just because a lawsuit is the American Way doesn't mean that it's the Internet Way.

If you are wronged by another person in a normal human way, resort to direct person-to-person communication to solve the misunderstanding.

If you are wronged intentionally by someone who's really Net savvy, get them where it hurts. Make a convincing case to their Net administrator to get their access revoked, so that they can't keep performing Net sabotage.

Arsenio Santos

No place to complain

When my Mom's birthday came, I ordered flowers for her through the Web page of a florist with a good reputation.

When I called Mom, the flowers hadn't arrived. I went back to the florist's Web page, but found no contact information. There was no company address or customer service phone number.

There was a Comments form, which I filled out but have not heard back on. So, my Mom and I are left wondering what happened. Were the flowers delivered to another address? Was the order ever received?

Right now, I'm waiting for my credit card statement, to see what shows up. If a city and state are listed for the charge, then hopefully I'll be able to get a phone listing for the florist.

Ellie Cutler

Software Publisher's Association
1730 M Street NW, Suite 700
Washington, DC 20036-4510
Voice: (800) 388-7478
        (202) 452-1600, extension 344
Fax: (202) 223-8756
World Wide Web: http://www.spa.org
Email: *piracy@spa.org*
CompuServe: *GO SPAForum*

To locate local law enforcement offices, your attorney general, the Postal Service, the Better Business Bureau, your congressional representative, and the local media, see your local telephone directory.

Quick Reference
if you get ripped off

The postmaster of my computer is _____

_____ .

I can contact the InterNIC Registration Services Center

by using the program _____

_____ .

I can look up the identity of another computer's post-

master by using the program _____

_____ .

I can look up Internet domains and administrative

contact information by using the program _____

_____ .

My local district attorney is _____

_____

and can be reached at the telephone number _____

_____ .

My state attorney general is _____

_____

and can be reached at the telephone number _____

_____ .

My local postal inspector is _____

_____

and can be reached at the telephone number _____

_____ .

The local telephone number for the Better Business

Bureau is _____ .

My closest congressional representative is _____

_____

and can be reached at the telephone number _____

_____ .

NOTES:

What will the future bring?

The Internet is constantly changing.

In the 1970s, few people would have guessed we'd have the worldwide computer network that is the Internet today. In fact, in 1985, the Internet didn't even formally exist. (Its predecessor was called the ARPAnet, and it was used mainly by government and academic organizations in the United States.) So what will the Internet be like in 10 or 20 years, or even in the near future? New technology, new laws, and the growing number of new users will all affect the Net in important ways.

In particular, the number of risks, and the kinds of risks, we encounter online will undoubtedly change. In the future, will we have more or less privacy on the Net than we do now? Will the number of scams increase or decrease? Will it get easier or harder to buy and sell safely over the Net? Will we get any better at seeing through people's false Net personalities? What will happen with junk email and spamming? How about sex-related material online? And how will perceptions of the Internet change in the public, in the media, in law, and in government? Will we see more restrictions or more freedom for users?

The biggest risk

The biggest risk that I face with the Internet is dilution of my proper use of time. Because I get so many email messages—often 100 to 150 a day—I spend all my time responding, and it's harder to stick to my priorities.

Tim O'Reilly

We've assembled a panel of expert users.

To help speculate on the future of Internet banditry, I've asked a group of experienced, well-known Internet users to share their thoughts with us. In alphabetical order, they are: Abby Franquemont-Guillory, Usenet news administrator for Tezcatlipoca, Inc., an Internet service provider in Chicago, and system programmer for *Encyclopedia Britannica*; Joel Furr, Internet journalist and moderator of *alt.folklore.suburban* and *comp.society.folklore* on Usenet; Dan King, maintainer of the Usenet Marketplace FAQ; Mike Meyer, an independent computer consultant in Silicon Valley; Tim O'Reilly, founder and president of O'Reilly & Associates, Inc.; and Brad Templeton, CEO of ClariNet Communications Corp., a respected electronic newspaper published on the Internet.

You'll see our panel members' wit and wisdom in the sidebars throughout this chapter. It's interesting to see how the panel members agree on some issues and disagree on others (including disagreeing with me). These differences of opinion can give us a broad appreciation for the various directions the Internet's growth might take in the years to come.

So, without further ado….

The public will become much more Net-aware.

Right now, there is a huge gap between people with online experience and people with none. This won't last. More and more people join the Internet every day. Eventually, Net awareness will be taught to school children at an early age. One generation from now, just about everybody will have online experience. The Internet (or whatever will come after it) will be so commonplace in people's lives that everybody will have at least basic online "street smarts." Users will be less likely to fall for scams that count on people's ignorance of the Net.

We'll also see glamorous phrases like "cyberspace" disappear from public vocabulary, once people realize that the Net isn't a mystical realm, but just a computer network. (An amazing and fun network, but a network all the same.)

What will the future bring?

There will be a constant war between more and less privacy.

Privacy is every user's friend, but every administrator's risk. If we don't have enough privacy on computers, the computers will be useless. If we have "too much" privacy, administrators (both computer and government related) can't watch for illegal activity that can harm our society.

As encryption schemes like PGP are becoming more widespread, we're able to encrypt our electronic conversations so they're completely private. (Well, as long as no packet sniffer is watching what we type.) The U.S. government has been battling to keep a lid on encryption methods (for example, not allowing them to be exported to other countries), and to retain the keys to whatever encryption methods people use (so they can decrypt our words in an "emergency"), and they will probably continue to do so. If these things alarm you, then follow the news in these areas, and maybe even get politically involved in the issue.

Ultimately, I think the answer is going to have to be better software that guarantees the identity of the sender of any message and uses encryption "invisibly" (so we won't even notice it's there) to guarantee the privacy of our communication.

Security violations will increase until better software is available.

Until more secure, sophisticated networking software is created, forgeries and spoofed messages will increase in number, as more and more users figure out how to do it. ("Security through obscurity" isn't going to last forever.) Also, expect to see more "turf wars" as more users learn how to cancel each other's electronic messages. In the meantime, before networking software gets more secure, we might see people migrating their discussions away from the more chaotic public discussion groups (like Usenet) into private electronic mailing lists.

The same solutions to Internet privacy also affect security. If we had unforgeable online identities for users and invisible encryption for communication, our words and actions online would be more secure.

Net etiquette

Sally Hambridge of Intel Corporation has drafted a set of guidelines for Net etiquette ("netiquette"). Known as "RFC 1855: Netiquette Guidelines," this document suggests minimum standards for online behavior that "organizations and individuals may take and adapt for their own use." Written in easy-to-understand language, RFC 1855 is full of helpful advice:

- For senders of email: "Remember that the recipient is a human being whose culture, language, and humor have different points of reference from your own."

- For advertisers: "Advertising is welcomed on some lists and Newsgroups, and abhorred on others! This is another example of knowing your audience before you post. Unsolicited advertising which is completely off-topic will most certainly guarantee that you get a lot of hate mail."

You can find a copy of RFC 1855 at the URL

http://www.cis.ohio-state.edu/htbin/rfc/rfc1855.html

What's the future of Internet privacy?

Brad Templeton:

Privacy is hard to predict. It will have trends in both directions. Computers have a greater ability to protect and invade our privacy than any other technology. It depends how we use them and how law allows us to use encryption and anonymity. Since the public is regularly willing to trade privacy for convenience (we'll tell somebody all about ourselves just to get a credit card or a cheap magazine subscription), that may continue—or computers may teach us what to keep private and what not.

Joel Furr:

I suspect that the U.S. government will eventually have to say "uncle" on the subject of computer privacy. It's simply too easy to come up with uncrackable encryption methods, and people are going to use them.

Mike Meyer:

The people putting up the money to create the software will largely decide how much privacy the users will have.

What's the future of Internet security?

Tim O'Reilly:

We are headed for a world with a lot more virtual transactions, where we will need some proof of identity online. That proof should be built into the software that we use on the Net. It makes a lot of sense to have a single, global mechanism for this. The biggest problem with PGP is just that it's not integrated into the software we use every day. Sure, some people will go through the trouble of obtaining a key and putting it in their email signatures, but this kind of ugliness should never be seen by users. It should be built right into the software. I think this is something that is very do-able, except for the political factors inhibiting the availability of encryption technology.

Joel Furr:

If you gave me two things: software that allows me to ignore jerks completely and software that makes absolutely sure that no one can eavesdrop on my communications, I'd be happy. Whenever I receive an annoying piece of email from some idiot, it would be marvelous if I could just add his name to a list of people that I never want to hear from again, and that would be it. Technically, this is possible now, but not for the average user.

Brad Templeton:

End-to-end digital signature and public key encryption can make the Net fully secure as far as we know. It's easy, we know how to do it; it's just a matter of arranging the laws, the licenses, and of course the protocols.

As security increases, though, risk will actually go up slightly because it will make us complacent.

Dan King:

We can use encryption methods, passwords, and robust filesystems, but unless computers become smarter than we are, no software can make it absolutely secure.

Abby Franquemont-Guillory:

I don't think software is as big a problem as social matters; in a way, that's too bad, because social matters are much, much harder to resolve.

Old scams will die out, but new ones will be harder to detect.

Right now, a large portion of the world's population is not on the Internet. So the "classic" scams and pranks—pyramid schemes, "credit repair" services, Craig Shergold get-well cards—have a constant supply of new, gullible users. Eventually, just about everybody will know about them, and they'll fade away, fondly remembered as part of Internet lore.

Also, as the general population becomes more familiar with the Internet, people will treat it with less mystery and awe. They won't be as quick to believe things just because "they were on the computer."

There will always be dishonest people, though, so new scams will undoubtedly arise. They'll be more subtle. Trickier. Scammers won't be able to play on people's unfamiliarity with the Internet any more, so they'll devise fresh schemes.

Buying and selling will get safer, at a price.

In the next 10 years, we'll see new standards of "digital cash" emerge, so that everybody can conveniently spend money on the Internet. There will be both credit services (similar to credit cards, where you borrow into the future) and debit services (similar to checks, where you already have the money). As a result, there will be less need for services like COD or escrow. Both Visa and MasterCard are working on some of these issues even as we speak.

I envision that people will be able to make some pretty fancy online purchasing arrangements. For example, suppose that I have a painting for sale; you want to buy it; and we live on opposite ends of the country. Before the sale, I'll show you the painting by transmitting a "live" video signal over the Internet, right to your computer screen, so you can see it, and we can see each other. I'll ship you the painting, and you'll send payment in digital cash directly to my bank. If I am a scammer, and I shipped you an empty box instead of a painting, you'll be able to contact the bank and put your digital cash "on hold" until you and I can settle the dispute. There will probably be all kinds of fancy arrangements we can do with digital cash,

Average users

The "average user" of a few years ago tended to be more interested in the hows and whys of computers and the Internet than is the average user of today. A lot of people who are brand-new to the Net are not going to find that it consumes a huge amount of their interest, once the novelty wears off. It's like using the telephone. While almost everyone has one, some people really like to use it to visit and socialize, some like to use it only as needed, some run up huge phone bills calling 900 numbers, and some use it exclusively for work.

Abby Franquemont-Guillory

What's the future of Internet scams and crime?

Mike Meyer:

Internet-related crimes will increase. The Internet is going to take off as the fax did, and everyone is going to be doing things on it. More users means more crime.

Abby Franquemont-Guillory:

I believe that crime that is strictly related to things on the Internet, like cracking passwords or running off with private information, will probably stay about the same. If you're talking about the use of Internet resources to commit real-world crimes that don't have any real bearing on computing, like fraud that happens to be committed by email, then those crimes will probably increase.

Brad Templeton:

It cannot help increasing because it is so low right now. In spite of the press, I am sure the crime rates online are minuscule compared to those among the general population.

Dan King:

New Internet users will always be available to fall prey to scams. It's our job to get them from "new" to "seasoned" as quickly as possible.

Someday, when it makes international news that someone broke into the Fed and bankrupted dozens of banks with a keystroke, everyone will become more aware, and then crime will drop.

Tim O'Reilly:

Today's Internet "alarmism" is more appropriate for the future, when we'll have more purely virtual interactions between people who have nothing in common in the physical world. I exchange email with all kinds of strangers, but typically they're strangers who move in the same circles that I do, and whom I might run into one day at a conference, for example, and who know and are known to other people in my circle. By contrast, these cases of kids being led astray on the Net... they're meeting people in a context that doesn't have any physical community associated with it.

Joel Furr:

There will continue to be crime on the Internet, but I think that the perception of crime will far outstrip the actual existence of crime online.

like give it an expiration date (so if we can't reach an agreement in a certain amount of time, it reverts to the buyer) or encrypt our cash with a password so it can't be used (or modified!) except by the owner.

All of the flexibility has a price. When our money is online, it will be more vulnerable to crackers. I shudder to think about the public outcry and backlash that will come the first time somebody breaks into the national digital cashbox.

Video will change the way we meet people.

When we meet people on the Net, current technology leaves a lot of room for error, since all we see are words on the screen. In the near future, don't expect this to change very much. But expect big changes as computer video teleconferencing becomes widespread, allowing people to view each other as they communicate. We'll be able to see each other's facial expressions and pick up on other subtleties that are currently not possible to observe in Net conversation.

After video becomes commonplace, people will still mislead each other on the Net (intentionally and unintentionally). But it will be harder, for example, for a man to pretend to be a woman. Or will it? Perhaps somebody will invent a way to project a different face and voice over the Net, completely disguising the speaker. It's science fiction now, but in 20 years, who knows?

In a way, all these changes will be sad, because Net culture has developed many endearing ways to assist communication using only written words. For instance, we use sideways "smiley faces" (the symbol :-)) to indicate humor, and write abbreviations like "IMHO" (In My Humble Opinion) and "ROTFL" (Roll On The Floor Laughing) to help express our views and actions. There's also a whole, rich culture in chat groups and MUDs. Once video arrives in full force, these practices might be lost, becoming a footnote in a history book somewhere.

Women are uncomfortable

The Internet has truly made the Earth a global village, where anyone can participate, discuss, laugh, chat, argue, fight, and do business with people around the globe. "Anyone," that is, who happens to be male. There are too many bozos who badger women online, trying to show what CyberStuds they are, and too many other guys whose apathy allows the situation to stay the way it is. If we want the world online to become a true community without frontiers, we must fight these attitudes.

Joel Furr

Junk email and spamming will increase, then die out.

Users can expect to have less privacy from advertisers, at least in the near future. As more and more companies get Internet access, expect to see the piles of junk mail grow larger in your electronic mailbox. Unless new laws are made, like the ones prohibiting junk faxing and certain types of phone solicitations, junk email will increase. In the long run, though, I think that companies will discover that junk email annoys more users than it attracts. (Although that hasn't stopped phone solicitors, has it...?)

We might also see federal regulation of junk email. Beginning in 1996, a new rule by the Federal Trade Commission will affect all telephone solicitors in the United States. The Telemarketing Sales Rule requires solicitors to identify themselves as salespeople, restricts their calling times, and makes it illegal for a solicitor to call somebody who has already asked not to be called. Maybe we'll see a similar law for email someday, making it illegal to send junk email to people who don't want it, or requiring companies to put the word "advertisement" in the Subject line of the message.

As mail-reading software gets more sophisticated, expect to see new features for filtering out junk email. It's like having an electronic secretary who screens your email before you see it. Some software has this feature now, but it's not very powerful yet.

Spamming is on the rise even now, though the cancelbots are extremely effective at deleting it from our sight. Eventually, news software will get sophisticated enough to prevent spamming from being done at all.

As of this writing, a new software solution, called *NoCeM* (pronounced, "No See 'Em"), has been proposed by *Cancelmoose* (see Chapter 7) and other concerned users as a Net-friendly antidote to spamming. NoCeM allows any user who sees a spam to send out a special "NoCeM message," which is basically an advisory that the user finds the message is objectionable. Other users and news administrators can configure their software to accept or reject NoCeM messages, based on the "Net reputation" of the sender. In other words, if you decide to trust Joe Smith's judgment about spamming, his

What's the future of junk email and spam?

Joel Furr:

Spamming is going to continue, but I see a developing public consciousness that spamming is bad. Once a person has actually spent time participating in Usenet rather than treating Usenet as a target, he or she is going to realize this. The problem is, most of our spammers these days don't actually use the discussion forums that they spam; if they did, they'd know how annoying it is to get ads for phone sex mixed in with discussions about child safety seats.

Dan King:

I believe we've already taken a stand. Junk email is not allowed. Spam is prohibited. Ninety percent of system administrators respond positively to angry Internet citizens who have been victimized by these forms of Internet crime. The other 10 percent don't remain system administrators for long.

Brad Templeton:

That's a tough one. There is a lot of resistance to a secure, verified Usenet and email network. People want a "fully open" Net. But with this comes junk email and spamming.

Mike Meyer:

I think it's going to die. Certain forms of solicitation by telephone, that are related to spamming, are already illegal in some areas.

Abby Franquemont-Guillory:

Eventually, as people develop strategies to deal with spam, more and more sites will block large crossposts and perhaps posts that look like they might be spam, just to be on the safe side. This will be a service that people will pay for and will take into account when selecting an Internet service provider.

I predict that eventually, the same kinds of laws will be passed about junk email that are in effect about postal mail, or those same laws will be extended to include the electronic world.

What's the future of Internet commercialism?

Abby Franquemont-Guillory:

The bulk of the people working in marketing in the U.S. these days don't know enough about the Internet. If you're dependent upon an audience, you've got to give them something worthwhile to keep them coming around, not just ads, ads, ads. Far more people watch actual shows on TV than watch the home shopping channel. If TV advertisers didn't understand this, eventually no one would watch TV. Internet advertising should be the same way.

There are numerous places for commerce on the Net, and I'd like to see them stay there. Just like cities have zoning laws so you can't open up a factory in a residential area of town, I'd like people to be unable to post commercial ads in a research or discussion-oriented newsgroup.

Dan King:

Advertising on the Internet will become big business, as common as TV, radio, fast food, and discount super-stores. To get there, it will suffer growing pains, the extent of which depends on you and me. The media of the past depended on a few rich magnates whose only goal was to promote their business. The Internet depends on the users, whose goal is to maximize useful information.

NoCeM messages will remove spam from your view. If you don't trust Joe, then your software will ignore his NoCeM messages, and you'll see the spam by choice.

NoCeM is already being used by a small community of Internet users. Time will tell whether NoCeM will be generally accepted and be added to future news software.

There will still be sex on the Net.

Whew. This issue will never be settled. As long as there's demand for sex on the Net, people will fill it. As long as people object to publicly available, sex-related material, there will be controversy.

Once people come to recognize that the Internet simply mirrors our society, I hope they'll realize that sex-related material and sex-related crimes should be treated the same way online as they already are offline. No additional laws are needed.

Political and legal issues will bear close watching.

I hesitate to guess what will happen with law on the Internet. In the short term, I think it's equally likely that we'll see brand new laws, or simply see new applications of existing laws. Since no existing government "owns" the Net, governments aren't quite sure what to make of it. Is the Net something that needs to be controlled? Or is it self-governing? Politicians have varying opinions, not to mention their own agendas, so it's anybody's guess whether we'll see more or fewer attempts at government regulation of the Internet.

How many politicians do you think have actually *used* the Internet for a significant amount of time? The average citizen probably has far more experience online than the average lawmaker. It's up to us to let the lawmakers know what the online world is all about and whether it needs "regulation" or not.

Other than privacy, the biggest Internet-related issue involving government and the law is probably free speech. In the media, you can hear people speaking passionately on both sides of the issue. On one side, there are people who believe that certain types of communications should not be permitted on the Internet. On the other side, people believe these communica-

What's the future of politics and the Internet?

Dan King:

We can't educate the government about the Internet. All we can do is wait for the Internet-proficient to move into government.

Brad Templeton:

By the time the government and lawmakers understand the Internet well enough to make reasonable judgments about it, it will have changed on them so that they don't understand it. The computer industry changes more in a long lunch hour than governments change in decades.

Tim O'Reilly:

I've spoken with people in the White House who say, "I can't give you details, but I will tell you that there are situations in which major terrorist activities have been stopped because we've intercepted electronic communications." So I'm not sure what you do with that.

I do believe that law-enforcement people have real issues to deal with. It's not just paranoia. So policies won't change because they suddenly "get religion" and realize that their concerns are inappropriate, but rather because the needs of electronic commerce will outweigh the disadvantages of criminals having secret communications. Jeff Schiller of MIT points out that horses were a real big advantage to criminals, and so are cars, but we don't outlaw them.

Joel Furr:

The only realistic way to educate politicians is to let them use the Net themselves long enough to feel like members of the Net community. So long as they think of themselves as outsiders trying to institute a little law and order, they're going to fail.

Abby Franquemont-Guillory:

I think that we are the ones to educate the politicians. If not us, then I don't see who it will be, and God forbid it should be someone with an agenda like turning the whole Net into a home shopping network. I'd like to see groups of Net experts run their own conferences, invite the government types, and offer seminars, using more traditional means of spreading information. If these activities don't sound like the home ground of the Internet type who maintains FAQs, answers questions, moderates newsgroups, and strives to assist, I don't know what does.

Mike Meyer:

As soon as the practicing lawyers and politicians are people who grew up with the Internet, they won't make any more of a hash of it than they do anything else.

What's the future of Internet legal issues?

Tim O'Reilly:

Most situations that I see seem to be covered by existing laws, like copyright, certainly. You have all these publishers crying, "Oh yes, if we don't get stronger copyright laws, we'll go out of business." And I say, "Wait a minute. Tell me about this $200 million a year Bible-publishing industry? You have lots of active players making lots of money peddling the same product, and it's all out of copyright! Tell me again why stronger copyright protection is so essential?"

Abby Franquemont-Guillory:

There will be more laws, if history is any example. I hope that there will not be censorship laws, decency acts, and the like, but rather laws regarding unsolicited mail, individuals' right to privacy and freedom of speech, and perhaps regulation of standards: fines for providers who don't care about their broken gateways spewing duplicate messages, or something along those lines.

Mike Meyer:

We need more intelligent application of existing laws, not new laws. The Internet doesn't let you do much that's new. It just makes some things easier.

The worst problem with any legal actions on the Internet is that of coordinating activities between police forces in a timely manner. Can police in seven countries on three continents cooperate together on what is essentially a phone trace? Will they?

Dan King:

Most laws, as we currently know them, are obsolete when applied to the Internet. I think written laws are needed, or at least their electronic counterparts, to lay down in stone the acceptable culture of the Net. I don't think this is feasible yet, because the Internet hasn't decided what its final culture will be, and it will likely be several years before it does so.

Brad Templeton:

Simple extensions of existing laws, plus technological security, are all we really need. Copyright law with a few minor tweaks à la the green paper should be fine to cover Net publishing. Defamation law is an interesting issue, though. The issue of anonymity will need to be addressed: how much anonymity will society want, and how much will it tolerate?

Joel Furr:

I don't think we can realistically design laws right now regarding the Internet. It's too much in flux and it won't settle down until everyone who's going to get online has gotten online.

tions are covered by the First Amendment of the Constitution. I believe that online censorship is not the answer. The Internet is simply a medium for communication. It's just very fast and cheap. We don't blame the phone company for obscene phone calls. Let's not blame the Internet for "objectionable" speech that flows over it.

The media will calm down.

Right now, the Internet is a super-hot topic in the media. They love to run stories about crackers and pornography, focusing on the actions of a tiny minority of users. A lot of these stories are written by people who have very little experience with the Internet. While the stories might increase in the next few years, expect them to die away after that, as the population becomes more Net-literate. Once a generation of reporters has grown up with the Net, they'll write more responsibly about it.

Then again, maybe there will be a newer, sexier replacement for the Internet that will get them all a-buzzing again.

You can get involved in the future of the Internet.

If you don't like the Internet-related laws that are being proposed and debated in the legislature, you can do something about it. Write to your congressional representatives and share your opinion. Contact the media if the issues aren't getting enough press.

An easy way to stay in touch with the Internet's future direction is to follow the Usenet newsgroups devoted to the topic. (See "For more information..." for a list of relevant newsgroups.) Participating in these newsgroups can have a tangible effect on the outside world. Look at what happened in the Martin Rimm case (see Chapter 9). By the time Rimm's study about online pornography was published, discussion on Usenet and other online services had already reached the media and influenced several articles that appeared in prominent newspapers. As a result of the criticism, *TIME* magazine printed a partial retraction of its coverage of the study, and Carnegie-Mellon University launched an investigation into the ethics surrounding the study.

Fear of the future

My grandfather, a ham radio operator, has convinced me that there's little difference between the Net-related stuff I do now, and the ham radio stuff he did when he was my age. "I never thought they'd regulate radio as they ended up doing," he told me once, "so enjoy what you've got now while you've got it. It won't last forever."

I fear that if we don't get together and really work on smoothing the transition of the Internet into mainstream life, then this transition will be done by people whom we don't respect, or don't approve of; and we'll be left with something radically different, and not necessarily better.

Abby Franquemont-Guillory

The Internet is built on the ideals of freedom of information exchange, entrepreneurship, and prosperity for anyone willing to work. Without regulation, though, I'm afraid that the Net may decompose into a worthless pile of irrelevant, annoying, useless information (an age that the spammers are ushering in). Maybe it's time for the Net to mature up and take responsibility for its integrity. Otherwise, leeching opportunists will abuse the Net and severely reduce its value as a tool of communication and a resource of value-rich information.

David Rahardja

The long-term solution to spamming is to create a mechanism where posts are authenticated to responsible individuals. This will probably require a new Usenet.

Peter da Silva

Get involved if you can. If you don't, then one day you might log in to find that the online protections you used to have are gone.

Thank you.

I hope that this book has served its purpose: to make you aware of the risks you might encounter online, and to help you identify and avoid them. If all went well, you now feel a little more cautious, and a little more confident, in your use of the Internet. Remember not to be paranoid: just be prepared. A few preventive measures and a critical eye can go a long way toward protecting you in the online world.

It's been my pleasure to guide you on this tour of the Internet's "dark side." I wish you a very enjoyable, productive, and safe time on the Net.

For more information…

On Usenet, *comp.society.futures* is for discussion of the future of computing as it relates to our society. It's not specifically related to Internet risks, but you'll find relevant, general information there. *comp.risks* is a fascinating newsgroup devoted to risks associated with computing, occasionally provides chilling insight into the future. *misc.news.internet.announce* is a moderated newsgroup for media coverage of the latest happenings on the Internet; followup discussions are held in *misc.news.internet.discuss*. *alt.internet.media-coverage* is also devoted to Internet-related issues that have appeared in the media. Finally, *news.admin.net-abuse* focuses on Internet abuse.

NoCeM, the proposed anti-spamming system, has its own newsgroup, *alt.nocem.misc*, for discussion and the posting of NoCeM messages. The NoCeM FAQ is posted there regularly and can also be found on *Cancelmoose*'s Web page,

```
http://www.cm.org
```

For more updated information about *Bandits on the Information Superhighway*, see the URL

```
http://www.ora.com
```

Understanding Internet addresses

If you are not familiar with Internet addresses, read this guide.

In this appendix, you'll find an overview of usernames, computer names, email addresses, and domains. You'll see just enough information to understand how these concepts are used in this book.

Do you need to read this appendix? Here is a quick quiz. Consider this funny-looking bunch of words and punctuation:

skink@swamp.ecs.uio.edu

Do you recognize what it is? If you said "an Internet email address," you are right. Can you identify the username, the computer name, the domains, and the sub-domains? Can you tell what kind of organization runs this computer: a company, a university, or a government agency? If you can do all of this, you can stop here: you already know enough about Internet addresses to read this book. Otherwise, continue. In any case, this chapter is very short, so it won't hurt you to read it. (The answers to the quiz are at the end of the chapter.)

Your username uniquely identifies you on a computer.

Before we talk about the Internet, let's start at the computer where you have your account. Every user on the computer has a *username* that identifies him or her uniquely on that computer. Your system administrator might assign a username to you, or you might be allowed to pick one yourself. Some examples of usernames are *jim, James_Smith, phantom, econ31,* and *91872.4412.*

Your username is unique on your computer, but it is probably not unique on the whole Internet. (Unless you choose a *very* weird one.) For example, different users on several Internet computers could all have the same username, *phantom.* This is no problem at all, as we'll see.

A user can have multiple usernames, called *nicknames* or *aliases,* that refer to him or her on the computer. For instance, a user named Jenny Smith, who logs in with the username *smith,* might also have a bunch of aliases, like *jenny, spike,* and *postmaster.*

Aliases are used for other purposes than logging in. For example, the *postmaster* name on an Internet computer is almost always an alias. This is helpful if somebody else becomes the postmaster, since the old postmaster doesn't have to change his or her username. Instead, the *postmaster* alias can simply be reassigned to forward email to the new postmaster's account.

Every Internet computer has a unique name.

Internet computers, like users, all have names. Each computer's name must be unique on the entire Internet.

Unfortunately, people do not agree on what to call "computer names." Some people call them *hostnames.* Others insist on the longer term *fully qualified hostnames* or *fully qualified domain names.* Users involved in networking sometimes use the word *domain* to mean a computer name. In this book, we'll just say "computer name" even though there might be a more technically accurate word.

A computer name on the Internet looks like words separated by dots.

Some sample Internet computer names are:

> *watson.ibm.com*
> *my-pc.cs.umass.edu*
> *informatik.uni-hamburg.de*

Notice how they all look like words separated by dots (periods). When you read a computer name out loud, you should speak the word "dot." So, for example, the computer name *watson.ibm.com* is pronounced "watson dot IBM dot comm."

Username + "@" + computer name = Internet email address

Your *email address* identifies you uniquely on the whole Internet. It begins with your username, is followed by an "at" sign (@), and ends with the computer name. So if your username is *jones* and your account is on the computer *my.machine.org*, your Internet email address is *jones@my.machine.org*. When speaking an email address out loud, you pronounce the "at" sign, like this: "jones at my dot machine dot org."

Now it should be clear why it's OK for two users on different computers to have the same username. If the computers *gatekeeper.dec.com* and *amiga.physik.unizh.ch* both have a user named *phantom*, there is no confusion, because the users have different email addresses: *phantom@gatekeeper.dec.com* and *phantom@amiga.physik.unizh.ch*.

At this point, you've seen what usernames, computer names, and email addresses look like. That's enough information to let you read this book comfortably. If you are interested in learning *why* things look this way, the rest of this appendix discusses the details.

The Internet is separated into domains.

Computer names aren't just random words and dots: they have meanings. To understand them, we have to discuss Internet domains.

With hundreds of thousands of computers on the Internet, it's important to keep things organized. To do this, the Internet is separated into *domains,* which are "areas" of the Net devoted to certain purposes or organizations. (These "areas" aren't physical places; they are just a helpful way to group things.) For example, there is a domain for colleges and universities, called *edu*; a domain for commercial businesses, called *com*; a domain for government organizations, called *gov*; and so on. These very general domains are called *top-level domains,* and they are listed in the table below.

Internet top-level domains

Domain	Meaning
gov	Government organization (nonmilitary)
mil	Military organization
net	Networking organization
nato	NATO organization
org	Nonprofit or not-for-profit organization

The top-level domains focus on the United States. Computers in other countries are usually found in other domains, organized by country. The names of these domains are called *country codes,* and a few are illustrated in the table below. Note that country codes are formed from the language of the country. For example, Germany is *de* because its name in German is *Deutschland.*

Country codes

Domain	Meaning
ca	Canada
ch	Switzerland
de	Germany
jp	Japan
se	Sweden
uk	United Kingdom

A complete set of country codes can be found on the World Wide Web at

```
http://www.ics.uci.edu/WebSoft/wwwstat/country-codes.txt
```

Domains are separated into sub-domains, and so on.

It would not be convenient to lump all corporate computers, for example, into a single domain. There are just too many computers to keep track of. So domains consist of *sub-domains,* and sub-domains consist of smaller sub-domains, and so on. For example, the top-level *edu* (educational) domain consists of sub-domains for each college or university (like *stanford, harvard,* and *princeton*), and each of those consists of sub-domains for departments (like *cs* for computer science and *psych* for psychology).

Each word of a computer name is a sub-domain. For example, in the computer name *watson.ibm.com,* the sub-domains are *watson, ibm,* and *com.* Each sub-domain name also defines a new domain. For example, *watson.ibm.com* is a domain (containing a single computer), and it's inside the *ibm.com* domain, which is itself inside the *com* domain.

Computer names are best understood from right to left.

Now that you've seen what sub-domains are, computer names should look less cryptic. In particular, a name gets more specific as you read its sub-domains from right to left. For example, the sub-domains of the computer name *watson.ibm.com* mean:

com	On the Internet, there are commercial businesses.
ibm	Inside the *com* domain, there's a computer company called IBM.
watson	Inside the *ibm.com* domain, there's a computer called "watson."

The sub-domains of *my-pc.cs.umass.edu* mean:

edu   On the Internet, there are educational institutions.

umass   Inside the *edu* domain, there's the University of Massachusetts.

cs   Inside the *umass.edu* domain, there's a Computer Science department.

my-pc   Inside the *cs.umass.edu* domain, there's a computer called "my-pc."

The figure below shows a picture of how these domains are "nested" inside one another.

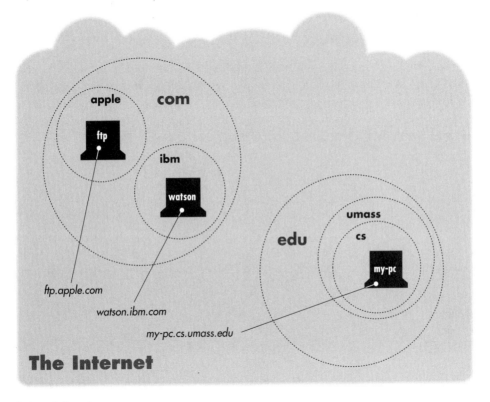

Internet domains

Computer names may have different numbers of sub-domains.

You'll notice that some of our example computer names have three sub-domains separated by dots, and some have four. In fact, computer names can consist of two sub-domains, or five, or even more. The reason is beyond the scope of this book, but it's perfectly normal, and the rule is still the same: the computer name gets more and more specific as you read from right to left.

Here are the answers to our quiz.

The first section of this appendix asked if you could identify the parts of the email address *skink@swamp.ecs.uio.edu*. Let's see if you got them right. The username is *skink*, and the computer name is *swamp.ecs.uio.edu*. There are four sub-domains in this name: *swamp*, *ecs*, *uio*, and *edu*. There are also four domain names: *edu*, *uio.edu*, *ecs.uio.edu*, and *swamp.ecs.uio.edu*. Since the top-level domain is *edu*, this machine is run by an educational institution.

How did you do?

For more information…

In this book, we've kept all the computer names and email addresses as simple as possible, and this appendix covers only what you need to know. In practice, however, email addresses can get pretty complicated and weird-looking. If you'd like to learn more, a comprehensive reference is *!%@:: A Directory of Electronic Mail Addressing & Networks* by Donnalyn Frey and Rick Adams (O'Reilly & Associates, 1994).

Index

About the Author

Dan Barrett likes to wear many hats, most of them electronic (with little beanie propellers). An active participant on the Internet and ARPAnet since 1985, Dan has worked as a UNIX system administrator, university instructor, software engineer, industry consultant, and Usenet newsgroup moderator. Currently, he's working on a Ph.D. in computer science at the University of Massachusetts.

In addition to *Bandits on the Information Superhighway*, Dan is the author of over 20 articles in *Compute!*, *Keyboard Magazine*, *AmigaWorld*, and other magazines. On Usenet, his BLAZEMONGER humor series ("the fastest computer game ever created") has vast legions of fans, both of whom were honored to be mentioned in this "About the Author" section.

When he's not flipping bits, Dan likes to compose and record progressive rock music, play competitive volleyball, read science fiction, and cook. He and his wife, Lisa, reside in State College, Pennsylvania.

You can write to Dan on the Internet at *dbarrett@ora.com*.

Colophon

Our look is the result of reader comments, our own experimentation, and feedback from distribution channels. Distinctive covers complement our distinctive approach to technical topics, breathing personality and life into potentially dry subjects.

In the What You Need to Know series, we look at technology in a personal way: how real people get something done and how they think about issues. The covers of the series reflect this personal, immediate approach to the subject. Inside the books, illustrations of the speakers in the sidebars give faces to those who have shared their experiences.

Edie Freedman designed the cover of this book, using an illustration by David White, in the style of 19th-century engravings. The cover layout was produced with Quark XPress 3.3 using the ITC Garamond and Futura fonts.

The inside layout was designed by Nancy Priest and implemented in FrameMaker 5.0 by Mike Sierra. The text and heading fonts are in the ITC Garamond and Garamond Condensed families. The sidebar text and headings are set in the Gill Sans font. The portraits were illustrated by Leslie Evans.

INTERNET

Books from O'Reilly & Associates, Inc.

FALL/WINTER 1995-96

The Whole Internet User's Guide & Catalog

By Ed Krol
2nd Edition April 1994
574 pages, ISBN 1-56592-063-5

Still the best book on the Internet! This is the second edition of our comprehensive—and bestselling—introduction to the Internet, the international network that includes virtually every major computer site in the world. In addition to email, file transfer, remote login, and network news, this book pays special attention to some new tools for helping you find information. Useful to beginners and veterans alike, this book will help you explore what's possible on the Net. Also includes a pull-out quick-reference card. For UNIX, PCs and the Macintosh.

"An ongoing classic."
—*Rochester Business Journal*

"The book against which all subsequent Internet guides are measured, Krol's work has emerged as an indispensable reference to beginners and seasoned travelers alike as they venture out on the data highway."
—*Microtimes*

"*The Whole Internet User's Guide & Catalog* will probably become the Internet user's bible because it provides comprehensive, easy instructions for those who want to get the most from this valuable electronic tool."
—David J. Buerger, Editor, *Communications Week*

The Whole Internet for Windows 95

By Ed Krol & Paula Ferguson
1st Edition October 1995
650 pages, ISBN 1-56592-155-0

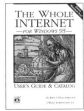

The best book on the Internet...now updated for Windows 95! *The Whole Internet for Windows 95* is the most comprehensive introduction to the Internet available today. For Windows users who in the past have struggled to take full advantage of the Internet's powerful utilities, Windows 95's built-in Internet support is a cause for celebration. And when you get online with Windows 95, this new edition of *The Whole Internet* will guide you every step of the way.

This book shows you how to use Microsoft Internet Explorer (the World Wide Web multimedia browser) and Microsoft Exchange (an email program). It also covers Netscape Navigator, the most popular Web browser on the market, and shows you how to use Usenet readers, file transfer tools, and database searching software.

But it does much more. You'll also want to take advantage of alternative popular free software programs that are downloadable from the Net. This book shows you where to find them and how to use them to save you time and money.

Bandits on the Information Superhighway

By Daniel J. Barrett
1st Edition February 1996
245 pages (est.), ISBN 1-56592-156-9

Most people on the Internet behave honestly, but there are always some troublemakers. What risks might you encounter online? And what practical steps can you take to keep yourself safe and happy?

With first-person anecdotes, technical tips, and the advice of experts from diverse fields, *Bandits on the Information Superhighway* helps you identify and avoid risks online, so you can have a more productive and enjoyable time on the Internet.

This book discusses how much privacy you have on the Net and how you can get more; how to spot common Internet scams and where to look for help if you get ripped off; and the "Ten Commandments"of buying and selling personal items on the Net when you don't know the people involved. You'll learn what every parent should know about the Internet—including the simple truth behind popular "scare stories"about pornography and pedophiles—as well as the risks of meeting, trusting, or falling in love with people that you've never met.

MH & xmh: Email for Users & Programmers

By Jerry Peek
3rd Edition April 1995
782 pages, ISBN 1-56592-093-7

There are lots of mail programs in use these days, but MH is one of the most durable and flexible. Best of all, it's available on almost all UNIX systems. It has spawned a number of interfaces that many users prefer. This book covers three popular interfaces: *xmh* (for the X environment), *exmh* (written with tcl/tk), and *mh-e* (for GNU Emacs users).

The book contains: a quick tour through MH, *xmh*, *exmh*, and *mh-e* for new users; configuration and customization information; lots of tips and techniques for programmers—and plenty of practical examples for everyone; information beyond the manual pages, explaining how to make MH do things you never thought an email program could do; and quick-reference pages in the back of the book.

In addition, the third edition describes the Multipurpose Internet Mail Extensions (MIME) and describes how to use it with these mail programs. MIME is an extension that allows users to send graphics, sound, and other multimedia formats through mail between otherwise incompatible systems.

Using Email Effectively

By Linda Lamb & Jerry Peek
1st Edition April 1995
160 pages, ISBN 1-56592-103-8

When you're new to email, you're usually shown what keystrokes to use to read and send a message. After using email for a few years, you learn from your own mistakes and from reading other people's mail. You learn:

- How to organize saved mail so that you can find it again

- When to include a previous message, and how much to include, so that your reader can quickly make sense of what's being discussed

- When a network address "looks right," so that more of your messages get through the first time

- When a "bounced" message will never be delivered and when the bounce merely indicates temporary network difficulties

- How to successfully subscribe and unsubscribe to a mailing list

With first-person anecdotes, examples, and general observations, *Using Email Effectively* shortens the learning-from-experience curve for all mailers, so you can quickly be productive and send email that looks intelligent to others.

The USENET Handbook

By Mark Harrison
1st Edition May 1995
388 pages, ISBN 1-56592-101-1

USENET, also called Netnews, is the world's largest discussion forum, encompassing the worldwide Internet and many other sites that aren't formally connected to any network. USENET provides a forum for asking and answering technical questions, arguing politics, religion, and society, or discussing most scientific, artistic, or humanistic disciplines. It's also a forum for distributing free software, as well as digitized pictures and sound.

This book unlocks USENET for you. It includes tutorials on the most popular newsreaders for UNIX and Windows (*tin, nn,* GNUS, and Trumpet). It's also a guide to the culture of the Net, giving you an introduction to etiquette, the private language, and some of the history.

WebSite™ 1.1

By O'Reilly & Associates, Inc.
Documentation by Susan Peck
2nd Edition January 1996
ISBN 1-56592-173-9, UPC 9-781565-921733
Includes four diskettes, 494-page book, and WebSite T-shirt

WebSite 1.1 now makes it easier than ever to start publishing on the Internet. WebSite is a 32-bit multi-threaded World Wide Web server that combines the power and flexibility of a UNIX server with the ease of use of a Windows application. Its intuitive graphical interface and easy install make it a natural for both Windows NT and Windows 95 users.

WebSite provides a tree-like display of all the documents and links on your server, with a simple solution for finding and fixing broken links. Using CGI, you can run a desktop application like Excel or Visual Basic from within a Web document on WebSite. Its access authentication lets you control which users have access to different parts of your Web server. WebSite is a product of O'Reilly & Associates, Inc. It is created in cooperation with Bob Denny and Enterprise Integration Technologies, Inc. (EIT).

New features of WebSite 1.1 include: HTML editor, multiple indexes, WebFind wizard, CGI with Visual Basic 4 framework and server push support, graphical interface for creating virtual servers, Windows 95 style install, logging reports for individual documents, HTML-2 and -3 support, external image map support, self-registration of users, and EMosaic 2.1 Web browser.

Marketing on the Internet

By Linda Lamb, Tim O'Reilly, Dale Dougherty & Brian Erwin
1st Edition May 1996 (est.)
170 pages (est.), ISBN 1-56592-105-4

Marketing on the Internet tells you what you need to know to successfully use this new communication and sales channel to put product and sales information online, build relationships with customers, send targeted announcements, and answer product support questions. In short, how to use the Internet as part of your overall marketing mix. Written from a marketing, not technical, perspective.

Internet In A Box,™ Version 2.0

Published by SPRY, Inc. (Product good only in U.S. and Canada)
2nd Edition June 1995
UPC 799364 012001
*Two diskettes & a 528-page version of **The Whole Internet Users Guide & Catalog** as documentation*

Now there are more ways to connect to the Internet—and you get to choose the most economical plan based on your dialing habits.

What will **Internet In A Box** do for me?

Internet In A Box is for PC users who want to connect to the Internet. Quite simply, it solves Internet access problems for individuals and small businesses without dedicated lines and/or UNIX machines. Internet In A Box provides instant connectivity, a multimedia Windows interface, and a full suite of applications. This product is so easy to use, you need to know only two things to get started: how to load software onto your PC and how to use a mouse.

New features of version 2.0 include:

- More connectivity options with the CompuServe Network.
- With Spry Mosaic and Progressive Image Rendering, browsing the Internet has never been easier.
- SPRY Mail provides MIME support and a built-in spell checker. Mail and News are now available within the Mosaic Toolbar.
- You'll enjoy safe and secure shopping online with Secure HTTP.
- SPRY News offers offline support for viewing and sending individual articles.
- A Network File Manager means there's an improved interface for dealing with various Internet hosts.

Designing for the Web: Basics for a New Medium

By Jennifer Niederst with Edie Freedman
1st Edition TBA
150 pages (est.), ISBN: 1-56592-165-8

This book is for designers who need to hone their skills for the Web. It explains how to work with HTML documents from a designer's point of view, outlines special problems with presenting information online, and walks through incorporating images into Web pages, with emphasis on resolution and improving efficiency. Also discusses the different browsers available and how to make sure a document is most effective for a broad spectrum of browsers and platforms.

Internet Security

PGP: Pretty Good Privacy

By Simson Garfinkel
1st Edition December 1994
430 pages, ISBN 1-56592-098-8

PGP is a freely available encryption program that protects the privacy of files and electronic mail. It uses powerful public key cryptography and works on virtually every platform. This book is both a readable technical user's guide and a fascinating behind-the-scenes look at cryptography and privacy. It describes how to use PGP and provides background on cryptography, PGP's history, battles over public key cryptography patents and U.S. government export restrictions, and public debates about privacy and free speech.

"I even learned a few things about PGP from Simson's informative book."—Phil Zimmermann, Author of PGP

"Since the release of PGP 2.0 from Europe in the fall of 1992, PGP's popularity and usage has grown to make it the de-facto standard for email encyrption. Simson's book is an excellent overview of PGP and the history of cryptography in general. It should prove a useful addition to the resource library for any computer user, from the UNIX wizard to the PC novice."
—Derek Atkins, PGP Development Team, MIT

Building Internet Firewalls

By D. Brent Chapman & Elizabeth D. Zwicky
1st Edition September 1995
544 pages, ISBN 1-56592-124-0

Everyone is jumping on the Internet bandwagon, despite the fact that the security risks associated with connecting to the Net have never been greater. This book is a practical guide to building firewalls on the Internet. It describes a variety of firewall approaches and architectures and discusses how you can build packet filtering and proxying solutions at your site. It also contains a full discussion of how to configure Internet services (e.g., FTP, SMTP, Telnet) to work with a firewall, as well as a complete list of resources, including the location of many publicly available firewall construction tools.

Practical UNIX and Internet Security

By Simson Garfinkel & Gene Spafford
2nd Edition April 1996 (est.)
800 pages (est.), ISBN 1-56592-148-8

A complete revision of the first edition, this new guide spells out the threats, system vulnerabilities, and counter-measures you can adopt to protect your UNIX system, network, and Internet connection. It's complete—covering both host and network security—and doesn't require that you be a programmer or a UNIX guru to use it. This edition contains hundreds of pages of new information on Internet security, including new security tools and approaches. Covers many platforms, both System V and Berkeley-based (i.e. Sun, DEC, HP, IBM, SCO, NeXT, Linux, and other UNIX systems).

Computer Crime

By David Icove, Karl Seger & William VonStorch
1st Edition August 1995
464 pages, ISBN 1-56592-086-4

Computer crime is a growing threat. Attacks on computers, networks, and data range from terrorist threats to financial crimes to pranks. *Computer Crime: A Crimefighters Handbook* is aimed at those who need to understand, investigate, and prosecute computer crimes of all kinds.

This book discusses computer crimes, criminals, and laws, and profiles the computer criminal (using techniques developed for the FBI and other law enforcement agencies). It outlines the the risks to computer systems and personnel, operational, physical, and communications measures that can be taken to prevent computer crimes. It also discusses how to plan for, investigate, and prosecute computer crimes, ranging from the supplies needed for criminal investigation, to the detection and audit tools used in investigation, to the presentation of evidence to a jury.

Contains a compendium of computer-related federal statutes, all statutes of individual states, a resource summary, and detailed papers on computer crime.

Providing Web Content

CGI Programming on the World Wide Web

By Shishir Gundavaram
1st Edition March 1996 (est.)
375 pages (est.), ISBN 1-56592-168-2

 As you traverse the vast frontier of the World Wide Web, you will come across certain documents that make you wonder, "How in the world did they create this?" These documents might consist of forms that ask for feedback or registration information, imagemaps that allow you to click on various parts of the image, counters that display the number of users that accessed the document, and search/index utilities. All of this magic can be achieved on the Web by using the Common Gateway Interface, commonly known as CGI.

This book offers a comprehensive explanation of CGI and related techniques for people who hold on to the dream of providing their own information servers on the Web. For most of the examples, the book uses the most common platform (UNIX) and the most popular language (Perl) used for CGI programming today. However, it also introduces the essentials of making CGI work with other platforms and languages.

Learning Perl

By Randal L. Schwartz, Foreword by Larry Wall
1st Edition November 1993
274 pages, ISBN 1-56592-042-2

 *Learning Perl* is a step-by-step, hands-on tutorial designed to get you writing useful Perl scripts as quickly as possible. In addition to countless code examples, there are numerous programming exercises, with full answers. For a comprehensive and detailed guide to advanced programming with Perl, read the companion book, *Programming perl*.

Programming perl

By Larry Wall & Randal L. Schwartz
1st Edition January 1991
482 pages, ISBN 0-937175-64-1

 An authoritative guide to the hottest new UNIX utility in years, coauthored by its creator, Larry Wall. Perl is a language for easily manipulating text, files, and processes. *Programming perl* Covers perl syntax, functions, debugging, efficiency, the Perl library, and more.

Using HTML: The Definitive Guide

By Chuck Musciano & Bill Kennedy
1st Edition April 1996 (est.)
350 pages (est.), ISBN 1-56592-175-5

 *Using HTML* helps you become fluent in HTML, fully versed in the language's syntax, semantics, and elements of style. The book covers the most up-to-date version of the HTML standard, plus all the common extensions and, in particular, Netscape extensions. The authors cover each and every element of the currently accepted version of the language in detail, explaining how each element works and how it interacts with all the other elements. They've also included a style guide that helps you decide how to best use HTML to accomplish a variety of tasks, from simple online documentation to complex marketing and sales presentations.

Java in a Nutshell: A Desktop Quick Reference for Java Programmers

By David Flanagan
1st Edition February 1996 (est.)
250 pages (est.), ISBN 1-56592-183-6

 *Java in a Nutshell* is a complete quick reference guide to the Java API, the hot new programming language from Sun Microsystems. This comprehensive volume contains descriptions of all of the Java classes and their related calls and an introduction to important Java concepts.

Exploring Expect

By Don Libes
1st Edition December 1994
602 pages, ISBN 1-56592-090-2

 Written by the author of Expect, this is the first book to explain how this new part of the UNIX toolbox can be used to automate Telnet, FTP, passwd, rlogin, and hundreds of other interactive applications. Based on Tcl (Tool Command Language), Expect lets you automate interactive applications that have previously been extremely difficult to handle with any scripting language.

Internet Administration

Getting Connected: The Internet at 56K and Up

By Kevin Dowd
1st Edition February 1996 (est.)
450 pages (est.), ISBN 1-56592-154-2

A complete guide for businesses, schools, and other organizations who want to connect their computers to the Internet. This book covers everything you need to know to make informed decisions, from helping you figure out which services you really need to providing down-to-earth explanations of telecommunication options, such as frame relay, ISDN, and leased lines. Once you're online, it shows you how to set up basic Internet services, such as a World Wide Web server. Tackles issues for the PC, Macintosh, and UNIX platforms.

DNS and BIND

By Paul Albitz & Cricket Liu
1st Edition October 1992
418 pages, ISBN 1-56592-010-4

DNS and BIND contains all you need to know about the Internet's Domain Name System (DNS) and the Berkeley Internet Name Domain (BIND), its UNIX implementation. The Domain Name System is the Internet's "phone book"; it's a database that tracks important information (in particular, names and addresses) for every computer on the Internet. If you're a system administrator, this book will show you how to set up and maintain the DNS software on your network.

sendmail

By Bryan Costales, with Eric Allman & Neil Rickert
1st Edition November 1993
830 pages, ISBN 1-56592-056-2

This Nutshell Handbook® is far and away the most comprehensive book ever written on sendmail, the program that acts like a traffic cop in routing and delivering mail on UNIX-based networks. Although sendmail is used on almost every UNIX system, it's one of the last great uncharted territories—and most difficult utilities to learn—in UNIX system administration. This book provides a complete sendmail tutorial, plus extensive reference material on every aspect of the program. It covers IDA sendmail, the latest version (V8) from Berkeley, and the standard versions available on most systems.

Managing Internet Information Services

By Cricket Liu, Jerry Peek, Russ Jones, Bryan Buus & Adrian Nye
1st Edition December 1994
668 pages, ISBN 1-56592-062-7

This comprehensive guide describes how to set up information services and make them available over the Internet. It discusses why a company would want to offer Internet services, provides complete coverage of all popular services, and tells how to select which ones to provide. Most of the book describes how to set up Gopher, World Wide Web, FTP, and WAIS servers and email services.

Networking Personal Computers with TCP/IP

By Craig Hunt
1st Edition July 1995
408 pages, ISBN 1-56592-123-2

This book offers practical information as well as detailed instructions for attaching PCs to a TCP/IP network and its UNIX servers. It discusses the challenges you'll face and offers general advice on how to deal with them, provides basic TCP/IP configuration information for some of the popular PC operating systems, covers advanced configuration topics and configuration of specific applications such as email, and includes a chapter on NetWare, the most popular PC LAN system software.

TCP/IP Network Administration

By Craig Hunt
1st Edition August 1992
502 pages, ISBN 0-937175-82-X

A complete guide to setting up and running a TCP/IP network for practicing system administrators. *TCP/IP Network Administration* covers setting up your network, configuring important network applications including sendmail, and issues in troubleshooting and security. It covers both BSD and System V TCP/IP implementations.

At Your Fingertips—

A COMPLETE GUIDE TO
O'REILLY'S ONLINE SERVICES

O'Reilly & Associates offers extensive product and customer service information online. We invite you to come and explore our little neck-of-the-woods.

For product information and insight into new technologies, visit the O'Reilly Online Center

Most comprehensive among our online offerings is the O'Reilly Online Center. You'll find detailed information on all O'Reilly products, including titles, prices, tables of contents, indexes, author bios, software contents, and reviews. You can also view images of all our products. In addition, watch for informative articles that provide perspective on the technologies we write about. Interviews, excerpts, and bibliographies are also included.

After browsing online, it's easy to order, too by sending email to **order@ora.com**. The O'Reilly Online Center shows you how. Here's how to visit us online:

👉 *Via the World Wide Web*

If you are connected to the Internet, point your Web browser (e.g., **mosaic, netscape,** or **lynx**) to:

http://www.ora.com/

For the plaintext version, **telnet** to:
www.ora.com (login: **oraweb**)

👉 *Via Gopher*

If you have a Gopher program, connect your **gopher** to:
gopher.ora.com
Or, point your Web browser to:
gopher://gopher.ora.com/

Or, you can **telnet** to: **gopher.ora.com**
(login: **gopher**)

A convenient way to stay informed: email mailing lists

An easy way to learn of the latest projects and products from O'Reilly & Associates is to subscribe to our mailing lists. We have email announcements and discussions on various topics. Subscribers receive email as soon as the information breaks.

👉 *To join a mailing list:*

Send email to:
listproc@online.ora.com

Leave the message "subject" empty if possible.

If you know the name of the mailing list you want to subscribe to, put the following information on the first line of your message: **subscribe** "listname" "your name" **of** "your company."

For example: **subscribe ora-news**
Kris Webber of Fine Enterprises

If you don't know the name of the mailing list, listproc will send you a listing of all the mailing lists. Put this word on the first line of the body: **lists**

To find out more about a particular list, send a message with this word as the first line of the body: **info** "listname"

For more information and help, send this message: **help**

For specific help, email to: **listmaster@online.ora.com**

The complete O'Reilly catalog is now available via email

You can now receive a text-only version of our complete catalog via email. It contains detailed information about all our products, so it's mighty big: over 200 kbytes, or 200,000 characters.

To get the whole catalog in one message, send an empty email message to: **catalog@online.ora.com**

If your email system can't handle large messages, you can get the catalog split into smaller messages. Send email to: **catalog-split@online.ora.com**

To receive a print catalog, send your snail mail address to: **catalog@ora.com**

Check out Web Review, our new publication on the Web

Web Review is our new magazine that offers fresh insights into the Web. The editorial mission of Web Review is to answer the question: How and where do you BEST spend your time online? Each issue contains reviews that look at the most interesting and creative sites on the Web. Visit us at **http://gnn.com/wr/**

Web Review is a product of the recently formed Songline Studios, a venture between O'Reilly and America Online.

Get the files you want with FTP

We have an archive of example files from our books, the covers of our books, and much more available by anonymous FTP.

ftp to:

ftp.ora.com (login: **anonymous** – use your email address as the password.)

Or, if you have a WWW browser, point it to:

ftp://ftp.ora.com/

FTPMAIL

The ftpmail service connects to O'Reilly's FTP server and sends the results (the files you want) by email. This service is for people who can't use FTP—but who can use email.

For help and examples, send an email message to:

ftpmail@online.ora.com

(In the message body, put the single word: **help**)

Helpful information is just an email message away

Many customer services are provided via email. Here are a few of the most popular and useful:

info@ora.com
For general questions and information.

bookquestions@ora.com
For technical questions, or corrections, concerning book contents.

order@ora.com
To order books online and for ordering questions.

catalog@online.ora.com
To receive an online copy of our catalog.

catalog@ora.com
To receive a free copy of *ora.com*, our combination magazine and catalog. Please include your snail mail address.

international@ora.com
Comments or questions about international ordering or distribution.

xresource@ora.com
To order or inquire about *The X Resource* journal.

proposals@ora.com
To submit book proposals.

O'Reilly & Associates, Inc.

103A Morris Street, Sebastopol, CA 95472
Inquiries: **707-829-0515, 800-998-9938**
Credit card orders: **800-889-8969** (Weekdays 6 A.M.- 5 P.M. PST)
FAX: **707-829-0104**

O'Reilly & Associates—
LISTING OF TITLES

INTERNET

CGI Programming on the World
  Wide Web (Winter '95-96 est.)
Getting Connected (Winter '95-96 est.)
Java in a Nutshell (Winter '95-96 est.)
Smileys
The USENET Handbook
The Whole Internet User's
  Guide & Catalog
The Whole Internet for Windows 95
Using HTML (Winter '95-96 est.)
Web Design for Designers
  (Winter '95-96 est.)
The World Wide Web Journal

SOFTWARE

Internet In A Box ™ Version 2.0
WebSite™ 1.1
WebBoard™ (Winter '95-96 est.)

WHAT YOU NEED TO KNOW SERIES

Bandits on the Information
  Superhighway
Marketing on the Internet
  (Spring '96 est.)
When You Can't Find Your
  System Administrator
Using Email Effectively

HEALTH, CAREER & BUSINESS

Building a Successful Software Business
The Computer User's Survival Guide
Dictionary of Computer Terms
  (Winter '95-96 est.)
The Future Does Not Compute
Love Your Job!
TWI Day Calendar - 1996

USING UNIX

BASICS

Learning GNU Emacs
Learning the bash Shell
Learning the Korn Shell
Learning the UNIX Operating System
Learning the vi Editor
MH & xmh: Email for Users &
  Programmers
PGP: Pretty Good Privacy
SCO UNIX in a Nutshell
UNIX in a Nutshell: System V Edition
Using and Managing UUCP
  (Spring '96 est.)
Using csh and tcsh

ADVANCED

Exploring Expect
The Frame Handbook
Learning Perl
Making TeX Work
Programming perl
Running Linux
Running Linux Companion CD-ROM
  (Winter '95-96 est.)
sed & awk
UNIX Power Tools (with CD-ROM)

SYSTEM ADMINISTRATION

Building Internet Firewalls
Computer Crime:
  A Crimefighter's Handbook
Computer Security Basics
DNS and BIND
Essential System Administration
Linux Network Administrator's Guide
Managing Internet Information Services
Managing NFS and NIS
Managing UUCP and Usenet
Networking Personal Computers
  with TCP/IP
Practical UNIX and Internet Security
  (Winter '95-96 est.)
 sendmail
System Performance Tuning
TCP/IP Network Administration
termcap & terminfo
Volume 8 : X Window System
  Administrator's Guide
The X Companion CD for R6

PROGRAMMING

Applying RCS and SCCS
C++: The Core Language
Checking C Programs with lint
DCE Security Programming
Distributing Applications Across DCE
  and Windows NT
Encyclopedia of Graphics File Formats
Guide to Writing DCE Applications
High Performance Computing
lex & yacc
Managing Projects with make
Microsoft RPC Programming Guide
Migrating to Fortran 90
Multi-Platform Code Management
ORACLE Performance Tuning
ORACLE PL/SQL Programming
Porting UNIX Software
POSIX Programmer's Guide
POSIX.4: Programming for
  the Real World
Power Programming with RPC
Practical C Programming
Practical C++ Programming
Programming with GNU Software
  (Winter '95-96 est.)
Programming with Pthreads
  (Winter '95-96 est.)
Software Portability with imake
Understanding DCE
Understanding Japanese Information
  Processing
UNIX Systems Programming for SVR4
  (Winter '95-96 est.)

BERKELEY 4.4 SOFTWARE DISTRIBUTION

4.4BSD System Manager's Manual
4.4BSD User's Reference Manual
4.4BSD User's Supplementary Docs.
4.4BSD Programmer's Reference Man.
4.4BSD Programmer's Supp. Docs.
4.4BSD-Lite CD Companion
4.4BSD-Lite CD Companion: Int. Ver.

X WINDOW SYSTEM

Volume 0: X Protocol Reference Manual
Volume 1: Xlib Programming Manual
Volume 2: Xlib Reference Manual
Volume 3: X Window System
  User's Guide
Volume. 3M: X Window System
  User's Guide, Motif Ed.
Volume 4M: X Toolkit Intrinsics
  Programming Manual, Motif Ed.
Volume 5: X Toolkit Intrinsics
  Reference Manual
Volume 6A: Motif Programming Man.
Volume 6B: Motif Reference Manual
Volume 6C: Motif Tools
Volume 8 : X Window System
  Administrator's Guide
Volume 9: X Window Window
  Programming Extentions
  (Winter '95-96 est.)
Programmer's Supplement for Release 6
X User Tools (with CD-ROM)
The X Window System in a Nutshell

THE X RESOURCE

*A QUARTERLY WORKING JOURNAL
FOR X PROGRAMMERS*

The X Resource: Issues 0 through 16

TRAVEL

Travelers' Tales France
Travelers' Tales Hong Kong
Travelers' Tales India
Travelers' Tales Mexico
Travelers' Tales Spain
Travelers' Tales Thailand
Travelers' Tales: A Woman's World

O'Reilly & Associates—
INTERNATIONAL DISTRIBUTORS

Customers outside North America can now order O'Reilly & Associates books through the following distributors. They offer our international customers faster order processing, more bookstores, increased representation at tradeshows worldwide, and the high-quality, responsive service our customers have come to expect.

EUROPE, MIDDLE EAST, AND AFRICA
(except Germany, Switzerland, and Austria)

INQUIRIES
International Thomson Publishing Europe
Berkshire House
168-173 High Holborn
London WC1V 7AA, United Kingdom
Telephone: 44-71-497-1422
Fax: 44-71-497-1426
Email: itpint@itps.co.uk

ORDERS
International Thomson Publishing Services, Ltd.
Cheriton House, North Way
Andover, Hampshire SP10 5BE, United Kingdom
Telephone: 44-264-342-832 (UK orders)
Telephone: 44-264-342-806 (outside UK)
Fax: 44-264-364418 (UK orders)
Fax: 44-264-342761 (outside UK)

GERMANY, SWITZERLAND, AND AUSTRIA

International Thomson Publishing GmbH
O'Reilly-International Thomson Verlag
Königswinterer Straße 418
53227 Bonn, Germany
Telephone: 49-228-97024 0
Fax: 49-228-441342
Email: anfragen@ora.de

ASIA *(except Japan)*
INQUIRIES
International Thomson Publishing Asia
221 Henderson Road
#08-03 Henderson Industrial Park
Singapore 0315
Telephone: 65-272-6496
Fax: 65-272-6498

ORDERS
Telephone: 65-268-7867
Fax: 65-268-6727

JAPAN
O'Reilly & Associates, Inc.
103A Morris Street
Sebastopol, CA 95472 U.S.A.
Telephone: 707-829-0515
Telephone: 800-998-9938 (U.S. & Canada)
Fax: 707-829-0104
Email: order@ora.com

AUSTRALIA
WoodsLane Pty. Ltd.
7/5 Vuko Place, Warriewood NSW 2102
P.O. Box 935, Mona Vale NSW 2103
Australia
Telephone: 02-970-5111
Fax: 02-970-5002
Email: woods@tmx.mhs.oz.au

NEW ZEALAND
WoodsLane New Zealand Ltd.
21 Cooks Street (P.O. Box 575)
Wanganui, New Zealand
Telephone: 64-6-347-6543
Fax: 64-6-345-4840
Email: woods@tmx.mhs.oz.au

THE AMERICAS
O'Reilly & Associates, Inc.
103A Morris Street
Sebastopol, CA 95472 U.S.A.
Telephone: 707-829-0515
Telephone: 800-998-9938 (U.S. & Canada)
Fax: 707-829-0104
Email: order@ora.com